PAID TO PLAY:

AN INSIDER'S GUIDE TO
VIDEO GAME CAREERS

D0071529

David SJ Hodgson
Bryan Stratton
Alice Rush, MA, RPCC, MCC

Published by Prima Games, a division of Random House, Inc.

 The Prima Games logo is a registered trademark of Random House, Inc., registered in the United States and other countries. Primagames.com is a registered trademark of Random House, Inc., registered in the United States.

Visit our website at www.primagames.com.

The advice, thoughts, and insights found herein are those of David SJ Hodgson, Bryan Stratton, and Alice Rush as individuals and not in any other capacity.

Product Manager: Mario De Govia
Editorial Supervisor: Christy Seifert
Copy Editor: Carrie Andrews
Book Design and Layout: Vanessa Perez
Illustrations: Penny Arcade

Interviews powered by the Chaos Engine: The Galaxy's Most Awesome Professional Game Developer forum.

Library of Congress Cataloging-in-Publication Data
David SJ Hodgson, Bryan Stratton, Alice Rush

Printed in the United States of America
ISBN: 0-7615-5284-7
Library of Congress Catalog Card Number: 2006903652

First edition

CONTENTS

DEDICATION

David would like to dedicate this book to Gary Harrod and Richard Leadbetter: Twin Masters, gaming savants, and my first end-of-game bosses. Thank you.

Bryan would like to dedicate this book to Patrick Baggatta and Bryn Williams, who didn't know any better; to Steve Stratton, who did know better but stuck by his brother anyway; and to Holly Hannam, who gave me the name of the book and other nice things.

Alice would like to dedicate this book to her children, Robby and Rebecca, whose passion for video gaming has allowed her to see how important it is to "do what we love."

She'd also like to thank her husband, her mother (who amazes her with her computer skills at 75), her dad (who's memory stays with her always), and her supportive family. Kim and Pattie, you rock! Jimmy, Chris, and Tim: Good luck with your careers in the video game industry!

ACKNOWLEDGMENTS

A giant thanks to everyone we interviewed in the process of making this book; we'd name you all, but we'd probably "out" most of our anonymous sources. We're sincerely and incredibly grateful that you took time out of what was mostly likely an insane schedule to write down your thoughts for us.

A large proportion of these interviews were rounded up and corralled from thechaosengine.com, an exceptional gaming forum where professional developers get to let off steam, and suited types aren't allowed through the door. Professor Shminky, in particular, should be available to collect "mad props" for his time and efforts.

Then there are folks like Iain Simons, who helped round up a load of UK contacts for us, and Alex Ward, who agreed to write our foreword. As always, cheers and salutations to Richard Leadbetter and everyone at digitalfoundry.org for their help and advice. Over on the U.S. side, Crispin Boyer and Demian Linn were instrumental in keeping us from going mental when no one wanted to return our e-mails. They gave us leads, words of encouragement, and e-mails that didn't end with "and don't bother me again." Rand Miller went far above and beyond the call of duty, Dennis Fong won the award for fastest response to the interview request, and both of them proved that their reputations as two of the nicest guys in the business are well-deserved.

Prostrate ground-hugging thanks should also be applicable to the good folks at Penny Arcade (penny-arcade.com), who agreed to illustrate our little book. And much gratitude and a mouthful of salty nuts to Seanbaby. And special thanks, as always, to Lord Viper Scorpion.

We'd also like to thank everybody at Prima Games and Random House for believing in the book concept. In particular, Julie Asbury and Jill Ellis for their help, and laughter/tears as they allowed us to work around dangerously hectic strategy guide deadlines. Editorial Team Mario De Govia, Christy Seifert, and Carrie Andrews, are an unbeatable team who looked out for our prose at every step of the way.

David thanks his wife, Melanie, who's always there, and always in his heart. Bryan thanks whoever that was that he woke up next to this morning. He'll call you, promise. And cheers to the Hodgson family back in Blighty and the Stratton clan, last seen in the wilds of Vermont.

And finally, thanks to you for buying this book.

— David S J Hodgson, Camas, Washington State
Bryan Stratton, Portland, Oregon
August 1, 2006

A special thanks goes to the UC Santa Cruz Career Center for their assistance.

— Alice Rush, MA, RPCC, MCC

Foreword

"IT ALL BEGINS HERE..."

In February 2000 I found myself in Makuhari, a small but futuristic town an hour outside Tokyo. I was attending an event called PlayStation Festival. This was the first real public showing of the PlayStation2. There were lots of new games on display. I milled around with assorted Europeans, mostly journalists sent to cover the event. Everyone knew that this event meant something. That this would somehow be important to us. I purchased a T-shirt at the merchandise booth. It came in a small matte-black box. Some of the press guys bought several, one to wear and a few to keep, boxed, pristine. It was a special shirt and was immediately a limited edition, only on sale at this event. On the long flight back to London, I opened the box and looked at the shirt. It said simply "PlayStation2. It all begins here...."

Flash forward. It is summer 2006. We are on the brink on a new generation in video gaming. I take a break from the screeching of tires, echoes of huge explosions, and the sound of automatic weapons. Just a regular day in the Criterion offices! It is an honor to be asked by David Hodgson, one of the most respected writers in video gaming on both sides of the Atlantic, to write the foreword to this exciting new book.

If you are serious about wanting a career in the ever-growing global video gaming business, then you have just discovered a great place to start. You can read how others got their start in the business as well as learn valuable lessons about how to join the industry itself. There are numerous opportunities waiting for you. The gaming business is now bigger than the movie business. But go to any bookstore or surf the Web and you will struggle to find concrete information to assist you in making your start. I think this is why David, Bryan, and Alice took on the task of writing this book. Other industries have traditionally done a much better job at taking time out and offering advice and a helping hand to others. In gaming, we're all much too busy designing the next game and spending too much time locked in a small, dark room reviewing the latest build. Or maybe that last one is just me!

We're on the brink of something new for all of us. This industry is always changing. And this is by far the most exciting period so far. The next generation of hardware is with us. Microsoft's Xbox 360 is already on sale, and this holiday season brings the launch of the eagerly awaited PlayStation3 from Sony and the innovative Wii from Nintendo. We're still in the infancy of the incredible rise of online global player, connecting players from around the world and shaping new gameplay experiences. This is also bringing new ways to distribute games. With downloadable content, there are games always waiting for you, and now you don't even have to leave the couch!

So there have never been so many opportunities for you to make your mark in the games industry. Holding this book in your hands is the start. So what are you waiting for?

Turn the page and let's get started. You can learn from the best in the business and then the rest is up to you!

It all begins here....

Alex Ward
Creative Director
Criterion Games
Guildford, England
July 2006

GETTING INTO THE GAME

"Video game players often display exceptional business skills."

—*Mike Antonucci*, San Jose Mercury News

"The people who play games are into technology, can handle more information, can synthesize more complex data, solve operational design problems, lead change, and bring organizations through change."

—*Chip Luman, Charles Schwab VP of Human Resources*

"Surgeons adept at video games were less likely to make mistakes during certain forms of operations and suturing."

—*Based on research from Dr. James Rosser, Director of the Advanced Medical Technology Institute*

"I recently learned something quite interesting about video games. Many young people have developed incredible hand, eye, and brain coordination in playing these games. The air force believes these kids will be our outstanding pilots should they fly our jets."

—*Ronald Reagan*

Game On: Welcome to the Book

Welcome to *Paid to Play: An Insider's Guide to Video Game Careers*. Now that Alex Ward has suitably pumped you up to read a series of thrilling revelations about what goes on behind the scenes at dozens of game development companies, we'd better honor our part of the bargain.

We're a couple of video game writers and a career counselor who have extensive industry experience. We've seen it all: company implosions, the launch of a dozen consoles (at least half of which included the words "game" and "boy" in their names), the birth of multimillion-dollar franchises, and the death of others. We've reviewed close to 1,000 games. We've interviewed industry legends like Toru Iwatani, the inventor of Pac-Man, and Gabe Newell, the founder of Valve software; and…er…James Best, Sheriff Roscoe P. Coltrane from *The Dukes of Hazzard*.[1] We've written close to 100 strategy guides. And we've worked with over 60 different video game development studios.

In all this time, there's one memorable line we've heard, above all others: "You get paid to play games for a living?! That's unreal!" It's also untrue, but we'll get to that later in this book.

---

1. Mr. Best was promoting a *Dukes of Hazzard* PS1 game at the time, which was far less entertaining than the man himself. Mr. Best is an accomplished painter, and *Counter-Strike* fan. Seriously.

Judging by the quotes at the start of this chapter, you can go into a variety of professions. However, judging by your purchase of this book, we know your first choice. We want to help you there, so read on my friend.

What Do You Want to Be When You Don't Want to Grow Up?

You're probably wondering what this book is about, how helpful it is, and how many jokes there are about pasty-faced, bearded men with hygiene difficulties. The answers in order are: "It's about getting a career in video games," "It's incredibly helpful," and "Loads." But the book's main purpose is to pass on the following information from over 100 gaming professionals:

- The main jobs you can do as a career in video games
- What goes on behind the scenes in most development studios
- How to turn a lifelong hobby into a lifelong career
- The good, bad, and ugly parts of each gaming job
- How to secure your first job in your particular field of interest

So, this book's for you if you are:

- thinking of subjects to study at school;
- thinking about which career discipline sounds the most entertaining;
- interested in what *really* goes on behind the scenes in the gaming industry;
- working, but the mundane drudgery is getting to you, and you're after a career change;
- parents. Thanks for everything!

Preparation: Over 100 Interviews, 50 Careers, One Book

Preparation for the book was intense. We crafted a finely honed, 22-question interview and sent it to everyone we knew who had even a passing interest in video games.

Something amazing happened. We were deluged with answers to our questions. Well over 100 of them, to be almost exact.

Around 60 of these interviews came in one week alone.

Three weeks later, we'd gathered the most comprehensive collection of video game answers ever assembled—or, at least, that we'd ever assembled.

Tome Raiders: What's in the Book?

We've segmented this manuscript into over a dozen meaty sections for you to digest at your leisure. Although we're convinced you know how to read a book, we thought we'd outline what each of the chapters contains, just to entice you further.

CHAPTER 2: CAREER TOOLS

Alice Rush has a lot of letters after her name. We're told that they mean good things in her world of career counseling. This chapter provides information on how to network with established professionals, write résumés, and conduct yourself properly during interviews...something about wearing pants. Anyway, it is useful information.

CHAPTER 3: GAME JOBS

The Big Idea—Game Design

This chapter deals with **game designers**, who come up with a game's original concept and shepherd the game through every stage of its development. You don't need artistic talent or technical skill, but you'd better have some good, creative ideas and a crazy work ethic.

Get with the Program—The Technical Department

When a game engine needs programming, bugs need to be fixed, and men with overly developed brains need to congregate in cubicles, they go to work in the technical department. **Programmers, technical directors,** and **engineers** should read this. Find out whether your HTML skills are strong enough to program the PS3. You may be disappointed.

Bugging Out—Quality Assurance

The starting point for many a career in the industry, the **tester's** lampooned and unappreciated life is revealed, in sometimes excruciating detail. Then there are the QA departments of software developers, who are much more valued but much less easy to work into a sensationalist introduction.

Pushing Pixels—Visual Art

Make your parents proud and prove to them that four years of art school wasn't just an advance on your inheritance. **Visual artists** create all of the visual components of a game, from concept art to 3-D character models. If you excel at any of the visual arts, you need to check out this chapter.

Stick It in Their Ear—Audio Artist

Audio artists include **soundtrack composers, sound designers** and other folks who create and implement all of the audio in a game. If you've got a trunk full of piano sonatas that you've been trying to unload, this might be your chance.

Production Values—Game Management

We interviewed **producers, directors, vice presidents,** and **presidents:** This chapter shows what you must do to get the highest-paid jobs around. It also reveals what exactly a producer does all day when the rest of the team is working.

Publish or Perish—Game Publishing

If you like the idea of having to be the tough-but-fair parent to creative types, or if you like people and want to buy them alcohol with someone else's money so that they'll like your games better, you might be cut out for a career in game publishing. It's like working for a record label, without having to deal with fevered rock star egos. Instead, you get to deal with fevered video game egos. Fun!

Write Angles—Writing for Games

Back in the day, writing for video games was limited to entering three initials after a particularly good game of *Missile Command*. Nowadays, with production values at an all-time high and every publisher wanting to add the word "cinematic" to a game's description, games need **scriptwriters.** They also need **translators** who can localize games for foreign markets, and they need **game manual writers.** And someone's got to write the strategy guides for these things.

The Write Stuff—Journalism

When game reviewers pan a game that a development studio has been working on for three years, are they then hunted down and killed? Do they receive huge gifts in return for favorable reviews? Are those free trips to Europe really necessary? We interview some of the best **video game journalists, editors in chief,** and **Web humorists** in the business.

Actually Paid to Actually Play—Professional Gamer

Some people really do get paid just to play games for a living. There are about four of them in the world, and their reflexes are so sharp that they can catch flies with chopsticks. If you think you've got what it takes to take them on, read this chapter and reconsider.

If You Want Something Done Right—DIY

Does your limitless genius bristle at the thought of being confined in the restrictive corporate culture of the video game industry? Have you tried working with The Man, only to get worked over by him instead? Or do you just want to mess around with coding and see where it gets you? If so, you might want to explore the do-it-yourself (DIY) options contained within this chapter.

Basic Cable Guys—Mass Media Personality

When you turn on the television and get to watch a program devoted to gaming culture, do you think to yourself, "I could do that!" If so, then you'll be pleased to know we're here to show you how difficult the job really is.

Shopping for a Career—Retail

Can you really parlay a part-time job testing partially eaten PS2 games and stacking shelves at a big-name game retailer into a bona fide gaming career? Or is the retail business exciting enough to stay in, what with the stacks and stacks of games surrounding you and all the customers you can punch. The conclusions probably won't surprise you.

Men Are from the Mushroom Kingdom, Women Are from Hyrule—Women in Gaming

Yes, women used to be prodded with a stick when they turned up at a development studio, expecting to work there. Now that stick has been replaced with a carrot of encouragement and the stick wielder replaced entirely. We get chatty with a dozen industry women and find out what it's really like working with socially awkward men.

CHAPTER 4: GETTING A JOB

After you find a career field that you'd like to try, this chapter will hopefully help you get your foot in the door. It's chock-full of time-tested strategies for landing your dream job, or at least the job that leads to your dream job (or was your dream job until you found out it took far more work than you expected).

NOTE

The one thing that you can count on in the video game industry is that you can't count on anything in the video game industry. Case in point: Just as this book was going to print, the story broke that E^3—the biggest trade event and hype fest in this business—might no longer continue to exist as an event, following the withdrawal of several major exhibitors. Or maybe E^3 will still be around, but it'll be scaled back. Or perhaps it's in the process of transforming into a delicious flaky pastry. At the moment, they're all equally probable.

This is especially hilarious to us and our editors, as there are references to the show throughout the rest of this book, and we don't have the time or the Wite-Out to go back and correct them all. So wherever you see the word "E^3," we'd appreciate it if you could cross it out and write "the show or shows formerly known as E^3, which might not exist in any recognizable form" in the margin. This is what we get for working in an antiquated medium like print. On the bright side, we now have an even stronger argument for releasing a Revised Edition in a year or two. Ka-ching!

What are you waiting for? Your dream career—or a series of difficult-to-accomplish hoops to leap through in pursuit of your dream career—awaits!

By the way, if you have any questions, comments, feedback, or offers of money that don't involve Nigerian princes or pyramid schemes, please direct them to vgcbook@randomhouse.com.

2

CAREER TOOLS

Self-Assessment

Sure, you love video games, and if you're reading this book, you'd like to make them a career and not just a hobby. But before you start picking out plasma monitors for your office, it's important to know *what kind* of job is right for you. And if we're doing *our* jobs, you'll have the answer to that question by the end of this chapter.

If you aren't sure which job is right for you, try completing what career counselors call a "self-assessment," which is designed to help you better understand your skills and interests.

GAME DEVELOPMENT FIELDS

When people think about jobs in the video game industry, they usually think about game development, the process of creating the games. Most game development jobs generally fit into five major categories:

1. Design
2. Art
3. Programming
4. Production
5. Testing

We've created some sample game development job descriptions, complete with lists of the skills that you need in order to be successful in each field. Read through them to figure out which area might fit you best. Remember, just because you don't have all the necessary skills right now doesn't mean you can't develop them.

Design

Game designers spend their days dreaming up fresh ideas for new games or looking at existing games and thinking of ways to improve upon them. They pay a great deal of attention to their surroundings, noticing details that others miss, and they draw inspiration from every facet of their daily lives. Analytical by nature, game designers also enjoy solving problems and tend to ask "why" a lot.

The best designers are creative visionaries who constantly devise new ways to do just about anything. They spend a lot of time in their heads creating new characters, worlds, and concepts, and they have strong written and verbal communication skills that allow them to share their ideas with the people who can implement them.

Obviously, game designers must also know and love a wide variety of games, and they must have an innate sense of what is fun and what isn't. It's pointless trying to get a concept made if there are already 10 other games out there that do the same thing better, or if it's an original idea that makes for a game no one wants to play.

Because game design is a constant tug-of-war between what you'd *like* to have in the game and what is technically and financially feasible, a good game designer must be able to strike the perfect balance between ideals and reality without getting frustrated or leaning too heavily toward one at the expense of the other. Designers must be flexible and adapt quickly to change, and a bit of tenacity and perseverance never hurt.

NOTE

Game designers don't actually *make* the game, and they don't have to possess any technical skills beyond a basic proficiency with word-processing and spreadsheet programs. All video game jobs that require specialized technical knowledge appear under the "Art" and "Programming" sections of this chapter.

Lead Game Designer

LOOKING FOR AN EXPERIENCED LEAD GAME DESIGNER with a strong design sense, excellent writing skills, and a deep understanding of games and mechanics. This is a unique opportunity to be a lead game designer with a progressive game developer working on blockbuster games.

Duties:
- Mentor members of the design team
- Develop new game components and ideas consistent with the company's design philosophy
- Work with programmers, artists, and other designers to get major portions of the game developed with minimal supervision
- Ensure the fun and proper function and balance of game systems
- Write and maintain design documentation and project schedules as required

Requirements:
- Minimum of 4 years of game industry experience in a design position
- Minimum of 1 year experience as a lead designer
- Strong analytical problem-solving skills
- Excellent written and verbal communication skills
- Ability to cooperate with others on shared projects
- Self-motivated and self-managed
- Passion for gaming
- Bachelor's degree in Game Design, Communications, English, Computer Science, or related field

Pluses:
- Familiarity with marketing
- Knowledge of game's time period

Please include the following:
- Résumé and cover letter
- Optional one- to three-page written analysis of specific games, discussing what you felt was done well, what was done poorly, and how you would improve the game

Art

While designers create the game's general concepts, the artists create the game's unique look and feel. The artist takes the game designer's design documents and creates original art assets that will be used in the game. Game designers sketch out the game's big-picture view, and artists use their specialized technical skills and creative vision to breathe life into every specific element.

Artists in the video game industry are much like artists in any other field. They have a strong eye for detail, they visualize what does not exist, and they use their tools to bring their ideas to life. In the software biz, those tools often include Adobe Photoshop, Maya, and 3D Studio Max. If you're planning on being a video game artist, it's important that you can learn new programs, as many studios use their own proprietary design tools as well.

Artists don't need to have the in-depth knowledge of games that designers do. In fact, many successful video game artists come from more traditional illustration or animation backgrounds before breaking into the video game industry. However, artists must be somewhat familiar with what's on the market in order to avoid creating unoriginal assets.

NOTE

Not all art in video games is visual. Audio engineers and sound track composers are just as vital to the game's creation as 3-D artists and animators.

Character Modeler/Texturer

TO MODEL IN-GAME CHARACTERS with effective use of a polygon budget, modeling high-poly characters to the required standard and level of detail. The role involves creating UV maps with good layout, use of space, and minimal texture distortion. The job also entails producing normal maps and surface bakes and creating textures to the appropriate style and standard. Previous experience in the games or similar industry is highly desirable, though not essential.

An intermediate to advanced level of proficiency with Maya/Max and Photoshop is essential, and an intermediate to advanced level of proficiency with ZBrush would be a distinct advantage. Applicants should also have a good understanding of underlying mesh construction techniques for joint deformation, facial animation, etc. Knowledge of human and animal anatomy plus cloth and drapery is beneficial.

Environment Artist

WE ARE LOOKING FOR SEVERAL ENVIRONMENT ARTISTS TO MODEL, texture, and light 3-D environments, and to model and texture additional props for environments. The ideal candidates possess 3-D modeling skills, including the ability to render detailed buildings, vehicles, props, weapons, etc., and lighting-technique knowledge.

Applicants must have an intermediate to advanced level of proficiency with Maya/Max and Photoshop. Knowledge of ZBrush and procedural geometry generation packages such as XFrog is desirable, as is knowledge of shader creation and techniques. Applicants should demonstrate a strong artistic background, though not necessarily academic. Please note that on the next-generation projects, artists will often specialize in just one of the areas mentioned above. If this is the case, please apply anyway—we would like to hear from you.

Technical Artist

WE ARE SEEKING A TECHNICAL ARTIST to assist the programmers and artists by investigating and solving art-related problems as they arise and by working on more technical areas of art production, special effects, scripts, and cutscenes. The technical artist will also investigate new techniques and methods and how they can be applied to a production environment. This role requires previous experience with game environment technical issues such as portalling and level of detail.

The artist must possess an intermediate to advanced level of proficiency with Maya/Max and Photoshop. It is desirable for applicants to have knowledge of normal, specular, and bump mapping techniques; shaders, CG, and other next-gen techniques; experience in creating particle systems, special FX, and scripts; and advanced lighting techniques such as global illumination, radiosity, and ambient occlusion mapping. A practical knowledge of MEL/MAX Script is also desired.

Programming

Programmers do all the game's behind-the-scenes work, from creating and implementing the artificial intelligence of computer-controlled characters to tweaking the physics engine. If programmers do their job right, you don't even notice their work—the game world they've helped create functions naturally and perfectly. Obviously, programmers must have a passion for technology and games, and they must pay attention to things like texture maps, light sources, and AI routines, all of which are probably lost on the average gamer.

Programmers are a breed apart from other developer types. They think in ones and zeroes, and when they gather together and discuss their projects, an outside observer might wonder if they're even speaking English. They are natural problem solvers with extremely high aptitudes in math and science. Programmers are capable of coding by themselves for hours on end—in fact, most great programmers choose to spend their time doing just that, even if there isn't a paycheck involved. Self-motivation and a strong work ethic are musts.

Game Programmer

WE ARE LOOKING FOR EXPERIENCED GAME PROGRAMMERS to join our project teams and perform high-level programming. This role requires previous games industry experience and structured C/C++ programming and debugging skills. Applicants should have knowledge of 3-D programming, and math/physics programming skills are desirable.

Tools Programmer

TOOLS PROGRAMMER NEEDED TO DEVELOP AND SUPPORT INTERNAL TOOLS and utilities. We are looking for professional programmers who have substantial experience developing complex graphical Windows applications in C++/MFC. Knowledge of 3-D math, physics, mechanics, and other game-related concepts is desirable, as is experience with 3-D graphics development using DirectX.

Online/Network Programmer

The online/network programmer will play a key role in creating the addition of a multiplayer component to a title currently in development for current and next-generation game systems.

Required Experience:
- Prior experience with network-related code for a published game
- Strong fundamental network knowledge with experience using TCP/IP and UDP protocols
- Experience dealing with bandwidth and latency issues
- Understanding of the implementation requirements of client-server and peer-to-peer networking models
- Strong C/C++ software engineering skills
- BS in computer science, engineering, mathematics, or equivalent
- At least 2 years of game-development experience
- Excellent communication skills
- Ability to work with multiple hardware platforms

Production

The days when a team of a half-dozen programmers and artists could crank out a professional-looking game are long past. Even the most modest modern game requires a full-time commitment by dozens of dedicated individuals. The larger the team gets, the harder it is to coordinate their efforts, and that's where producers come in. Just as with programmers, producers are the unseen forces behind the entire process of game development. Almost nothing they do on a day-to-day basis actually makes it into the game, but without them, the game itself would never exist. They must ensure that everything gets done on time and on budget, and they must be able to anticipate and solve small problems before they become big ones.

Producers must have strong leadership and management skills and must be willing and able to step up and run the show. Their whole job is making sure that their team has everything necessary to do their jobs; therefore, producers must be able to multitask like mad and not lose their cool when they're pulled in several directions at once. The best producers are always in control but resist the temptation to micromanage, instead trusting that their team can handle what's thrown at them.

Because the game development process is stressful (especially close to deadline), producers absolutely must have well-developed people skills. They must be able to criticize constructively without offending; build strong relationships with people with very different personalities; and maintain a positive, supportive attitude. As the point person for the development process, the producer sets the tone for the team. If the producer can't deal with the pressure, the whole project's going to wind up in the toilet.

NOTE

An often-overlooked cog in the great gears of game production is the tester, whose job entails playing the game over and over, finding bugs and passing them along to the rest of the team. This is an entry-level position that can open doors to low-level production and design jobs. It is often one of the first things on any aspiring professional's résumé.

Associate Project Manager

ASSOCIATE PROJECT MANAGERS PLAY A CENTRAL LEADERSHIP ROLE in the entertainment team. They provide online information and establish a community related to video games, music, television, and more. Reporting to the director of operations and business relations, the associate project manager participates in every aspect of product management, including overseeing website content, syndication, co-branding efforts, and other relationships in the industry. The associate project manager's sphere of influence may include hands-on product management and planning, management of the technology development team, client relationship management, and a range of other issues.

Other examples of associate project managers' responsibilities include, but are not limited to, the following:

- Independently and collaboratively execute long-term product plans for aspects of website functionality, as dictated by both short- and long-term business goals
- Serve as a contact for external clients, internal departments, and partners within the industry
- Must be an effective representative for the entertainment business unit
- Must be able to eliminate barriers to effective work by using internal departments and external resources
- Work independently and with the entertainment product team, development team, and production team on site enhancements, including developing detailed specifications and requirements, resource management, and seeing game functionality all the way from inception to launch

Associate Project Manager (cont.)

- Proactively identify areas of potential weakness or opportunities for improvement, including translating findings into actionable plans and seeing those plans through to realization
- Working closely with Quality Assurance to maintain a positive end-user experience and to ensure the successful rollout of any new site developments

This is a position of substantial responsibility that demands an experienced and proven professional capable of handling complex and strategically important products and initiatives.

To be successful, the associate project manager must:

- function independently, with little oversight, for certain areas of responsibility;
- demonstrate professional expertise with and have a clear understanding of the online product management business, processes, and procedures;
- be very familiar with content and usability issues on the Web; be very comfortable with technology; be detail-oriented; and show a strong interest in video games, music, television, and other forms of entertainment;
- multitask and simultaneously manage multiple projects, both big and small;
- have a proven ability to work with groups at all levels within an organization, including members of Sales, Editorial, Development, IT, Customer Support, and beyond;
- be outgoing, friendly, and a true "people person" who thoroughly enjoys working with many different people and groups on any given day.

Qualifications:
Candidates should have a minimum of 2 years' experience working on and responsible for game product/content-related issues. Familiarity with ad-serving technologies and Flash is a plus. A bachelor's degree or equivalent professional experience is required.

Tester

IMMEDIATE NEED FOR MOBILE AND CONSOLE GAME TESTERS at $10 per hour.

Primary responsibilities:
- Review/double-check and correct collected data
- Report bugs to database and the lead QA analyst
- Assure new patches and updates are functional
- Assure shipping product is fully functional

Qualifications:
- 18 years of age or older
- High school diploma or equivalent
- Superb work ethic
- Sharp attention to detail
- Strong interest in video games
- Aptitude to learn quickly and effectively
- Ability to remain focused in a team-oriented environment
- Basic PC knowledge, as well as being familiar with Microsoft programs such as Word, Excel, and Outlook
- Excellent interpersonal, written, and oral communication skills
- Ability to work a designated schedule

Desired Qualifications:
- Hardcore gamer
- Previous testing experience
- Understanding of the software test cycle process
- PC and console game troubleshooting
- Experience and familiarity with multiple gaming platforms and genres

OTHER CAREER OPTIONS

If none of the preceding career fields sound interesting to you, or if you're not a good fit for any of them, check out the "Detailed Career Assessment" section to help determine where your strengths and interests lie. If you're still not convinced that game development is for you, don't despair. There are plenty of non-development careers in the industry:

- Finance
- Marketing
- Customer support
- Video game journalism

- Public affairs/legal
- Planning
- Information Technology (IT)
- Manufacturing and distribution

If you have a good idea what field you'd like to move into, you can skip the rest of this self-assessment section and head to "Networking."

SKILLS ASSESSMENT

For a more detailed assessment of yourself, start by thinking about the skills, interests, values, and personality style that makes you who you are. Ask yourself the following questions:

What Skills Energize Me When I Use Them?

We're talking about the skills you're good at and that get you pumped when you apply them. What are these skills? Solving problems? Troubleshooting? Researching? Making physical or mechanical things better? Maybe you get turned on by creating something new that never existed before. Does art, music, or sound energize you? Or is it influencing, educating, or motivating people? Is it writing or creating characters? Is it using your imagination in everything you do?

Whatever your energizing skills, you can bet there's a job in the video game industry that uses them. But you must find your best area of focus, based on the skills you enjoy using the most. If you haven't assessed your skills yet, here are a few exercises to choose from:

1. Go to www.skillscan.net and complete an online skills assessment to help determine your "motivated skills"—what you love to do and skills you possess and enjoy using the most. (Note: Skillscan charges a small fee for the assessment.)
2. If you're in junior high, high school, college, or are a college grad, visit your school's career center and ask the career counselor to complete a skills assessment with you. Most schools and colleges have tried-and-true skill exercises you can complete, typically for free. Customized and advanced career counseling services may ask you to complete an "accomplishment inventory," where the counselor listens for recurring themes and patterns of strengths and motivated skills.
3. One of your humble authors (Alice) has a website, www.careeru.com, where you can complete a "Rewarding Experiences Assessment." Instead of hiring a career counselor, you can use this to share your most rewarding experiences with a friend or parent and ask them to listen for recurring patterns of skills in your experiences. This will help you determine which skills you enjoy using the most.

What Am I Interested in Most?

What are (or were) your favorite classes? What books or magazines do you like to read? What corner of the bookstore do you find yourself in most often? Is it fiction, computers, psychology, or finance?

It's also worth visiting your school's or alma mater's career center and completing a Strong Interest Inventory (see sidebar). The Strong will connect you with popular occupations, but don't expect it to list many jobs in the video game industry. (That's why we're here.)

WHAT'S A STRONG INTEREST INVENTORY?

For over 25 years, the "Strong" has been used in virtually all U.S. high school and college career centers. It's also offered in classes in high school and college that relate to major or career decision making. The Strong is designed to give a clear understanding of whether the respondent is "enterprising" (has business interests), "social" (relationship focused), "artistic" (creative, aesthetically focused), "investigative" (analytical, scientific, inclined toward programming and problem solving), or "conventional" (traditional, organized, likes routine and paperwork).

Here's a brief rundown of what kinds of jobs your Strong results might push you toward:

- "Social" and "enterprising" gamers make good producers, product managers, and business types.
- "Conventional" and "investigative" gamers are well-suited for programming and research analyst jobs.
- "Artistic" gamers should consider art jobs such as 3-D modeling, enviromental design, or audio engineering. They make for good game designers as well.

NOTE

Your interests may change every couple of years, but these results can help you now in determining how you want to work with video games.

What Are Your Values?

Knowing your values helps you understand why certain kinds of work satisfy you the most. For example, if you value autonomy and independence, then you may prefer video game careers that allow you to work from home, such as a strategy guide writer, game journalist, or programmer. If you value monetary rewards highly, then you may have a hard time working for free, which often happens in a video game career's early stages.

Being aware of your values at the start of your career search will help you make the right decisions and hopefully fend off the dreaded midlife crisis. Review the following values and check which *10* are most important to you. Then, note the top five values you want more of in your life. Use these values as a guide as you make decisions about your video game career.

NOTE

This assessment is only a partial list of values, so feel free to add any you wish!

CareerU® Values Assessment Exercise

VALUE	DEFINITION
❏ Accuracy	Paying attention to detail, avoiding errors, focusing on quality
❏ Adventure	Traveling and/or risk-taking, enjoying change
❏ Balance	Flexibility, spending more time with family, having leisure time
❏ Challenge	Activities that require an element of risk, stretching beyond your comfort zone
❏ Creativity	Creating new ideas, designs, methods, using your imagination to improve things
❏ Decision making	Having your input and ideas applied within the organization
❏ Expert	Being known as one of the most knowledgeable in your field
❏ Expression	Flexible work allowing for original and/or artistic thought
❏ Feedback	Receiving helpful guidance in both what you do well and how to improve
❏ Flexibility	Controlling your own work flow, environment, and schedule
❏ Helping others	Supporting individuals or groups through advice, information, or counseling
❏ Honesty	Sincerity, standing up for your beliefs and convictions
❏ Independence	The freedom to shape your own work
❏ Influence	The ability to change ideas or have an impact on the way others think and/or behave

VALUE	DEFINITION
☐ Integrity	Able to be yourself at work and in your work, without politics or pretense
☐ Knowledge	Learning and advancing your intellectual abilities through your work
☐ Leadership	Directing and influencing others in their work
☐ Learning	Enjoying a variety of experiences that result in learning new skills
☐ Loyalty	Being dutiful to your work, always following through
☐ Making a difference	Feeling your work positively impacts society in some way
☐ Monetary rewards	Being able to afford an affluent lifestyle and high standard of living
☐ Personal growth	Developing your sense of self and how you impact the world, continuing to improve
☐ Physical & mental health	Maintaining a sense of well-being
☐ Practicality	Hands-on work that makes a tangible difference and uses common sense
☐ Public contact	Meeting and greeting the public
☐ Recognition	Receiving validation from superiors or peers at work
☐ Relationships	Having strong connections and bonding with people at work
☐ Results	Seeing tangible results of your efforts at work
☐ Security	Earning a steady paycheck from constant, reliable employment
☐ Status	Prestigious job, well respected by others
☐ Structure	Clear direction, predictable work environment
☐ Teamwork	Belonging, being part of a group, working together
☐ Variety	Consistent changes and unexpected challenges, work requiring multiple aptitudes
☐ Working alone	Autonomous work, where you can concentrate with minimal interruptions

TOP FIVE VALUES LIST

Enter five of the values you checked above, including any you added to the list. The first should be the value that is most important to you.

1. _____
2. _____
3. _____
4. _____
5. _____

When looking at job descriptions, consider if your values will be satisfied in the jobs you are attracted to. This is a good exercise to use at the start of your career search, and it's helpful to visit it every couple of years to see how your values have changed and how that impacts any career choices you might make in the near future.

Consider also conducting your own information interviews with professionals in the field, to further "reality-test" the jobs that most interest you. This helps determine if various jobs and company cultures will satisfy your values. For example, if you're a writer and "recognition" is a value that matters to you, jobs with bylines and author photos might matter more to you than for someone who does video game script writing, where only your mom will look for your name in the tiny type at the back of the instruction manual.

What's Your Personality Style?

Finally, assess your personality style to determine your best fit within the video game industry. Your school's career center or a certified private practice career counselor can help you complete a Myers-Briggs Type Indicator (MBTI).

The Myers-Briggs is a personality inventory that has been utilized in the United States for over 50 years for career decision making. It helps people understand their natural style. For example:

- Extroverts are energized by people; introverts are energized by time alone.
- Sensing types prefer specifics and practical matters; intuitive types go in for the big-picture vision and are drained by details.
- Thinking types are logical, critical, and excel in technical jobs; feeling types value harmony and relationships above all else.
- Judging types are more product-focused, preferring closure and immediate results; perceiving types enjoy spontaneity and leaving options open, and they tend to procrastinate and enjoy thinking on their feet.

Knowing your natural personality (or Myers-Briggs results) helps you answer questions such as:

- Do I prefer to work alone on projects or with people?
- Am I detail- or idea-oriented?
- Do I solve problems logically or through relationships and communication?
- Do I thrive on deadlines and tangible results or on process improvements— leaving options open with plenty of flexibility?

Unlike all your other assessment results, a properly administered and validated Myers-Briggs does not change much throughout your life, because—barring any dramatic, life-altering events—your personality remains relatively unchanged. Therefore, it's important to consider your personality traits when looking at a career path. For example, if you are introverted, a producer position would probably be draining; if you were an extrovert, you'd probably go stir-crazy as a programmer. A feeling type probably wouldn't enjoy the criticism and conflict inherent in a game designer's day-to-day life, while thinking types might be too exasperated dealing with interpersonal dynamics to effectively lead a design team.

NOTE

Do What You Are, by Paul and Barbara Tieger, is one of the best books for understanding your Myers-Briggs results.

SUMMARY

Every potential career in the video game industry requires a set of skills. You can either choose a job that matches the skills you have, or you can develop the skills necessary to get the job you want.

Your values and personality type influence the amount of satisfaction you'll get from your job. Matching the right job to your personality and values ensures that you'll enjoy what you do, and it increases the probability that your natural enthusiasm for the work will carry you to greater success in your field.

There are plenty of ways to get paid to play. Make sure you're doing it in a way that satisfies you.

ADDITIONAL ASSESSMENT RESOURCES

www.careerdesignguide.com: Good for career advice for those age 17 and up. It measures values, skills, and interest inventories in one unique tool. A personal favorite of ours.

www.elevateyourcareer.com: Includes values, skills, and interest inventories.

www.skillscan.net: An online tool to help assess your skills.

www.ncda.org: A national resource to find a certified or master career counselor in your area.

Education and Training

Courses and colleges in video game study are starting to appear on the radar. If you're in high school now, or if you're thinking about returning to school in order to continue your studies, consider choosing a school that offers programs in video games.

The following is a partial list of colleges and sources of training information for the video game field. It is not an endorsement of any school or course of study. College programs and reputations change on an annual basis, so do some investigating when selecting a school. It's best to go directly to your dream employers for their advice on which schools would be most advantageous to your future career plans.

Video Game Schools and Programs of Study

Name	Location(s)	Website
American Film Institute	Los Angeles, CA	www.afionline.org
Art Center College of Design	Pasadena, CA	www.artcenter.edu
The Art Institute	Thirty-two campuses across the United States	www.artinstitutes.edu
California Design College	Los Angeles, CA	www.allartschools.com/schools/ID1046/
Carnegie Mellon, Entertainment Technology Center MA Program	Pittsburgh, PA	www.etc.cmu.edu/about.html
Collins College	Tempe, AZ; Phoenix, AZ	www.collinscollege.com
DigiPen Institute of Technology	Redmond, WA	www.digipen.edu
Full Sail	Winter Park, FL	www.fullsail.com
Georgia Institute of Technology	Atlanta, GA	www.gatech.edu
The Guildhall at Southern Methodist University (SMU)	Plano, TX	http://guildhall.smu.edu
New York University	New York, NY	www.nyu.edu
Parsons School of Design	New York, NY	www.parsons.edu
Rhode Island School of Design	Providence, RI	www.risd.edu
University of Advancing Technology	Tempe, AZ; online	www.uat.edu/graduate
University of California, Irvine	Irvine, CA	www.uci.edu

Name	Location(s)	Website
University of California, Los Angeles	Los Angeles, CA	www.ucla.edu
University of California, Santa Cruz	Santa Cruz, CA	www.ucsc.edu
University of Massachusetts, Lowell	Lowell, MA	www.uml.edu
University of Southern California	Los Angeles, CA	www.usc.edu

NOTE

For additional colleges and courses of study, click the "Education" tab at www.gamasutra.com. Game Discovery (www.gamediscovery.com) and David Perry's website (www.dperry.com) are also excellent sources of educational information.

Video Game Company Websites

NAME	WEBSITES
Activision Publishing, Inc.	www.activision.com
Agetec, Inc.	www.agetec.com
Alchemic Dream, Inc.	www.alchemicdream.net
AOL Games	www.aol.com
Atari, Inc.	www.ATARI.com
Atlus U.S.A., Inc.	www.atlus.com
Bandai	www.bandai.com
Bethesda Softworks	www.bethsoft.com
BioWare/Pandemic Studios	bioware.pandemicstudios.com/
Blitz Games	www.BlitzGames.com
Blizzard Entertainment	www.blizzard.com
Blue Shift	www.blueshiftgames.com
BradyGames	www.bradygames.com
Buena Vista Games, Inc.	www.buenavistagames.com
CAPCOM Entertainment, Inc.	www.capcom.com
Carbon6	carbon6.com
CNET Networks Games	www.gamespot.com
Codemasters	www.codemasters.com

NAME	WEBSITES
Computer Games Magazine	www.cgonline.com
Crave Entertainment	www.cravegames.com
Cyberlore Studios, Inc	www.cyberlore.com
Eidos, Inc.	www.eidos.com
Electronic Arts	www.ea.com
Ensemble Studios	www.ensemblestudios.com
Foundation 9 Entertainment	www.f9e.com
Fugitive Interactive	www.fugitive-interactive.com
Future US, Inc.	www.futureus-inc.com
G4	www.g4tv.com
The Game Factory	www.gamefactorygames.com
Game Informer Magazine	www.gameinformer.com
GameDaily	www.gamedaily.com
GameINSTINCT	www.gameinstinct.com
Gameloft	www.gameloft.com
GamesIndustry.biz	www.gamesindustry.biz
GameSpot	www.gamespot.com
GameTap	www.gametap.com
GameTrailers	www.Gametrailers.com
Global Gaming League	www.ggl.com
Glu	www.glu.com
Greenstreet Software, Ltd.	www.greenstreetsoftware.com
Hardcore Gamer Magazine	luv2game.com
Her Interactive	www.herinteractive.com
High Moon Studios	www.highmoonstudios.com
Hudson Entertainment	www.HudsonEntertainment.com
Humagade	www.humagade.com
I-play	www.iplay.com
iBeta Quality Assurance	www.iBeta.com
Id Software	www.idsoftware.com
IGN Entertainment	www.ign.com
IronMonkey Studios	www.ironmonkeystudios.com

NAME	WEBSITES
Kemco USA, Inc.	www.kemcogames.com
KOEI Corporation	www.koei.com
Konami Digital Entertainment	www.konami.com/gs
Krome Studios	www.kromestudios.com.au
Kukan Studio	www.kukanstudio.com
Left Behind Games	www.leftbehindgames.com
LucasArts	www.lucasarts.com
Majesco Entertainment	www.majescoentertainment.com
Marjacq	www.marjacq.com
Massive Entertainment	www.massive.se
MCV	www.mcvuk.com
Microsoft Corporation	www.microsoft.com
Midway	www.midway.com
Mythic Entertainment	www.mythicentertainment.com
Namco Bandai Games America	www.namcobandaigames.com
Natsume	www.natsume.com
NCsoft	www.plaync.com
Nexus Entertainment	www.nexusent.com
Neversoft Entertainment	www.neversoft.com
Nintendo of America, Inc.	www.nintendo.com
Novalogic, Inc.	www.novalogic.com
Oddworld Inhabitants	www.oddworld.com
Orbital Frog Production	www.orbitalfrog.com
Pandemic Studios	www.pandemicstudios.com
Prima Games	www.primagames.com
Radical Entertainment	www.radical.ca
Real Time Worlds	www.realtimeworlds.com
Rebellion	www.rebellion.co.uk
Red Mile Entertainment	www.redmileentertainment.com
Rockstar Software	www.rockstar.com
SEGA of America	www.sega.com
Sierra Entertainment	www.sierra.com

NAME	WEBSITES
Sigil Games Online	www.sigilgames.com
Simutronics Corporation	www.play.net
SNK PLAYMORE USA CORP.	www.snkplaymoreusa.com
Sony Computer Entertainment America, Inc.	www.playstation.com
Sony Online Entertainment	www.soe.sony.com
Square Enix	www.square-enix.com
Superscape.com	www.superscape.com
Swordfish Studios	www.swordfishstudios.com
Take-Two Interactive Software, Inc.	www.take2games.com
Tantalus Interactive	www.tantalus.com.au
Tecmo, Inc.	www.tecmogames.com
THQ	www.thq.com
Thunderbird Games	www.thunderbirdgames.com
TimeGate Studios	www.timegate.com
Tips & Tricks Magazine	www.tipstricks.com
Treyarch	www.treyarch.com
Turbine, Inc.	www.turbine.com
Ubisoft Entertainment	www.ubisoftgroup.com
UGO Networks, Inc.	www.UGO.com
Vicarious Vision	www.vvisions.com
Vivendi Games	www.vivendigames.com
VMC Game Labs	www.vmcgamelabs.com
Volition	www.volition-inc.com
WildTangent, Inc.	www.wildtangent.com
Ziff Davis Media	www.ziffdavis.com

3

GAME JOBS

Okay, so here's the meat of the book, where we tell you about a whole slew of jobs in the video game industry. Actually, it's where real video game professionals tell you about them. We just cleaned up their spelling and stuck in a bunch of quotation marks while downing margaritas.

You could skip directly to the jobs that interest you most, but we suggest reading all the chapters to see if you come across that perfect job, which may turn out to be one you hadn't even thought of. Also, we worked really hard on this stuff, doing way more research than we thought we were going to have to do (after we drank all those margaritas, which didn't help) and scientifically infusing hilarity into each and every page.[1] But you know what? Read it however you want. It's yours now!

---

1. Well, most pages. The Audio Artist chapter's a little light on the yucks, especially after our editors removed our wacky sidebar on creating the perfect fart sound and banned the use of the word [CENSORED].

*Game Designer * Creative Consultant * Creative Manager
Lead Designer*

THE BIG IDEA: GAME DESIGN
How to get paid to play with game concepts and ideas.
Becoming a video game designer.

"See first that the design is wise and just: that ascertained, pursue it resolutely; do not for one repulse forego the purpose that you resolved to effect."
—William Shakespeare[2]

"Design is not just what it looks like and feels like. Design is how it works."
—Steve Jobs

GAME DESIGN IS WHERE IT ALL BEGINS,

where every video game is conceived and nurtured in a womb of brainstorming sessions and "blue sky" planning.[3] Design documents are a formative game's DNA, spelling out in precise detail how every facet should develop and come together to form a perfect, beautiful whole. And then the real world intrudes, and it's a constant struggle to keep it all from going to hell.

Game design requires a deep passion for games and a comprehensive knowledge of the best games out there. Even more important than that is knowing what exactly makes those games so great, what separates the great from the good, the good from the mediocre, and the "holy crap, that's god-awful!" from the merely poorly designed and executed.

One thing that game design does *not* require is specialized technical skill. You don't need a background in art or programming or scriptwriting to be a game designer, although none of those could hurt. So if you're someone who's full of ideas for games, and if you're constantly thinking of ways to improve the ones that you play, this might be the job for you.

We've rounded up more than a half dozen game designers with wide varieties of experience, from those just starting out to those who were dreaming up games back in the days when a line attached to a square was commonly understood to be a knight holding a sword.

A Day in the Life

Because every game starts with the designers, most designers are full-time employees of a game development company, or at least exclusively contracted freelancers. Doing design work for more than one company simultaneously is both a big no-no and a surefire recipe for career suicide. Working on small outside projects unrelated to game design is generally acceptable, but you'd better clear it with your producer first. Even if your other work isn't a conflict of interest, they might not be thrilled with anything that diverts your attention from the full-time commitment of game design.[4]

And because game design requires that you coordinate with all the other creative departments, from art to programming, most developers prefer that their designers work in the office, rather than from home. Michael Becker, a creative consultant for THQ's World Wrestling Entertainment franchise, is one of the few exceptions to this rule, but he's been in the business for over 20 years and has a list of credentials longer than your arm.[5] Once you can count *The Lord of the*

---

2. From *The Tempest*. Thanks, Middlebury College! Your six-figure tuition now seems like a bargain!

3. A term derived from the illusion of an open horizon's limitlessness. Also, it's the last time most designers will get to leave the office and see the sun before the production cycle takes over their lives.

4. Fortunately, they are legally prohibited from physically chaining you to your desk.

5. And we don't care how long your arms are. It's a very long list.

Rings, *Harry Potter*, and *Madden* on your résumé, you might be entitled to the same flexibility. Until then, we expect you in the office at 8:00 a.m. sharp.[6]

TELECOMMUTING

It's becoming increasingly more common for development studios and publishers to contract out work to third-party animators, modelers, scriptwriters, and the like. And with many jobs, this makes sense. If you spend the majority of your day working alone on a specific aspect of the game, it's not a big deal if you're working from home.

But game design is a different beast entirely. Sometimes instant messaging and conference calls and e-mail aren't good enough substitutes for a good old-fashioned face-to-face meeting. If you're considering a career in game design, be prepared to work on-site. If you somehow manage to land a design job that doesn't require you to work from an office, offer up a prayer of thanks to whatever deity you recognize. And don't screw it up.

Design titles are generally straightforward and tend to describe exactly what the job entails. A **lead designer** (sometimes called a *design lead*) manages the design team and coordinates design and development with the heads of the other departments. Oli Clark Smith, a lead designer with Circle Studio, spends his time "writing design documentation, implementing gameplay in levels, managing the team, and discussing the project with the relevant people in other teams to communicate my design."

Working directly under the lead designer are the other designers, whose titles often have an adjective that describes their relative positions on the totem pole. A **senior designer,** such as Dan Teasdale of Harmonix Music Systems, wears many of the same hats as a lead designer, and in some companies, the two positions are synonymous. Nick Dry is a **designer** who plans and implements game mechanics and double-checks each new build of the game, "playing through the product to make sure everything should be as we have suggested."

Christa Morse is a **junior game designer** at Pronto Games, but because she works for a smaller company, she takes on many more responsibilities than her title suggests: "I do a wide variety of design-related tasks, ranging from constructing levels (all aspects—building, scripting, placing spawners, etc.) to creating game design documents and pitches, attending production meetings, and more. I handle design-related questions on projects from producers, programmers, artists, and QA testers."

Sometimes game designers specialize in specific elements of game design, such as Derek Daniels, who is a senior designer in charge of combat design at Sony Computer Entertainment America. You might have heard of a little title he worked on, the critically-acclaimed smash-hit *God of War*. His fingerprints can be found in all of the combat elements of the game, including the boss battles and

---

6. Or at least by 10:00. This is the video game industry, after all.

AI scenarios. As a senior designer, he's also responsible for communicating with the rest of the development team. "The most important aspect of the job is communicating with each department so that everyone knows what is going on."

Straddling the line between design and production, Bryan Williams is an **associate creative manager** who is part of the team that creates and documents gameplay features for a major sports game franchise. However, he also works closely with the PR and marketing departments on media coverage, "among a bazillion other things."

In any game design job, you can count on never knowing exactly what you'll have to deal with from one week to the next. Complex gameplay features that you're sure will need heavy guidance might wind up being implemented without a fuss, while the simplest aspect of a game might turn out to be an unexpected nightmare. As Dan Teasdale puts it, "Generally, my responsibilities are all focused around making sure the game is fun and making sure the team as a whole is all on the same page in terms of our direction. But the day to day [usually] doesn't share much resemblance to what happened the day or week before."

SUMMARY

Game designers are usually exclusively contracted to a single company and work on one game at a time. They usually work from an office, unless their résumé earns them some latitude or they gnaw their own leg off and escape from their shackles.

Game designers conceive every aspect of gameplay, and they work together with the other departments to implement it and make sure it works. Their specific day-to-day tasks are often unpredictable.

The Good, the Bad, and the Ugly

Being a game designer has plenty of perks, not the least of which is having the opportunity to bring your concepts to life on game consoles across the world. However, like most "dream jobs," there are plenty of nightmare aspects to it as well.

PAYMENT FOR PLAYMENT

Game designer salaries vary, depending on the person's experience level, their position on the design team, and the game being designed. If you're the lead designer on a blockbuster holiday release, you'll take home a much larger Christmas bonus (to the family you never see) than will a junior game designer working on an obscure game for a small company.

The typical starting salary for an entry-level game designer is about $40,000 per year. Senior and lead designers can expect to top out in the high five figures, around $80,000. These figures can also vary, depending on things like the cost of living in the studio's community and how well you negotiate when the job is offered to you.

IT'S ALIVE! ALIVE!

Most game designers count the excitement of creation as the major perk of the job, the Frankensteinesque thrill when the switch is flipped and the game comes to life. "Obviously, the best part of the job is that you get to make video games," says Derek Daniels. "I mean that in all seriousness. You get to be part of pop culture, and it's a wonderful feeling, after the game is done and published, to see how people react and what fun things they found that you didn't even plan on."

Dan Teasdale says that "the best part of this job is when the team achieves 'critical mass' on something. These are the moments where something comes online for the first time, and everyone in the office congregates around the programmer/designer/artist that was working on it and plays with the new feature on their machines. It's such a morale boost and buzz to see these things that you've theorized about not only alive, but also capturing the imagination of your peers and critics."

Bryan Williams echoes that sentiment: "Coming up with new ideas for the game is without a doubt the best part of my job. It's equally challenging and fun at the same time."

Design veteran Michael Becker has seen games grow in complexity over the years, with development teams growing exponentially larger with every new generation of hardware. And with larger teams comes the reality that it's increasingly more difficult for a single designer to have their vision fully realized. "So many hands touch the work before it is finished," he says. But that doesn't dim his enthusiasm one bit: "When the general spark that inspired the vision is finally seen in an interactive product, then there is a tremendous sense of satisfaction."

If you're a team-oriented person, game design can be incredibly rewarding. "I enjoy pushing my ideas and convincing the team that they will actually work and then seeing them implemented and being proved right," says Oli Clark Smith. Michael Lubker, designer and founder of Zeolite Studios, explains it well, "The best parts of the job are getting to make neat things happen, and getting to connect with neat people."

And whatever else you might say about the job, it certainly isn't dull. "I don't feel like my job is repetitive," says Christa Morse. "And since I have several projects running simultaneously, I can easily switch gears if I get bored or stuck with one task and still remain productive."

LATE HOURS AND REALITY CHECKS

Very, very few of the best jobs in the video game industry are nine-to-five gigs, and game design is no exception. Because most game designers are salaried employees, they don't get paid overtime for working above and beyond the eight-hour work day.[7] "This job demands long hours," says Bryan Williams, who typically works up to 14 hours a day. Fifty- to sixty-hour weeks are common in game design, and the days only get longer as milestones draw near.[8] For a single person, this can lead to a reduced social schedule. For family men and women, the pressure's even worse. As Oli Clark Smith puts it, "Coming home at five in the morning is a surefire way of getting into trouble with loved ones."

THAT'S GOLD, JERRY! SOLID GOLD!

Dan Teasdale shares the following anecdote about a particularly low point in his career: "At a previous developer I was working at, our lead designer decided to leave mid-project to dance around the world and become an Internet dancing sensation.

"Our business director decided that, since he played games, he would be the perfect person to take his place. His vision for our destruction-focused game was to add a stealth mechanic in. Why? Because he loved the *Thief* series of games, and wanted to do the same thing here. Any designer will tell you that putting a stealth mechanic into a game that's balanced and geared around lots of enemies coming at you and a player character that can level city blocks probably isn't going to be easy to make fun or entertaining; however, we had to struggle with it for a year before the higher-ups realized what was going on and fired him.

"While we did manage to recover the project and release something that we were proud of, that year could have been used expanding the core vision of the game instead of trying to make someone's random ideas work with a design vision. If we had hired a person who was thinking about the design mechanics rather than "cool game ideas," that year could have also been used making this title a critical success in terms of design."

Derek Daniels laments the necessary evils of milestones, describing them as a "dog and pony show once a month just to make sure that everyone gets paid. This relationship seems to be slowly changing, but it is still one of the worst things about the video game industry as a whole." He also wishes that games didn't spend so long in development. "*God of War* was three years in the making! That's a long time to spend working on the same project."

The unpredictability and dynamic nature of game design can keep you from being bored, but it can also pull you in a thousand directions at once and burn you out. "Getting swamped with stuff is not the most fun thing, especially when it happens at midnight," says Michael Lubker. And because the designer is so central to the development process, everyone who comes to them with a question or request gets the same deadline as a response: ASAP.

---

7. Most are compensated with "comp time," extra vacation time that can be cashed in when the dev cycle slows down a bit.

8. Milestones are waypoints along the development cycle that measure whether the dev team is on schedule or not.

When you're depending upon a large development team with diverse personalities, interpersonal conflict is inevitable. You might have a great idea for a gameplay feature, and you know the programming team can implement it with minimal fuss, but you just can't sell them on it, no matter how hard you try. That's when things get ugly, and you've got only two options: Grit your teeth and drop your killer idea (something no designer ever wants to do) or lean on the code monkeys and make them do your bidding, an equally unpleasant route. "The worst part [of the job] is trying to communicate new ideas to negative team members who don't agree with you," says Oli Clark Smith. "Having to pull rank and just tell them to do it isn't nice and leads to substandard work."

But the worst part of any designer's job comes when outside forces that are completely out of the designer's control encroach on the development process and sabotage the project they've sunk their blood, sweat, and tears into. Usually these forces are financial in nature and imposed by management due to a lack of funding or a need to ship the product to meet the end of a fiscal year.

"There are several bad things that a designer can hear," says Michael Becker. "Most of them don't lead to a really happy outcome. Examples include: 'We are going to have to scope the game down. Way down.' Or: 'The executives met yesterday and they want us to make some major changes.' Or: 'We're going to have to bring the schedule in, and we're going to have to cut features.' Or: 'We've just had a reduction of force.'" At that point, the designer's job goes from dreaming up cool new concepts and getting them into the game to performing triage on the project and salvaging whatever they can.

SUMMARY

The best parts of being a game designer are taking a game from concept to reality, working with (and being central to) a team, and the unpredictability and variety of the work. Drawing a steady paycheck is also a nice perk.

The downsides of game design are the long hours, the hectic schedule, the creative differences, and having to gut your own project when management's priorities shift—which is kind of like having to decide which of your child's legs is more expendable.

Take This Job and Love It

You've made it this far, and *game designer* still sounds like a pair of words you'd like to have on your business card. Now's the time to take a look at what it takes to land the job.

EDUCATION

Many game designers have a four-year undergraduate degree, but it's uncommon for them to do graduate studies. Most designers have at least some college under their belts. Being able to attend a school where there's a course of study in game development is probably the best possible academic preparation you can have, but don't expect book-learnin' alone to prepare you. "Right now, there's no degree that I've seen that relates to what a designer would do at a professional studio," says Dan Teasdale. "They don't teach the core tenets of design—mainly because we're still establishing them as an industry."

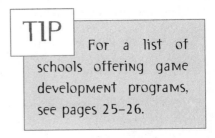

TIP For a list of schools offering game development programs, see pages 25–26.

Game design requires so many different elements that anything you study can come in handy for someone. History majors might find that they're attractive candidates for a company that specializes in historical strategy games. The critical skills that come with a bachelor's degree in fine art or film will be put to good use in game design. And being able to communicate effectively via the spoken and written word means that your English major might not have been as big a waste of money as you thought.[9] "For a designer, I would suggest either a strong computer science background or a strong English literature background," says Derek Daniels.

But if you're in the right place at the right time and have enough to offer a developer, you might be able to land a game design job with only a high school degree. Oli Clark Smith did, but he also extols the virtues of more specialized post-secondary education: "There are a number of game design college courses available, and these are the best academic preparation for the job," he says. "Reading as much game design theory as possible also helps, as well as playing as many games as possible as much as possible."[10]

PRIOR EXPERIENCE

Many game designers start out in QA as testers. That's how Oli Clark Smith, Christa Morse, and Bryan Williams all got their start in game design. But simply holding the job wasn't enough: "I worked as a tester for a little over a year," says Williams, "and throughout that time, I was fortunate enough to have met and made good impressions on the right people. People within the company recognized my hard work and dedication and offered me my current position."

Nick Dry broke into game design in an almost storybook way: "I designed and pitched a product to a game developer who saw potential and gave me a shot at it." He counts his portfolio of previous work as his most important asset when going for the job, something Morse seconds.

One of the items in Dan Teasdale's portfolio was a *Quake* mod: "It wasn't a mod that anyone would know. In fact, it was just a simple weapons-only mod-

9. Seriously, Middlebury. Total bargain.
10. You were waiting to hear someone say that, weren't you?

ification that about three people downloaded. But the mod was the thing that sealed the deal. It showed not only that I could complete something, but it also communicated my design strengths and my abilities in other fields."

And Derek Daniels' history proves that any experience in the video game industry looks good on an aspiring designer's résumé: "Prior to getting my game design job, I was also contributing to strategy guides for a few large publishers. This helped create a few contacts that would have been extremely hard to obtain otherwise."

DON'T BURN BRIDGES

The video game industry is smaller than you think, and people have long memories. It's very likely that the impression you make on them will affect your career—for better or for worse—for a long time to come. According to Michael Becker, "It is always a mistake to burn bridges or make enemies. You never know which logo you will be standing under at the next trade show." Christa Morse agrees: "Don't burn bridges. The game industry is a surprisingly small world."

There's a reason game professionals hold grudges, and it's not entirely because of the abuse they suffered at the hands of larger children during adolescence. The process of game development is so frantic and stressful and interdependent that if the wrong person snaps or walks off the job or is just simply a pain to deal with, they might jeopardize the whole project. Developers also don't have to deal with unprofessionalism, because the demand for game design jobs is always high. So be a professional at all times, even when you don't think that the favor is being returned.

Prior game design experience is the best possible thing you can have on a résumé, especially if you're looking for non-entry-level design jobs. And obviously, the prestige of the products you've previously designed counts for a great deal. "Having them be big sellers is always a plus," says Michael Becker. "Your track record counts." However, even if you don't have prior video game experience, any employment experience in the entertainment or pop-culture field can make you a more attractive candidate for a job in game design. You might even find that previous work experience that you never thought would translate to the video game world is actually just what your prospective employer is looking for. "Comic books, illustration, board game design, ad agency writing, and print pre-production are all useful background skills that help me do a better job," says Becker. Derek Daniels agrees, "Being a video game designer in particular is perhaps the most abstract job in the video game industry right now. For a programmer, it easy to say they need to have a strong background in programming. For an artist, it's easy to look at their portfolio and see how good they are. But for a designer it is much more esoteric."

NETWORKING

"Almost every designer I know has come into the industry through a different door," says Derek Daniels. "However, the one common anecdote in all of the stories is, 'I knew this one guy who knew about an opening....'"

Yes, as with most video game jobs, networking is vital to getting your game design career off the ground. "Meet all the game developers you can meet," stresses Michael Lubker. Creating and maintaining positive professional relationships with game producers or anyone else on a dev team is the best networking you can possibly do when going for a design gig.

Even if you don't know someone on the development team, you might know someone who does, if you've been networking well enough. Dan Teasdale made good use of "the interconnectedness of everyone in the games industry. Even though I was in Australia and they were on the East Coast of the United States, there were still people with one or two degrees of separation between us that could not only vouch for me, but also provide me with the real working conditions at the company."

Industry events are a golden opportunity to meet professionals to network with. Christa Morse found that the Game Developer's Conference (GDC) gave her the best chance to network with other professionals. But in the end, she didn't make her most valuable connections at industry events. "Ultimately, it was networking I'd done on my own that landed me my job."

Certain professional organizations can help too. After founding his own game development company, Michael Lubker discovered that membership in the International Game Developers Association (IGDA) opened doors for him.

SKILLS

A good game designer must be able to thoroughly deconstruct a game and understand why and how it works—or doesn't. "You need to be able to look at a game and quickly identify its fundamentals and what makes it tick," says Oli Clark Smith. "Being able to analyze and pick apart games is a must." Christa Morse sums it up as "having a solid understanding of what's fun."

Because a game designer has to deal with every other department directly, it's also important that they have strong organization and communication skills. "Communication skills, both written and verbal, are key to this industry," says Bryan Williams. "It's imperative that you be able to translate your thoughts and ideas to paper. That's what a design document is. You brainstorm a really terrific idea and then create a document so that others can read it and comprehend exactly what it is you had envisioned."

"But most of all," says Michael Becker, "you have to embrace your own creative nature and trust in it at all times."

OTHER ADVICE

If you're going to attempt a career in game design, perseverance is the most valuable quality you can have. This is one of the most competitive jobs in the industry, and you must pay some dues if you want to land it. "In this business, you often have to start at the bottom and work your way up," says Bryan Williams. "I won't lie to you—it sucks! But if you make the most of your time at the bottom and absorb as much knowledge as possible and have the necessary drive to succeed, you will."

THE GOOD ONES BORROW, THE GREAT ONES STEAL

No good idea ever comes from a vacuum. Concepts are based on concepts that were based on other concepts, and so on. There's no shame in lifting a good idea from another game for use in your own. It all comes down to how (and how well) you do it.

Ripping off an existing game wholesale and making a seemingly major but ultimately irrelevant change to it is lazy and gutless. If you're not going to improve on *Grand Theft Auto*, don't just change the setting to Mars in the year 2350 and expect that gamers will be satisfied with stealing hoverbikes and beating up space hookers.

But if you've played *GTA* and taken it apart in your mind and broken down what makes an open-ended game work and what its limitations are and how you can incorporate these concepts into the title you're developing, you're starting to understand how a real game designer thinks. And we need more of you.

A detailed knowledge of the game's subject matter is critical for success. Being able to list the signature moves of every professional wrestler from the last decade might get you kicked out of fancy cocktail parties, but it might be exactly what you need to get a WWE video game design job. "The important thing is to always do your homework on any project you get involved with," says Michael Becker. "Assume you are going to have to conduct a master's thesis worth of research before you can make valuable contributions. Otherwise you're probably just copying what others have done before you."

Don't be inflexible and assume there's only one way to design games. The design process, structure, and titles vary from company to company, and even within the same company; no two games ever go through the exact same development process. "From my experience, every company has their own working practices," says Nick Dry. "It's what you bring to the table that helps."

That being said, even if you've never held a design job, get all the information you can about it and practice the skills you'll need. That's what Christa Morse did: "With the help of various mentors, I started writing down my own game ideas and shaping them into something similar to real-world design documents." Even though those games never got beyond the design stage, Morse was able to use them to prove that she could get the job done.

And this can't be stressed heavily enough: know your games. "Play as many games as you can and quote mechanics and features from them when you are describing your ideas," says Oli Clark Smith. Having a wealth of game knowledge "immediately puts you at a massive advantage in discussions."

Of course, there's always the chance that your job will crush your love of games. It's a tough business. The hours are long, and the danger of burnout is real. Think twice before turning your hobby into your full-time job. Or, as Nick Dry says, "Don't do it! Go out and get a proper job. Don't go to college to study games; play games to relax."

But Michael Becker is a little more optimistic: "You have to follow your passion. Game design should be regarded as an art form, and one who practices it should be ready for a lot of emotional ups and downs along the way. But at the end of the day, doing good work and making good friends in the trenches is more important than collecting trophies on the wall. Remember that human existence is really about living a fulfilling life, and this particular field allows you to help entertain others through mass-market communication in the process. Believe it or not, it's a big responsibility. Don't let your ego get in the way."

SUMMARY

Most designers have at least some postsecondary education. Having gone to college, period, is more important than what you studied.

QA testing is an effective in for game design, as are just about any other jobs in the video game industry. A portfolio of quality amateur work also helps.

Network thoroughly and be ready to pay some dues. Know the subject matter of the games you're hoping to design.

Conclusion

If you want to get a job in game design, learn as much as you can about everything, especially games. Think about how and why they work, and figure out what exactly makes them fun. Network like a fiend and snap up any entry-level video game job possible—all of it looks good on the résumé. Once you get your shot, you're the one who must come up with the big ideas, communicate them effectively to the people who will be implementing them, and follow through to make sure that everything works. Be ready for long hours, butting of heads, and a job that changes day to day.

HANDS ON, NECK DEEP: TECHNICAL JOBS

How to Get Paid to Play with Long Strings of Numbers, Long Strings of Repetitive Days, and Possibly Long Strings of Obscenities

" Technical Jobs" is a wide umbrella that covers a lot of different career paths. Generally, the people under this category have a lot of hands-on time with the inner workings of a game...caffeine shaking, cheese-puff stained hands-on time. The range of skill level can be wild, too. Programmers are strange savants who know how to link together letters and numbers that will create digital, realistically bouncing breasts, amongst other things. Testers are maniacally persistent gamers who can concentrate on playing one game so hard for so long it's a wonder they can't simply move control sticks with their minds.

And there are divisions within those categories explored in this section. So if you're looking to get neck-deep in code, or neck-deep in running characters into walls for weeks on end, perhaps a technical job is for you.

*Programmer * Quality Assurance * Technical Director * Engineer Tester * QA Manager*

GET WITH THE PROGRAM: THE TECHNICAL DEPARTMENT

How to Get Paid to Play with Game Engines and Complex Calculations: Becoming Part of the Technical Team

"A programmer is a person who passes as an exacting expert on the basis of being able to turn out, after innumerable punching, an infinite series of incomprehensive answers calculated with micrometric precisions from vague assumptions based on debatable figures taken from inconclusive documents and carried out on instruments of problematical accuracy by persons of dubious reliability and questionable mentality for the avowed purpose of annoying and confounding a hopelessly defenseless department that was unfortunate enough to ask for the information in the first place."

—*IEEE Grid newsmagazine*[1]

"Pessimists, we're told, look at a glass containing 50% air and 50% water and see it as half-empty. Optimists, in contrast, see it as half-full. Engineers, of course, understand the glass is twice as big as it needs to be."

—*Bob Lewis*[2]

"Be nice to nerds. Chances are you'll end up working for one."

—*Bill Gates*[3]

"There's an old android saying which I feel is particularly relevant to this situation. It goes, '0010101011010010110100111100101010100101011000101010,' which, roughly translated, means, 'Don't stand around jabbering when your life is in dang...hey, wait for me, you guys!

—*Kryten*[4]

---

1. This magazine follows one of the first grammatical rules: "i" before "eee" except after "c."
2. Bob Lewis offers an advice line at weblog.infoworld.com/lewis.
3. Whereas, if you're nice to geeks, expect to listen to a rambling diatribe on which Doctor Who's assistant was the most useful *and* a badass. It's got to be Leela, really, hasn't it?
4. Any *Red Dwarf* fans in the house? No? Then smeg off.

DO YOU CONSISTENTLY WOW (OR WORRY)

your parents with precise and calculated answers to seemingly impossible equations? Are the hardest Sudoku puzzles a joyful diversion during English class? Are you currently learning computer programming and taking your work home with you? Are you able to survive on a steady diet of pizza and soda? Can you arrange those derelict pizza boxes and soda cans into an interesting edifice that surrounds your desk so that the rest of the real world can leave you alone to (a) finish painting your Citadel miniatures or (b) knock out that final code to the MUD[5] you're completing in Fortran?[6] Then you should be thinking about a career in video game programming.

We put out a call to anyone with a technical background in the video game industry and amassed over 20 responses from programmers of every type. There are software developers and technical directors who speak about grand schemes and how the programmers interact with the less-geeky members of the team. And there are a range of quality assurance folks, or "testers" as most people call them, to tell us what it's like to be on the first rung of the video game career ladder.

Let's start with the technical stuff first, though, shall we?

LET'S NOT GET TECHNICAL FOR A SECOND

C++.[7] Renderware.[8] Game Engines.[9] We're not here to explain the intricacies of game programming; we're here to show what it's like being a programmer, and the mind-set you need to be one. We'll give some clues so nonprogramming types can cross this career off their list, but if you're headed for a programming job, some vague definitions of Lisp,[10] Haskell,[11] and Miranda[12] we stole from Wikipedia just aren't necessary. We're writers, not programmers, you know.

---

5. Look, if we have to tell you that MUD stands for Multi User Dungeon, and then explain that these are text-based adventures that eventually paved the way for *Elder Scrolls: Oblivion*, then you're obviously reading the wrong book.

6. Fortran is a general-purpose, procedural, imperative programming language that is especially suited to numeric computation and scientific computing. Invented in the 1950s, it's good for a laugh.

7. C++: An object-oriented programming (OOP) language that is viewed by many as the best language for creating large-scale applications.

8. Renderware: A 3-D API (application programming interface) and graphics-rendering engine developed by Criterion Software.

9. Game Engine: A core software component that simplifies development, like Renderware.

10. Lisp: A family of computer programming languages that began in the 1950s, originally for artificial intelligence research.

11. Haskell: A standardized, purely functional programming language with nonstrict semantics. We'd elaborate, but our brains would explode.

12. Miranda: The first purely functional language intended as a commercial tool, rather than for academic purposes.

A Day in the Life

Once you've learned the language of computers, which is a bit like coding in HTML but several billion times more complex, and you've won over your video game studio interviewer with some hilarious banter about the perils of Assembly language and landed a job as a programmer, what do you do all day?

CODE MONKEY BUSINESS: THE PROGRAMMER

When Richard Fine worked as a junior programmer at Rebellion Software, his job consisted of "programming tasks. In the strictest sense, my 'responsibility' [was] to do the jobs my lead [told] me to do; these usually [involved] writing new code or modifying existing code, both from the game engine and the tools used by the development team. Examples of specific tasks [included] rewriting the particle system in SSE assembly to make it more performant, modifying the model tools to export geometry in a compressed format, and creating a build fingerprinting tool." Got that? Because if you're only pretending to know what a "build fingerprinting tool" is, it might be time to hit the books.

Being brought on as a junior programmer, you're helping on the periphery of the programming team. In the case of Tamir Nadav, an associate programmer at KingsIsle Entertainment, her job includes "assisting the other programmers, and doing smaller tasks that aren't mission critical for the project." If you're Andy Firth, an engine programmer at Neversoft, your day might encompass the "management of code and systems mostly self-written, but in some cases written by other programmers." Then there's the "generation of schedule information for myself and other people (though I don't manage anyone)," not to mention the "design and implementation of new systems, optimization of existing systems, and research and development into new hardware, software, and algorithms."

If you're an animation programmer, such as Y Salmi of Evolution Studios, you're veering in a slightly different direction: "On a daily basis, [my job] consists of maintaining an updated list of features, bugs, and requests, dealing with various issues as they arise, planning for new features, implementing said features, fixing bugs, and assisting others in whichever ways possible."

But if you're working for a start-up or tiny company, such as David May of Spiral House Ltd., your plate is much bigger: "I tend to work on anything and everything. In the last year I have worked on things such as collision, gameplay, tools, exporter, etc. I guess my responsibilities are 'whatever needs doing, I give it a go.'"

For others, such as Leon Hartwig, a programmer at BottleRocket Entertainment, your job may take on a variety of roles such as "computer programming [and] software and systems design" or, as is the case for Peter Blackburn, graduate programmer at SEGA Driving Studios, "developing midlevel systems for the core technology group at the studio."

When you get to the middle-level programmer, or what Electronic Arts has christened "Programmer II," you're "somewhere between a 'code monkey' and a senior programmer," according to Michael Davies, a mid-level programmer at Eletronic Arts. "My duties involve taking responsibility for large chunks of programming work (e.g., developing a game subsystem such as AI or physics) under supervision of the project lead. Normally I would not have people working under me, but would work with other programmers at the lead's discretion."

Jason LaCroix, who is a specialized programmer and a software developer at Electronic Arts Montreal, cites the "development of new features and maintenance of existing software on a daily basis" as his reasons for getting up in the morning. When you've gained more experience and can claim the title of lead programmer, such as Paul Robinson of Neversoft, you can focus on "creating technical design, optimizing, profiling, planning budgets, assigning tasks, [and being] responsible for the overall architecture of the project."

Or there's the senior programmer, like Richard Crockford at Embyonic Studios, whose responsibilities are like Paul's, only greater and less focused. For example, Richard is "responsible for improving and maintaining the game engine, in particular the platform-specific functionality. On a day-to-day basis, this means covering widely different areas depending on what needs doing for the current project. I generally work mostly on graphics and rendering, but collision, physics, level loading, sound, and even gameplay are also significant parts of my role." At this level of programming, you'll likely be dabbling in everything.

Richard's role of overseeing a particular platform is similar to those often taken on by freelance programmers, who make up a small portion of the overall talent pool. For many companies, once their main console games are almost ready, they call in freelancers, such as lead programmer Rune Braathen, who's currently "designing and implementing the DS version of a well-known SKU."[13] There's a healthy market for talented folk who can work at home, on the slightly less complete port-overs (a game on a certain console that's not as finished as the same game on another console) of your favorite video games.

TECHNICALLY BRILLIANT: THE DIRECTOR

Do most senior members of technical development enjoy their jobs? They do. Jamie Fristrom,[14] a technical director at Torpex Games, whose previous work included *Spider-Man 2* and *Tony Hawk*, has even more hats to wear: "Since we're a start-up, I do whatever I can to help bootstrap the company. Lately, that's been helping pitch documents and going to pitch meetings; showing publishers that we have the technical chops to tackle the projects they might give us; evaluating technology and middleware; and even getting homebrew code running on my PSP so we can have something to demo."

---

13. SKU means "stock keeping unit" but has taken on a wider meaning in recent years and now encompasses anything from "a game" to a "game on a particular platform."
14. Whose current plans are to work "on a next-generation console and handheld game involving great big guns," which is pretty much the most splendid job advertisement ever.

IN THE PINK: PART 1—WHAT A TECHNICAL DIRECTOR DOES ALL DAY

Chris Pink is the technical director for HB Studios, a Canadian arm of Electronic Arts. He is partly responsible for their cricket, rugby, and street soccer games. Here's the list he made, most of which he gets done before lunch:

1. Check up on the status of all projects.
2. Hire and fire people in the engineering and networking departments.
3. Deal with the publisher on any technical issues.
4. Prepare and deliver yearly assessments, including deciding on any pay raises and bonuses that are to be handed out.
5. Obtain and maintain developer status on any and all platforms we have interest in.
6. Decide the technical direction the company should move in. Generate own tech, use middleware, [decide] which source control software to use (Perforce, Subversion, etc.), and so on.
7. Write feasibility reports for management meetings with regards to potential projects.
8. Travel to local universities and colleges when asked to promote the company. This is lately also entailing the assisting in preparing courses that will turn out better candidates for our company.
9. Be one of the public faces of the company. In this regard I've been on local television and in a local magazine and the local newspaper recently.
10. Teach and mentor. As the staff grows, my ability to do this has reduced but it's still something I enjoy (I have 26 people I manage these days).
11. Assist in the debugging and coding of our projects. Again, this has been greatly reduced because of our growth, but I still do it from time to time. But also again it's something I like to do and something that my experience helps me do better than most of my current staff.

Once Torpex Games becomes Seattle's newest powerhouse dev studio, Jamie's role should stabilize into what he's trained to become: "responsible for the quality and timeliness of engineering at Torpex. To that end, I'm responsible for recruiting, interviewing, and testing programmers; I help make decisions on what middleware and third-party technology to use; choose and create the processes which the company follows in its engineering efforts; decide which programmer attacks what problem; lay down the guidelines for how code is written; and probably a bunch of other stuff that I'm forgetting right now."

But there are some things Jamie just won't do: "I won't look at every programmer's code and give feedback—I'll maybe do a spot check here and there, but we hire people who are so good, that kind of micromanaging isn't necessary."[15]

Mark Fisher, a technical director at MAD 4 Games, illuminates his role in "programming, technology design, and implementation." He is also a bit of a bookworm: "I do lots of reading to keep up-to-date with current trends and technologies."

Paul Bonner, a technical director at Streamline Studios, has a similar role, but he relies more on acronyms: "I manage the coders in the company, as well as evaluating [the] SDK,[16] writing TDD[17] for all game ideas, [and] doing risk reports on game designs from a technical point of view." Streamline Studios is also an interesting development in the industry, as they work on their own games but are also part of the flourishing "content providers" who create buildings, weapons, vehicles, and characters for other companies.

JUST ANOTHER DAY (AND NIGHT) AT THE OFFICE

With all this highly technical work going on, you'd expect everyone to be on site, with the ability to quickly team up and talk about problems. And you'd mostly be right. Freelancing, the ability to roll out of bed and straight into the latest bug-fixing lists, is a skill developer studios would prefer you did at the office. "In theory, you *could* [work at home]," says Richard Fine, "but the lack of 'face time' with the rest of the team would have quite a negative impact on the speed and accuracy with which you could work."

Andy Firth does both, and at home, it's "via VPN,[18] which isn't common," but he's secured his computers and is trusted enough to take his work home with him. In practice, however, this is very rare.

---

15. If your first programming job involves some man peering over your shoulder while you work, prodding you, it's either the janitor taking an unhealthy interest in your collection of *Space Channel 5* memorabilia, or it's the technical director making sure you're actually competent. If he keeps this up, *and* you're competent, it might be time to look for other work. Usually your competence is thoroughly tested during the interviews for the job.

16. SDK (software development kit): includes programs to aid in the development of a particular console, and usually comes with full-on development stations, but most testers use "debug" versions of the final console: The PlayStations were bright blue. The GameCubes were turquoise. The PlayStation 2s looked the same but with "Test" written on the side. The Xbox debug was green, like the limited-edition Halo Xbox. And the Xbox 360s have a large hard drive bulging out of the top, but otherwise look the same. Fascinating, eh?

17. TDD (test-driven development), also known as "prebugging" instead of "debugging"; it basically (and theoretically) removes loads of bugs before the game goes to testing.

18. VPN: virtual private network

"It's theoretically possible to work from home, with a PC borrowed from work and communicating over VPN. Plus, you would eventually need access to dev kits, and under no circumstances would you be allowed to take one home (although I have heard that this has happened at other companies)." Because if there's one thing liable to freak out a publisher, it's members of the team waddling off the premises with a working prototype of a game that's due out in six months.

Richard Crockford agrees: "Working from home with consoles is possible, but uncommon. While there's nothing inherently preventing it, moving dev kits can be awkward due to both technical issues and for reasons of security. Generally it's easier to work in an office unless you're only working on PC content or tools."

TIME TO PAY, OR TIME TO PLAY?

We think Y Salmi said it best when he explained his workload is "usually 45 hours a week, but during crunch periods, can vary from anywhere from 50 to 80." And the numbers we received from our respondents backed up this claim: around 75 percent of those polled usually worked between 40 to 50 hours on an average week. Around 15 percent were in the 30- to 40-hour range, but there were a few, usually more senior folks, who managed 50 to 60 or more. One poor guy consistently does more than 70 hours a week, but with some freelance thrown in, he's likely to be making enough money to pay the hospital bills for mental exhaustion.

So, you can take work home with you if there's extra coding to complete, and this is often the case, but the vast majority of work is done at the office. But when does this cool, calm collection of highly brilliant technicians turn into a mass of unwashed, grimy freaks with wild eyes, wilder hair, and the wildest odor? We're talking crunch time, folks, when schedules take a turn for the hectic, when "milestones"[19] have to be met. This depends, says Richard Fine, "100 percent on the project schedule. Things get busy the week before a milestone, and cool down afterward; and the baseline level ramps gradually up as the project nears completion."

"Every so often (around once a month) we have a hard-core week," says Andy Firth. "These are used to catch up on schedule issues and involve four 12-hour days followed by a normal Friday. During the release season (around August or September), there are more hard-core weeks, but nowhere near as many hours are worked at our company as with other companies."

Programmers aren't immune to the regulation times of year when the entire gaming industry freaks out—the weeks leading up to GDC, E[3], and the holiday season. "E[3] and other conferences are the busiest, because usually you need to make functional demos, and require a lot of crunch mode," says Tamir Nadav, enforcing this point.

---

19. *Milestones* is a term used to describe the stages in software development that must be met, on pain of death.

Y Salmi agrees, but adds there's also long hours "before deadlines such as [a game going] alpha [or] beta. Usually this is a two- to three-week busy period, but can be longer when approaching important deadlines. The slowest are after milestones, and at the beginning of a new project (or the first couple months after the end of one)."

But this schedule isn't the same for everyone. Peter Blackburn's biggest headaches occur "around prototyping time," a particular milestone he must hit. An anonymous lead programmer at a large game company concurs: "[The] busiest [times] are just prior to a product review and [are] least busy just afterward, while people recover."

And if you're working on cell-phone games, like Mark Fisher, "it really does vary. Given the nature of the mobile business, opportunities crop up all the time, and the time scales are quite short. So essentially all the time is our busiest time."

When you get to head your own department, there's a few extra layers of work that pile up, too. Chris Pink explains, "April is busy in that I do the yearly assessments then, so this means taking the budget that my department is given and deciding salary increases, bonus payments, etc. Reviewing the engineer's self-assessment form, generating my own based on my opinion of the employee and their assessment form, delivering that to them (I never look forward to these because invariably one or two will argue with you even if they don't have a leg to stand on)."

When embroiled in the game preproduction, the technical director also tries "to ensure the documentation delivered to the publisher is up to the quality expected from our company. Also determining the staffing for that project can take time, as does making the choices of if we upgrade the tech on a yearly title or not (very easy for current gen titles right now)."

IN THE PINK: PART 2—CHRIS GOES SHOPPING

What does Chris Pink do instead of sleeping during the most horrendous of deadlines? He attempts to have some semblance of a family life.

"The week leading up to when a milestone is due can get very hectic. Our worst milestone nights saw us going to work normally on Friday at 9:15 a.m. and not leaving work until 3:00 p.m. on Saturday afternoon. Personally, I went home, picked up the wife and kids, drove into the city to my in-laws, dropped off the kids, and went shopping. I wouldn't end up going to bed until past midnight [on Sunday morning]." We worked out that, assuming an hour's commute, with Chris getting up around 7:00 a.m. on the Friday, he worked a total of 30 hours straight, then took another 9 hours until bed. That sort of stamina would even impress an all-night raver with an addiciton to Bawls.

SUMMARY

- To become a programmer, it helps to love programming. In fact, it's pretty much vital.
- Programmers fiddle with code and compile lists; the number of ways this fiddling can occur is limitless.
- Junior programmers take orders from lead programmers or technical directors.
- Programmers also take orders from lead programmers or technical directors, then sometimes grumble about it afterward.
- There can be a wide variety of programmers with specific skill sets.
- There are a few freelance programmers out there, but they usually work on less-important versions of key software releases.
- You'll be taking your work home with you, but probably not the game that you're working on.
- Expect a 40- to 50-hour week, with a side-splittingly humorous increase in hours before milestones, trade shows, and when the game is about ready.

The Good, the Bad, and the Ugly

You're committed, aren't you? Assuming you're not continuing to read this section for the hilarious prose alone[20], and you're actually still considering making complex changes to lines of code your life's work, read on to discover how great, crappy, and odd all of this can be.

THE GOOD

What's the best part of being a programmer, then? For Junior Programmer Richard Fine, it was learning to cope with a lack of control: "You can make suggestions to the designers, but it's ultimately their call—so instead I choose to take pride in writing the best systems I can, given the requirements. Making some changes and discovering that you've halved the amount of space a level takes up in memory (thereby allowing the designers to pack that much more stuff in), or that the speed of a system has quadrupled, can give you a great sense of achievement. For tools work, it's always nice to get positive feedback from other people on the team— being told that what you've done has made someone else's job easier or more efficient can really make you feel like you've made a difference to the project."

This pride in being a small cog of a larger man-machine sometimes results in benefits as you prove yourself time and time again. Richard said, "There was also that one time my lead gave me a task that was just, 'We need a visual effect for this particular game mode. Go make something cool-looking with lots of shaders.' That was a fun week."

---

20. Sorry, we're all out of hilarious prose.

PAYMENT FOR PLAYMENT

We've gone online, spoken to dozens of folks, and figured out how much money you'll be accruing in the bank during the time most people leave work and go shopping. The results are rather interesting; entry-level candidates or those with less experience usually make between $40,000 to $60,000 a year, but after a couple of years, a "regular" code-monkey can expect an annual salary between $60,000 and $80,000. The senior guys make closer to $100,000, and once you hit director level, at least in the bigger companies making next-gen console titles, up that to $150,000. Or over $200,000...with enough experience and some damn fine titles under your belt.

If you're extremely technically minded, you'll probably really enjoy kicking around code. Andy Firth does. He says, "Being able to design and implement on code on [the] latest hardware is enough for me. I also *really* like optimizing, which is a *large* part of my job...I do what I love."

Peter Blackburn loves the cutting-edge nature of game programming, too: "Getting to work with the latest technology, which people will only get in a few years' time!" Our anonymous lead programmer loves the way the technical and creative processes combine: "This is not a nine-to-five job where you do mundane, repetitive tasks. You need to think and invent clever solutions to complicated problems under some serious time pressure. Oftentimes you need to work in areas you previously had no experience in, so you learn, and you learn a lot. This is not an industry where you can accept the status quo; you need to innovate and constantly push the limits."

Y Salmi agrees, and he should know—he works for Evolution Studios, which is deep in development on the PS3 game *MotorStorm*. "The freedom to innovate, working on bleeding edge hardware/software (this is a double-edged sword), and the camaraderie" are the best reasons for taking this job. "Depending on your position within a company, you will at times get a lot of flexibility on how to implement a solution to a given problem. In our company, we are trusted to come up with effective solutions. Large problems are discussed in groups, but individuals are trusted with solving problems in their areas. As long as things are coordinated properly, it gives us a lot of freedom to try new techniques and solutions to the challenges we encounter."

And as for the technology? "It's great to be able to work on the latest hardware. It is especially satisfying at the beginning of next-generation cycle. You get to work with hardware very few other people have seen yet. Personally, it's quite exciting. Of course, it's a double-edged sword in that with new hardware comes new problems [that] very few people have encountered. So it can become a struggle to work with the latest hardware and try to make sense of APIs[21], which are constantly changing, and hardware [that] is in flux."

One of Jamie Fristrom's greatest achievements came during his stay at Treyarch, working on *Spider-Man 2*: "[One of my] favorite parts of the job is when I actually see my ideas in the final game. A programmer can have lots of influence on the design of the games—sometimes it's up to us to prove that things are possible that nobody believes in. My favorite accomplishment in the games industry so far was back on *Spider-Man 2*; nobody believed that we could make a physics-based swinging system for Spider-Man that would still be controllable, so I went in and prototyped something and proved it could be done. It's a fantastic feeling to pull off something like that." And of course, when your game's done, published, and getting great reviews? "Finally seeing your game on the shelf, and seeing people buying it" is Paul Robinson's finest hour.

This feeling of accomplishment never wanes, but for technical directors like Chris Pink, "seeing another product shipped is always great, but for me these days the most enjoyment I get is from watching people I've hired into the company fresh from university get their feet under them, and then become solid (and sometimes spectacular) contributors to the company."

Another benefit from a job in programming, according to Tamir Nadav, is the fact that you're in the best industry around: "Being able to wake up in the morning and say 'I make video games.' Also, I work with some of the most creative and entertaining people in the world. Everyone else around me loves video games, too." Yes, job satisfaction is tremendously high in the world of video game programmers. Leon Hartwig, for example, thoroughly enjoys "the work, [the] good geographical location, the laid-back attitude, and perks as compared to other kinds of companies."

Your colleagues are likely to be one of the reasons you're working sometimes ludicrous hours. For Kain Shin of Breakway Games in Austin, Texas, "the best part of this job is the cross-mixing of people from all disciplines that run the spectrum from creative to technical in a perpetual state of R&D as they continue to push the envelope with every new project. This attracts a certain type of personality and is conducive to a high-energy creative atmosphere that you don't necessarily find outside the entertainment industry, because non-entertainment jobs are not always motivated by people's passions."

In fact, a team of like-minded individuals, plunging into passionate debate and overcoming obstacles in gaming development, is a huge part of many programmers' decisions to stay in the gaming industry. "This tends to be much stronger in small companies and small tightly knit teams, which is why I prefer working in them," says Richard Crockford. "The ability to have a laugh and generally relax with your colleagues is good for relieving stress, and without it the job starts to feel too much like a grind." For Michael Davies, his job is a mixture of entertaining work and positive reinforcement. There's a "fun atmos-

---

21. API (application programming interface): usually plug-ins showing how other functions interact. Still clueless? Try the chapter on working at a game store. Then read some programming books.

phere, being paid to play games; [there's also] decent pay, good people to work with, and [development of] a product that entertains people; and seeing feedback on websites, game stores, etc., is always positive."

After mentioning the usual reasons for liking his job, such as interactions with talented people, Jason LaCroix says, "We also get games for cheap, so that's an added bonus. All of the other perks are nice, too (i.e., stock options, bonuses, etc.)." Yes, some of the more gargantuan software corporations lay on the amenities like a holiday camp.

THE BAD

So, in case you're thinking that a programmer's job is to work with incredibly talented, highly motivated teammates on a spectacular next-gen title and solve crazy problems, let's get this job placed firmly in perspective: "Like most work places, there are downsides but...I can't think of any." Okay, looks like Andy Firth won the lottery when he started working at Neversoft.

Crunch Mode

Ah, the infamous time period when exercise, sleep, and one's social life are seen as annoyances that stand between your team and software salvation. According to Michael Davies, "crunch times and deadlines, debugging vague or hard-to-reproduce bugs, being unfamiliar with code, and being expected to produce results quickly" are all problems you'll need to be aware of.

David May says, "Coming to the end of one project at a previous company, I worked 18-hour days for about a month." And our unnamed lead programmer isn't too happy about the "industry standard concept of overtime. Too often, schedules are overly aggressive and can turn into death marches."

For one of Richard Crockford's ex-colleagues, this was almost literally the case: "[We worked] long hours, particularly as a result of publishers and/or management moving the goalposts midproject. Although people are becoming more aware of the issues of crunch, it's still common in the industry and can be very damaging to developers. I've seen people literally driven to the edge of madness or beyond by excessive crunch—we had one programmer leave and be committed to a mental asylum at a previous company."

This should clear up any illusions you may have that this is a stress-free, nine-to-five lark.

WHY CAN'T I BE YOU, Y? SALMI'S IN FOR THE LONG HAUL

Y Salmi works long hours, and he runs down the reasons why:

WHY CAN'T I BE YOU, Y? SALMI'S IN FOR THE LONG HAUL (CONT.)

Most of the time these are a consequence of poor management, but not always. Sometimes it can't be helped; there simply isn't enough time left or something has gone completely broken but has to be fixed.

Long hours are the most frustrating aspect of this job for several reasons. First, they're unproductive. After 1 to 2 weeks of 60 hours, your productivity plummets, and you're working less efficiently than when you're working normal hours. Errors and frustration increase. People get cranky. Second, everything else goes out the window. Plans get ignored; your home life gets ignored. Chores get ignored. You have to fight to get anything done when you get home because you're exhausted.

Third, the mentality that it's okay to work long hours is still very well present in the industry. Companies like mine make quite a bit of an effort to minimize crunch periods, but it is seen externally (by publishers) that companies aren't working hard enough if they're not driving their workers to the bone. The industry still has a long way to go before crunch hours are done away with.

Fourth, you're expected to work longer hours for the love of the game. In other industries, you either get paid overtime or receive holiday time in compensation. In the games industry, you do it because 'you love to make games.' Sadly, too few people are willing to stand up and demand to be treated like professionals for this attitude to change anytime soon. Again, I'm generalizing, and there has been a general effort to slowly move toward saner working hours, but it is still widely prevalent through the industry.

Hopefully, with more effective planning techniques such as agile development, and further publications on quality of life in the industry, the move toward respectable hours will continue.

The downsides to a programming career vary wildly, depending on whether you're just starting or are an old hand. For Junior Programmer Richard Fine, bug-hunting was his biggest peeve: "Some of the really obscure crash bugs and networking bugs are incredibly frustrating to track down, usually because they're not repeatable; I hate having to tell my lead, 'I can't find this one,' especially if we end up having to waive it as a result. A lot of this can be avoided by improving one's test platform to do things like automatically capture crash dumps, but we didn't have that." Testers often videotape bugs, but oddly, a lot of U.S. and European companies still haven't figured out how helpful this is.

When you reach the dizzying heights of technical director or lead programmer, you're faced with a different set of downers: "Increasing team size means less and less [of a] connection to the project as a whole," remarks Paul Robinson. For Chris Pink, it's "firing someone [and] informing a team that their project has been cancelled." For an anonymous high-ranking member of a technical department, "fixing problems for my team, whether it's finding a better way to do something, or they need me to explain a technical process or problem to the rest of management" comes at the top of his list of headaches. And Jamie Fristrom simply misses the good old days: "Once you end up in management, you do a lot less of the stuff you love to do. In my case it's programming. I delegate almost all of it to everyone else. Sure, I got a prototype [of Spider-Man's web-maneuvering] up and running, but then I handed it off to other coders to improve. Part of me would have liked to keep working on it, but it was more important that I spend time leading, and those other guys that worked on it did a great job—they made it much better than it would have been if it was just me."

Then there are the publishers and producers. An uneasy truce sometimes exists between the technical and publishing side of the business, and this can lead to nasty flare-ups from time to time, as one anonymous source tells us: "Dealing with publishers, for me, is the worst part of the job. I've never worked with a producer to this day that has managed to make a decision.[22] [We sometimes make] all the changes they demand, [then they] turn around after a week's work and say they preferred it the way it was before!"

Another programmer explains that he "always seems to have mindless meetings that only take up time from fixing or producing the game…[it is also hard] trying to find good staff and then trying to talk the CFO into making an offer that is competative."

If you're going into programming for the money, then find another industry. Kain Inshin explains that "average salaries for programmers will always be below the average salaries of less exciting positions outside the industry. I know for a fact that I could easily get at least an instant 25 percent raise by leaving the games industry and entering the non-entertainment sector with my current skillset." Grumbles about payment irked at least a third of our respondants, but this was quickly tempered by the fact that they get to create video games rather than tweak *Quicken*.

THE UGLY

Before you're turned into a shivering husk of your former self, thanks to overwork and 25 percent less cash than your programming brethren in other industries, here's some stereotypical viewpoints from industry outsiders. If you end up in the game industry, you'll spend the rest of your career explaining to others that these viewpoints aren't actually true.

---

22. See the producers' take on this situation in the "Game Management" section.

According to Richard Fine, for all the technical control over a project, it's a misnomer "that the programmers have creative control over the project. It's true to a small extent, in that we tend to make the calls about things that the designers have not specified, but it's more accurate to say that we have creative *input* instead—i.e., we can give the designers our ideas and feedback, and they can choose to change the game accordingly. It's a necessary approach to things because without the designers acting as a 'focal point,' the game would lose cohesion."

At the top end of the technical departments, most people think technical directors "don't do any work," says Chris Pink. But if you read Chris's tale of crunch time shenanigans in the nearby sidebar, you'll see he's never in the pink for long; in fact, most days he's deluged with responsibilities for managing his team.

Those on the outside looking in sometimes think games are all built from scratch. "Almost nobody writes an engine from scratch anymore, so most of those decisions have already been made," says Jamie Fristrom. However, the team has a lot to do with making the game unique: "For the smaller-scale decisions that need to be made going forward, I prefer to let the individual programmers working on the tasks create their own architecture, as long as it fits with the rest of the project and they keep to a few guidelines."

Michael Davies says, "A lot of people simply don't understand what it is a programmer does (yet grasp what an artist or game designer does very quickly). And some people think it's highly introverted and nerdy," a horrific and slanderous accusation that really gets some programmers' goats.

But by far the most common misconception from outsiders is that programmers "sit around playing games all day." A good 90 percent of our respondents said this. "Everyone I speak to who has no experience [in the industry] immediately jumps to this conclusion," Andy Firth explains.

"People underestimate the amount of work required to develop a title," says Tamir Nadav. David May agrees: "People don't seem to understand that we can be working on one game for 18 months, so the last thing I want to do is play it all day, every day."[23]

Not that programmers have time to play any games: "I spend the majority of my time programming, followed by meetings," explains an anonymous lead programmer. "At odd times, maybe 1 to 2 hours a month, I might check out a competitor's product at work, but all my game-playing happens after hours at home." And that home is likely to be an apartment a couple hours away from the development studio, and not a mansion in Malibu.

Another popular myth is that "we all earn incredibly large amounts of money and drive Ferraris," Richard Crockford tells us. "Unfortunately only the lucky few make it big in that way. Most developers live much more modest lives."

---

23. A sentiment shared by almost every tester in the industry, and, alas, that's their job.

SUMMARY

The Good

- There's a great sense of achievement, even at the most junior of programming positions.
- You're likely to be working on the latest gaming hardware, which is pretty much the most exciting type of programming outside of MIT's black-ops sex-robot project.
- You're constantly learning new tricks and tips, and are working in areas you need to learn from scratch.
- When you invent a method of, for example, getting Spider-Man to zip around a city without it looking terrible, there's an immense feeling of pride—which increases as other team members take this idea and run with it, and when the game ships and becomes a gigantic success.

The Bad and the Ugly

- Unfortunately, you will be faced with crunch times, which can be very unpleasant, especially if a project is mismanaged. (Fortunately, companies are at last attempting to decrease the long hours.)
- There are infuriatingly difficult-to-find crash bugs to weed out.
- The pay sucks compared to your programming buddies in other IT industries.

Take This Job and Love It

We like your chutzpah—you still seem to be reading this chapter, having ignored all previous warnings. Well, your reward is a few nuggets of information about how to go from a dark room full of gaming and anime posters in your parent's house to a dark room full of gaming and anime posters in the programming department of your first software company.

LANDING THE JOB

Getting a job as a programmer involves determination and offering up your free time to a video game company. It certainly worked for Richard Fine: "While I was still in school, I approached the company to discuss the possibility of doing some unpaid work experience. I did two weeks QA for them, and got to know the producer. Come the summer, I got in touch with the producer and asked if I could get a paid position for a couple of months, which he was fine with. Then, once I'd finished at school, I got in touch with the CTO (chief technical officer) and asked for a full year's contract—pointing out that I was already familiar with their methods of operation, tools, and people. That got me the job."

So, while other folk take on a job at a games store, the more enterprising of you should parlay the college course you're taking into an internship at a software company, gradually familiarizing yourself with the way they work and using this knowledge to get the job. Richard's method is a great way of networking without previous connections in the industry.

Of course, everyone's got a story about how they landed a job as a game programmer. Andy Firth wasn't always at Neversoft. In fact, he wasn't even on the same continent as Neversoft: "I started as a 'games programmer' after a degree in mathematical computation.[24] It soon became obvious that my skill set was more technical in nature, so I switched to engine and eventually worked up to lead and then senior programmer. That company [Attention to Detail] started a bout of redundancies, so I looked around again and moved to Muckyfoot and wrote their GameCube engine from scratch in just a few months. Muckyfoot hit financial issues later that year, which is when I applied to Neversoft. My experience on GameCube, and PPC[25] in general, and the fact that I'd had experience developing entire engines, made me a good candidate for their position." Andy was laid off twice in 12 months in the UK and saw the job posting on the developer website The Chaos Engine.[26] He PMed (private messaged) the human resources rep and "got the job three days later; [he] got offered two other jobs as well, but decided LA was the best of the three locations."

Paul Robinson, another British programmer working at Neversoft, halted a promising career in the food-service industry to fulfill a programming dream: "Unless you count a paper route or working at a fish and chip shop, my first job was in the video game industry. I left school in England at 16 with 6 GCSEs[27], and went to a local tech college for about a year; but [that] was basically a waste of time. I ended up getting a job at a local developer by showing game and tech demos I'd done." He jetted across the pond to the US after utilizing the services of a recruiter, Digital Artist Management.[28] Since he didn't have a degree, it was Paul's prior work that made Neversoft nab him.

Tamir Nadav explains how she got into the industry: "I met two people at Disney World two years ago who lived where I wanted to move to get a job once I graduated college. We kept in touch, and once moving down here to Austin, it turned out that one of their friends knew John Romero. I was put in touch with him, and then he sent me to my current boss to interview. I was a student at Full Sail, studying video game development. By the time I graduated, I had enough experience to enter the industry. I've also been attending conferences for a few

---

24. Get one of these or a degree in software engineering and/or computer science, work on a *Half-Life* mod, and as long as you're sociable enough and haven't got two heads, you'll find it incredibly difficult *not* to land a programming job.
25. PPC means production process characterization.
26. We found at least 60 respondents for *Paid to Play* at the Chaos Engine. It's simply one of the best resources for game developers.
27. General Certificate of Secondary Education. What kids get at 16.
28. We've heard mostly excellent murmurings about these guys. Check out the list of resources at the end of this book for more options.

years, which helped me build a large network. I believe this made a *very* big difference in my ability to get a job right after college."

Leon Hartwig got started without the benefit of a college degree, plunging into the world of modding. This led to his first real job, "working at a very high-profile game developer." Then, he scoured adverts "on Gamasutra, sent in a résumé, did a phone interview followed by an on-site interview, and was hired."

These interviews usually take the form of a technical interview, a personality interview, and sometimes a meeting with the team to ensure you can gel together without resorting to fisticuffs.

Kain Inshin passed both types of interviews, but "before games, I worked in programming jobs outside the industry, and any programming job is useful experience." Our anonymous lead programmer says, "[I had] numerous years of professional programming experience, and prior to working on games full time, I was always working with mod projects for fun. A few of them garnered some publisher attention, which got me some extra contract work. This led to published game experience, so I took that and interviewed with a local developer. Been here since."

FROM PSYCH MAJOR TO PARTNER

Jamie Fristrom tells you how to get a job without a relevant degree:

I dove into the games industry right after college, so I haven't really had any other jobs. In college I was a psychology major, which you'd think would be totally useless for a technical job, but it actually has some value; we're managing people to make games for people, so understanding people actually is a big help—my classes on behaviorism and social psychology actually did contain a useful nugget of wisdom or two!

To get that very first programming job in the industry, I had friends. One, Dogan Koslu, talked my first boss into hiring me. When he said he didn't have the money, [my friend] told him he was making a really big mistake. So he relented and brought me on for marginally more than minimum wage—for the first couple of months I could barely afford my apartment. But he quickly realized I was valuable and started rapidly giving me raises.

[However], after that company went under, I moved around some and finally landed at Treyarch, the company Dogan Koslu was now running. I worked my way up from programmer to lead programmer to what they called 'technical director,' which at Treyarch meant 'a lead with subleads,' which is a somewhat different position than I am in now.

After nine years at Treyarch, I decided I wanted to try something entrepreneurial myself, so I quit. I looked for people to partner with in a start-up venture and came upon my friend Bill Dugan at Torpex Games. He agreed to bring me on as a partner, and here we are!

GETTING SCHOOLED: WHAT TO LEARN AND WHAT SKILLS YOU NEED

Those in the technical field of video gaming are in high demand; there are fewer people who can program in C++ than who can work an Excel document and manage deadlines. Therefore, more than the other disciplines, programmers can gain a sigificant advantage if they attend college (to learn a host of programs, like C++). Almost 70 percent of our respondents have a college degree, around half have a masters, and each of them, with the exception of one, has a degree that's extremely relevant to his or her work.

What degrees do most of our programmer respondants recommend? "I suppose that computer sciences would go a long way to helping you secure a job in the games industry," replies David May; then he adds, "but not actually having a degree myself, I have to say that qualifications are preferred but not essential."

Michael Davies recommends "studying software engineering or computer science augmented with some kind of multimedia or 3-D graphics education; [that's] a very good start. There are now a few courses focusing on game development (such as at the Academy of Interactive Entertainment in Australia), which tailor the education specifically for games."

If you're looking for a college, Paul Robinson recommends getting "a computer science degree at almost any college, and I think the courses at Digipen, SMU, and Full Sail[29] are excellent. Lots of companies are accepting summer interns, so I'd recommend looking."

You could also just turn to the books, as did Jamie Fristrom: "I've learned just about everything I know from reading books and experience in the trenches. Programming books, software engineering books, project management books, and management books were all a big help to me in my career. I suppose you can learn this stuff in college or in MBA programs, but book learning gets you most of the way there and is a heck of a lot cheaper."

PHONING IN YOUR WORK

It's a little easier to learn the ropes if you're willing to work in the cell-phone games field, as Mark Fisher attests to:

I guess having a computer science degree helps, but there isn't anything like real-world experience. You need to get your hands dirty in the real world with real projects. Fortunately, because of the open nature of Java and J2ME, all the development tools and resources are freely available online. So it essentially doesn't cost anything to get started with.

29. These are but three of many credible universities; be careful of those institutions that are recommended only on TV adverts. Check the list of resources at the back of this book.

PHONING IN YOUR WORK (CONT.)

First off, get all the tools and development resources. If you have limited programming experience, then get hold of a good book, in this case something along the lines of one of the Dummies series of books for Java or J2ME. All my programming knowledge was self-taught (at the age of 13), so it really isn't all that difficult.

Then take a look around at some of the mobile gaming websites to see what kind of stuff people are producing. Then dive straight in and have a go.

As for the job itself? David May "honestly believes that you have either got it or you haven't. But you've got to have a good math background, good communications skills, and, obviously, fantastic programming skills."

Richard Fine also knows a good programmer when he sees one; they need the following traits:

"Primarily, the ability to think analytically and logically, and to break a problem down into component parts (to 'think top-down'). This is a pretty fundamental trait for any kind of programmer, let alone one in the games industry.

"Second, the ability to find information—a lot of people think they have to memorize programming languages or APIs. That's a fallacy; you will memorize the things you most commonly use automatically, but for everything else, keep references at your fingertips. MSDN has been particularly helpful in this regard.

"Related to this is the ability to understand documentation. Learn to speed-read and 'eyeball' docs to get a quick overview of what they're talking about, and then go back for a second pass to get the details that you really need.

"Lastly, [you need] curiosity and a desire to learn. Lots of people seem to have contempt for tools and techniques beyond the ones they already know (particularly when it comes to programming languages); yet each new piece of information is another potential string to your bow. The games industry is so fast-moving in terms of technology that you really need to stay informed of developments, or you'll become obsolete."

Michael Davies also recommends "a solid knowledge of video games (you need to know what you're trying to create), C++, C, and some assembler, good basic 3-D and 2-D math (geometry, calculus, matrices, vectors, trigonometry, pythag), some scripting languages like Python or Ruby are always useful for off-line tools, and knowledge of DirectX or OpenGL would be a bonus." Looks like it's time to break open those textbooks and start that learning in earnest.

WHY CAN'T I BE YOU, Y? PART 2: PROGRAMMING YOUR CAREER

Y Salmi contains a wealth of knowledge and gives you *his* methods of breaking into the industry:

Taking a one-year degree in game programming is how I broke into the industry. It helped strengthen my programming skills and helped me focus when writing demos. I highly recommend it, but it's not the only way to get in the industry.

Make a few small (or one big) impressive demos highlighting a certain interesting technique. It doesn't have to be novel; it just needs to be well executed. If you don't have work experience, you absolutely need a portfolio.

Fix up your CV/résumé. It needs to be clear and concise. Highlight any work you've done and skills that are relevant to the job.

Have some source code examples you can show off. Even a simple class doing something neat would do. Make sure it's well formatted, commented, and does something kinda cool. Perhaps use a piece of code you're especially proud of, clean it up, and package it. Then, include that in your portfolio.

In my experience, putting all these things on a simple website is quite effective. Alternatively, mail a CD with your portfolio when applying. A good résumé and some nice simple demos go a long way.

Leon Hartwig thinks that your mod hobby should also really start encroaching into your day-to-day life: "Working on a mod project for a few months to a year and having a result to show (and be able to discuss) is really just as good as the same amount of experience at an actual game company. Plus, it is likely the only time you will be able to make exactly the game that you want to, so have fun doing it."

Jason LaCroix says, "Never quit trying. Be persistent, read up on industry goings-on, join the IGDA, and make contacts there. Eventually, following these avenues will get you what you want."

Paul Robinson warns, "There are no shortcuts. Education is important, motivation is important, and experience is essential."

And once you get a job? "Expect to be the first in and the last to leave, and never lie to your team. Ever." Paul Bonner is emphatic about this. As is Andy Firth with his final piece of advice: "Be a geek; it's gonna happen anyways so may as well embrace it early."

Conclusion

Programming is one part of the gaming industry where a degree carries much more weight. Try one of the following college degrees:

Computer science

Software engineering

Computer programming

And perhaps consider a minor in psychology, or some subject that teaches you how to function within a team without freaking out yourself or your teammates.

Can't afford college tuition? Then buy all the books on programming you can, and read them until the information sticks in your brain.

Whichever path you take, make sure you learn a variety of programming languages. HTML only allows you to make websites, and the coffee, at most development houses.

Visit all those industry-friendly websites we refer to throughout this book. Get yourself a recruiter if you're having problems.

Network by offering to work for free, intern, and make friends by visiting all the game developer conferences you can. A good start would be the Game Developer Conference. These friends are key in getting you a job.

Get on with that modding you've been putting off, and use it to showcase your talents with an interactive résumé. Then make yourself a rosette and pin it to yourself with pride—you're about to embark on the geekiest profession in the geek-filled world of video games: Shine on, you crazy, corduroy-pants-wearing diamond.

Tester ∗ Embedded Tester ∗ QA Technician ∗ QA Manager

BUGGING OUT: QUALITY ASSURANCE

How to Get Paid to Play the Same Game Again and Again and Again: Welcome to the Test Department

"All work and no play makes Jack a dull boy.
All work and no play makes Jack a dull boy.
All work and no play makes Jack a dull boy...."

—*Excerpt from Jack Torrance's typewriter in* The Shining

"I was in the Virgin Islands once. I met a girl. We ate lobster and drank piña coladas. At sunset we made love like sea otters. **That** *was a pretty good day. Why couldn't I get that day over and over and over...?"*

—*Phil Connors,* Groundhog Day[1]

READY TO BREAK INTO THE VIDEO GAME

industry but don't have any qualifications? Do you have a breezy disposition and aren't easily depressed? Are you ready to run into every wall in a game to ensure your character can't plummet through a seam to his death? Have you mastered the art of the Excel document? Or is this just a means to an end, and you need *some* way to gain entry into the world of video games? Then you might consider the much maligned, almost never entertaining, world of the tester.

We interviewed several people from test, or QA (quality assurance), departments across the industry. One was a manager (or "lifer" as one anonymous respondent referred to the role), some were QA technicians, and one was an "embedded tester." A few wanted anonymity. But all had the same overall role: to break games before they got shipped to the general public. Sometimes the testers broke first. This is their story.[2]

---

1. Bill Murray's character gets caught repeating the same day over and over. What kind of analogy to the life of a tester are we trying to convey here?

2. A tester's life isn't all doom and gloom. Some people thrive in this department, and there are elements of the job that many people find entertaining. But prepare for the stigma to stick; you'll definitely find out why testing games gets no respect in the video game industry.

A Day in the Life

We've got our own little test for you. Study your game collection. Pick out your favorite game. You know, the one involving giant guns and giant environments. Now find another game in your collection from the same genre but one with slightly less entertaining guns/environments. Start playing the first level and instead of completing it, stand in the first room and hit every object. Now run into every wall. From every angle. Now pick up every object and throw it into every wall. Now do this while rolling. Now do this while jumping. Now do this while pressing the Pause Menu button over and over. Now attack the first foe you meet with your favorite weapon. Then do it again with your next favorite weapon, and the next one. And the next....

Now repeat this for 10 to 14 hours a day for six months, and pay yourself $9 an hour. Still want to get paid to play? Good. This is what you're getting yourself prepared for.

TESTING, TESTING, ONE, TWO, THREE... MONTHS AT A TIME

Christa Morse is now a designer, but she used to be a QA tester and has worked on projects for LucasArts and Sega. She says, "QA has best been described as 'the last line of defense between the company and the public.' By going through and finding bugs, you are making whatever game it is you are testing a superior product. Very few people can say that their work guarantees that a game will be better, other than QA." She describes a typical tester's day in the "Testing Times" sidebar. When she was in QA, she was brought in by a publisher and was "mainly a beta tester either ad hoc[3] testing or running through premade plans." This is common.

There are many types of testers, but they can be split into two main groups: those hired by the developer (these people are usually paid better,[4] have a closer understanding of the game they're testing, and aren't seasonal workers) and those hired by the publisher, either via internal job adverts or through an agency specializing in sending testers into the field (these people are usually hourly workers, with less knowledge of the game they're testing, and may work away from the developers, sometimes in a different state or country). This second group of game nomads drops in on a project as it nears completion, then leaves after a game is shipped. They then descend on another game the agency has lined up for them or a game the contacts they made at the first job have mentioned to them.

---

3. *Ad hoc* simply means you can run through a game, going anywhere you want...well, until you glitch through a wall and tumble out of the game space.
4. Unlike the $9-an-hour wage of most entry-level freelance testers.

TESTING TIMES

Christa Morse has worked for LucasArts and Sega helping play-test a game, and her day followed an all too predictable pattern:

- Arrive at work at the start of shift. Grab a cup of tea or coffee; start out by checking e-mail.
- Once done with checking and responding to e-mails, check the bug database. If a new build is in, see which bugs have been marked "fixed" within the last 24 hours or so. Start verifying if bugs are fixed or not.
- Ask the lead tester if there are any specific areas he or she wants checked or test plans to run through.
- Run through tasks assigned through by the lead tester until completed. Enter bugs as lead specifies. Some leads may ask testers to keep notes and wait first or enter as encountered.
- Once complete, ask the lead tester if there are any other unfinished tasks. If there are, finish them. If not, then ad hoc/play test until shift is over.

Matt Ibbs informs us what he does on a daily basis: "We also check all the technical requirements that need to be adhered to when we submit the game for approval. We create all the test plans, [and] we write the walkthrough guides for the games...the list goes on."

Christa Morse says, "When I tested at a game development company, builds came very often. I was in charge of making my own test plans, and I was able to contribute suggestions to improve gameplay." Usually, though, when you're first summoned to the test department's domain, expect to follow your lead's directions to the letter.

When you sit down, staring in disbelief at the 1995 13-inch Zenith TV you'll be squinting at for the next few months, you'll be asked to play through a game ad hoc, or in a specific area. You'll spend days or weeks investigating every nook and cranny of a small portion of the game to ensure nothing weird is happening—for example, if the save points are too far away, beasts keep resurrecting themselves, and your hero keeps glitching in the crouched position instead of firing his bow, then you make a note of when, where, and how this happened. Usually you take note of these sorts of things on a bug-testing form that's part of the company's intranet or wiki (an internal intranet, with game information on it, accessible to the team).

These bugs are tagged with an explanation, such as "magical sword of Sharoo turns bright purple and loses all textures when hitting an orc." Bugs are also flagged based on their severity. Then the programmers, producers, designers, and artists attempt to solve them. This is the main reason for crunch time at the end of a development cycle: the game's thousands of bugs, ranging from the tiny ("the pixie's left wing isn't fluttering correctly") to the monumental ("the entire game crashes, the screen turns blue, and all my save games are wiped"), are fixed in order of importance.

Nick Scurr, a QA technician with Blitz Games, spends his days "checking the game for bugs; gameplay testing; giving the design team feedback, suggestions or improvements; and watching over focus tests." This, and Christa's job, is the more entertaining side of testing. And if you're a full-time employee, working down the hall from the designers, programmers, and artists, you're actually seen as one of the most valued members of the team.

Emmeline Dobson, a QA technician working for Ninja Theory, developers of *Heavenly Sword* for the PS3, was also seen as part of the game. "QA was a support and feedback role on our project," she says. "There is a lot of communication on a daily basis with people from all disciplines—art, design, coding, and management. Day-to-day duties would usually be playing the game, being the first line of defense if the build stops working. Then the issues need to be logged and communicated in a helpful, levelheaded manner. Sometimes the work will involve discussing how to improve an aspect of the game. Many developers comment that they can get so close to their work that it becomes hard to have an objective opinion. In such a situation, it is useful to be able to find a second opinion from an in-house QA department. All issues are logged in an issue-tracking database, and keeping the information held therein up-to-date and useful is a significant duty." QA departments are just that: they assure a gamer that the game's quality will be up to par.

This is another reason why the "QA farms" that publishers use are sometimes helpful—they provide a fresh pair of eyes to find bugs the developers miss or can provide several people to test a game at a much quicker pace.

Speaking of quickening the pace, David Doherty, an **embedded tester** for Electronic Arts Europe, is currently "testing a new piece of software used to speed up and improve the testing process of games. This is a slightly more technical role than tester, as it requires programming and scripting knowledge." There's a large variety of test staff, and sometimes they merge or work closely with other departments. Embedded testers are usually part tester and part programmer. Although their roles vary somewhat in different companies (their role isn't clearly defined in many), these guys are here to assist the main programming core of the team.

Leading the charge of testers is the **QA manager**, such as Matt Ibbs, who works at Rockpool Games Ltd. He says, "[I do] a bit of everything, really…I coordinate my test team and make sure they're working (they always are; they're that kind of team). I liase with the porting/certification team[5] and the production team to find out what's happening on certain games. We create all the documentation

---

5. These guys are on teams consisting of the different disciplines needed to create each game's console ver. These teams communicate with the developer, publisher, and ESRB ratings board.

for our department from scratch and we maintain it so it's up-to-date. I create a weekly report document that details exactly what QA are doing each week for the management team to read. I'll help out when the producers are busy and [will] contact publishers for information. And I am about to start handling the P&L (profit and loss)[6] for my department. It keeps me busy and keeps me on my toes."

Finally, there's some crazy half-tester, half–customer service hybrids, who Christa Morse has encountered, too: "Lead testers, QA engineers, and managers are often permanent employees of a company while regular testers are often contract. Some [companies] will employ people as a combination of **tester/customer service**,[7] but this is fairly rare."

ON CONTRACT VS. ON THE CLOCK

There's a difference between working from home and being a freelancer. Entry-level testers are almost exclusively freelance contract workers[8] that flit from job to job and are usually working at a company for not longer than six months before moving on to the next job. Unlike a freelance programmer, who does most of his work from a home office, "QA is rarely done from home, excluding voluntary online stress tests," says Christa Morse. Yes, the only real time you get to play a preproduction game from your own home is if you're a journalist or you're spending extra (and sometimes unpaid) time ensuring Internet connectivity, online bantering between players is lag-free, and nothing bizarre or odd is going on.

BUSY, BUSY

Testers are busier than Donald Trump and usually sport a hairstyle that's just as perplexingly outlandish. But when will you be busiest? "The three- to six-month period before a product ships will usually be the most hectic time for a tester," Christa Morse informs us. "This is where testers usually have to run through the critical path of a game quickly and without cheats.[9] In a very short period of time, they must simulate the myriad of conditions that users across the board will face." Embedded Tester David Doherty says, "It's usually towards the game's milestone or deadline dates that we become busier. There is no real 'least busy' time, as we're always busy."

---

6. That's a checklist of all the expenses the department has accrued. Every late-night pizza delivered, every hour of overtime, and every game pad that gets thrown against a television, breaks, and is replaced is listed in these documents.

7. Customer service personnel have to answer calls from the general public, politely explaining that the reason the caller's tiny game disc isn't playing on the PlayStation2 is because the disc is for the Nintendo GameCube.

8. If you're on contract, the company you're working for doesn't have to pay for needless little additions like health care, 401Ks, or anything a salaried staff sees. Of course, contract workers can expect overtime, which is usually used to pay for the bouts of eye strain, nervous exhaustion, or gamer's thumb.

9. There are often large debug menus for most games. These menus have almost everything you could wish for: instant teleportation to anywhere in the game world; all weapons, vehicles, and level-ups; instant mission completion, and much more. This is then made inaccessible before the game ships. Boooo!

If you're part of a game launch scheduled for the third or fourth quarter, like over 80 percent of games usually are, then "around summer is busiest," says Nick Scurr. Emmeline Dobson's schedule ramps up "in the lead-up to E^3, as studios prepare demos for this all-important trade show. Then, at the end of the project, which often occurs in August and September in anticipation of releasing in time for Christmas, there is often another season when work becomes urgent."

TESTING AT THE CELLULAR LEVEL

What is it like working for a cell-phone game company? Almost constantly crazy, says Matt Ibbs. But there's an upside, too: "Because we have a very short development time for mobile games, we don't always have longer periods of downtime like, say, the console industry. We maybe have the odd week here and there where we're not completey maxed out. Any time we're not flat-out testing the games, we're usually catching up on documentation or helping out the design department or the art department. We're lucky here because my team are offered the opportunity to get really involved in that kind of thing—and that's rare for the industry."

TIME TO PAY, OR TIME TO PLAY?

If you're an entry-level freelance tester working for a publisher, you'll be expected to pull 60 to 70 hours a week for about three to six months prior to the game shipping. At $9 an hour, that works out at just over $7,000 to $14,000. Ah. "Other companies will staff up slowly to try and keep testers at a 40-hour week unless absolutely necessary. There are a select few companies that are dedicated to avoiding crunch time for everyone," says Christa Morse. For in-house, dedicated team members from the QA department, expect to work between 40 to 50 hours a week, until you hit the dreaded crunch time, when sanity, cramp-free thumbs, and washing become things of the past.

SUMMARY

- Broadly speaking, there are two types of testers: one employed by the developer, and the other by the publisher.
- The in-house tester has a career that works with the rest of the team and makes a great contribution to the quality of the game.
- The publishing company's tester usually migrates from game to game, either staying at a company headquarters or trailing developers around the country.

- Testing is pretty straightforward; check absolutely everything that's in the game, and make sure it's working properly.
- Each time a bug is found, the severity is noted and compiled into a giant database that the development team then tries correcting.
- The last three to six months of a game's gestation period are when most freelance testers make more than minimum wage. Although, if a project drags on, the hourly wage and overtime can increase this to something approaching what a developer makes, which tends to annoy in-house testers and developers.

The Good, the Bad, and the Ugly

The real test to determine whether you're cut out for QA has only just begun. By now you've realized that being a tester isn't a cross between having free pizza and soda on speed dial and having 10 hours to kick back in your recliner and play games on a 50-inch plasma screen. In fact, it's more like a cross between having free pizza and soda arriving after a 14-hour marathon play session, with you hunched over a portable CRT TV and writing about every single thing that goes wrong.

THE GOOD

There are some plus points for this ceaseless, thankless toil. The great bands of testers who flit from company to company certainly have their fair share of hopeless cases. But, if we're being needlessly romantic for a moment, these task forces of testers are like the immigration boats docking at Ellis Island at the turn of the twentieth century. Christa Morse says, "As a tester, I came across many fellow testers with aspirations of something better and [with] immense amounts of talent." Christa is now a designer at Pronto Games; she's living the dream, and one of the few who managed to enter the gaming industry, gain a foothold in QA, and land a much more entertaining job. "Test is a good place to start net-working with other professionals within the game industry, and you are also earning 'industry experience.' Experience is like money in the bank, and it can be used [to get] better jobs when you have a lot of it."

David Doherty says, "I get to work doing something I love; I've always been interested in games and now I'm helping to create them."

Meanwhile, Nick Scurr, who has scored his first industry job, gives a thumbs-up to being a tester because it allowed him to get into the industry, which in itself is no mean feat. "All the teams I have worked with here are friendly, and [I] have made some good friends. I generally enjoy my job, even if the tasks can be a little tedious. I still wouldn't want to do anything else at the minute really. Getting an inside view of the industry (my first job 'inside'!) has also been interesting."

So, what is so good about the "inside view"? For British-based QA Manager Matt Ibbs, it's the people he works with: "Your colleagues will either inspire you to work to the best of your abilities or they'll drag you down to their level. Or a bit of both."

"Playing games for money should always be enviable," states Emmeline Dobson before running us through with a few home truths: "Even though the reality of playing buggy software over and over until boredom grips you in its clutches can be far from fun." (Remember, we asked about the best parts of the job!) But there's a glimmer of light in the darkness and despair of the QA department. Emmeline Dobson adds, "There are some moments when some feature that has been worked on heavily suddenly reaches the threshold from functional implementation to a polished, fun, and artistic implementation, when you have the pleasure of enjoying a new moment in gaming! This is even more rewarding if you have been working on the game in some capacity as a source of feedback for the team. Working in QA on the final stages of a game can be a fun job, as near-finished games, if you are lucky to be working on a great product, are as fun to play as a tester as they are as a consumer. Just remember to keep your professional mind-set and strain out the remaining issues!"

THE BAD

When "the good" part of a career in testing contains warnings rather than a deluge of excitement, expect "the bad" parts of the job to be real bad. Christa Morse left the world of testing and not soon enough, it seems, as testers are "treated as a disposable thing, not a person," she says. Emmeline Dobson agrees, "QA staff can be undervalued by other team members, as people in game development may come to a company with a preconception of testers as unskilled, lazy, disposable labor."

And why would development team members think that? Well, because, according to Emmeline, "some companies *do* hire unskilled, lazy, disposable, short-contract testers!"

But it isn't just the great unwashed masses of testers descending into a software company to do the minimum amount of test work for minimum pay. There's a load of "precious" development staff, too. "Nobody likes to have their work 'criticized,'" says Emmeline, "so there are some challenging personalities, like the guy who always passes the buck for an issue arising in a system he oversees to another department, or the girl who believes her work is so important that she has no time to listen to the concerns of the QA department."

It's all part of testers getting no respect, as we mentioned earlier. Emmeline again: "Sometimes as a tester, I believe I have done great work persisting towards accurate information on a problem, but rarely seem to be thanked for the efforts. Some think that quality assurance leads to a career dead-end, too. In particular, it can be a frustrating place to be for someone who is creative at heart."

For one anonymous tester, the job "can be hell on your social life, especially during 'crunch' where you are expected to put in a lot of extra [effort] to make sure the product ships on time."

Nick Scurr concurs, "The hours can sometimes be long (and the overtime unpaid) and the pay itself is not that great, considering I have to travel a bit to get here." Ah, the old commuting problem: You might be longing to visit that incredible, space-age gaming studio in San Francisco, and you will, but even if you get to work there, you still have to find a place to live. Rents near many development studios are outrageously expensive, meaning you'll end up living an hour (and sometimes longer) away. And when you've spent 14 hours staring at a monitor, the last thing you want to do is drive home. You just want to crash—which is, ironically, what your game's been doing all day.

PAYMENT FOR PLAYMENT

Testers don't get paid squat. Contract testers are paid hourly, and $9–$10 an hour is pretty much the standard. You'd be lucky to pull in $28,000 a year, with constant work, which is difficult to get. In-house, entry-level testers don't fare much better; expect a salary that's less than $25,000 a year. When you're a more seasoned in-house tester, this rises to the dizzying heights of around $40,000, and a little more for managers, but don't expect to trade in that 1991 Suzuki Sidekick for that Porsche any time soon.

THE UGLY

So, we've sent you reeling with a swift flurry of one-two punches that describe a once dream job as little more than indentured servitude. Add to that the biggest delusion people have about a career in testing, according to pretty much everyone in the industry: "That we just sit there and play different games all day long!"

"People think that it's easy and fun to play games and test software all day," says David Doherty. "It's not. You have to play the same game for a number of months, and sometimes you *have* to play the same level over and over until all the bugs are gone. The software you're testing is nowhere near the polished product that ends up on the selves, and can be prone to crashing every five minutes. However, that's all part of the job."

Emmeline Dobson has some words of discouragement for publishers hoping that throwing more bodies at a problem is going to help: "The most common misconception is that contracting 250 low-skilled emergency testers in the final month of a game's development is an effective way of finding and fixing all the bugs." It isn't. In fact, it usually fries the QA managers and causes a huge number of already-fixed bugs to be logged, which makes new bugs more difficult to find.

"Many workers in the games industry choose a career in games because we have found excellent games to be of real significance to us. An industry that prizes excellent games should be putting quality in the midst of the development process!" We wholeheartedly agree.

And yet, there's a faint glimmer of hope. Although opinion is divided, even among our respondants, Christa Morse is proof positive that game testing isn't a dead end: "While I wouldn't want to be a game tester for years and years, much like others wouldn't want to be a burger flipper for ages, testing did lead to something better for me. You have to do a lot of extra work on your own, but testing can lead to bigger and better things!"

To discover what these "better things" are, read on and you'll find out.

SUMMARY

THE GOOD

- The tester pool contains some great characters. Align yourself with the entertaining and driven ones, and you can hopefully begin to network.
- Being a tester can be a foot in the door to the gaming industry. It's a good place to network and get industry experience.
- You get to offer an alternative to a bug fix that actually makes it into the game, and you've made a difference.
- You can say you're an important part of the process of making video games.
- The best games are a hoot to play no matter how close to completion they are.

THE BAD AND THE UGLY

- Games are fun for minutes, hours, or days, but you're playing them for months.
- The pay scale is on par with a well-paid fast-food outlet, or game store.
- You're seen as disposable, annoying, or annoyingly disposable.
- You're also seen as lazy and unskilled, which some testers are. Break the mold, please.
- And don't you *dare* criticize the ultrahip designer god who's creating a really lame block puzzle. Your opinion doesn't matter.
- Make these people listen. They'll respect you. Or fire you.
- For many, QA is a dead end. For others, it's a wake-up call to finish that design document, mod, or degree, and interview at a company properly.
- Of course, if you're great at QA, the company could keep you, even if QA isn't your career goal.
- Don't expect to afford an apartment close to work or have much of a social life.
- And you don't get paid to play games. You get paid to play one game. One unfinished game. With blocks instead of enemies and gray untextured walls.

Take This Job and Love it

Out of every career in this book, it's going to be most difficult to take *this* job and love it. But think of it as the first rung on your ladder to success. A tester's job can be tough, but it can be rewarding and can lead to better jobs within the industry, assuming you persevere. Here's how to bag your first QA position:

CONVENTIONS, COOPERATION, AND KISMET

Christa Morse decided on a discipline early, which we encourage also. She says, "I jumped into testing right after college to pursue my dream of becoming a game designer. I did get a technical (but not computer science) major, which helped shape my analytical skills.[10] I was able to network with other professionals in various small industry events such as the Women in Games International conference, which got me some interviews. However, ultimately, the game design documents I prepared during my spare time are what led to employment." Scan the industry websites for developer conferences, befriend[11] anyone you can, and work on that portfolio. Christa did, and she went from the test department to the design department. While she was working on her design documents, she accepted her first testing jobs: "I e-mailed my résumé directly to the company that hired me. In the case of the second [testing job], I responded to an ad on craigslist. A recruiter I sent my résumé to a long time ago contacted me about the third testing job." So, whatever anyone tells you, a good résumé is still vital to your job-hunting tools.

Emmeline Dobson also got her enviable position at Ninja Theory through a recruiter:[12] "I had worked for 18 months as a junior designer in one of the largest developers of video games in the UK. Also, previously I had a job as a QA technician in the localization department of a major Japanese developer's European branch." But she credits her efforts coordinating with an IGDA chapter on a volunteer basis for putting her in touch with the right people. She also used conferences as networking opportunities. The moral of this tale? Don't rely on fate alone: "None of the connections that helped me get this job were chances that appeared for me 'out of the blue.' There are no opportunities I had that anyone else could not get with perseverance and resourcefulness."

STAY A WHILE...STAY FOREVER!

Recently, *EDGE* magazine ran a feature called "A Bug's Life," which detailed the life and times of testers in the industry. They presented one particularly horrific story about how QA personnel can be treated if a deadline needs to be met and the company can't afford time for the tester to take a break. Ex-tester Jai Kristjan brought *EDGE* the story:

---

10. Check the chapter on designers to figure out the best way to spend that college tuition.

11. Do: meet, shake hands, strike up a conversation about their game, politely ask for a business card, exchange cards, and thank them for their time.
Don't: Meet, lie prostrate in front of them, talk loudly at them, ask them for their IM information, look up their studio, and set up camp across the street.

12. Use the IGDA, or any of the other websites we recommend at the back of this book, to locate a recruiter who can help you—providing you have the correct mixture of skills and chutzpah.

TIME TO PAY, OR TIME TO PLAY?

"At one compa-ny, I stepped into a vital role as the only senior tester, and my managers did everything to keep me on site and organizing the test team. My boss bought me a hammock, which he installed while I was at lunch, that I would sleep in almost every night. When I complained about needing clean clothing, they had the secretary buy me a new wardrobe. A cell phone was bought for me, to get a hold of me wherever I was, even in the bathroom; when I complained about not seeing my girlfriend in two weeks—I lived with her—they paid for a hotel room for us twice a week to see each other. I did this almost straight seven days a week for seven months. When it was done I spent three months decompressing from the ordeal."[13]

For anyone who's currently employed at a games store, you'll be ecstatic to learn that Matt Ibbs once worked at one, too: "They say that if you want to be an actor, you should work in a theater. I think the same applies if you want to work on games. Apart from the working in a theater bit. I mean, get a job in a video game store." Naturally, a developer walked in off the street, and Matt struck up a conversation and got his first interview from this chance encounter. "My first interview for my first ever job in the industry—it was purely down to luck and getting along famously with the guy that interviewed me." Then came a period of hard work and dedication. "I spent the last six years working as a tester, lead tester, and then a senior tester…and I got lucky. Very lucky. I was fortunate enough to get a boss that saw I had potential and he gave me the opportunity to prove that."

We can't really recommend Matt Ibbs's methods of getting that first industry job. Matt is based in the UK, which is the size of California, and even the likelihood of living near a software studio was miniscule. As for the United States? Well, the chance of bumping into John Romero is about the same as bumping into John Travolta, unless you live in a particular part of the country where Romero's office is. Or Travolta's compound/spacecraft. Check a developer's website to see where the closest one is to you. If that's within a half hour, drive to the nearest game store, ask the clerk if any developers frequent the place, then get a job there. This is a silly plan, but it's crazy that it has worked.

However, we really recommend Matt Ibbs's work ethic: It's imperative for this industry. Slackers need not apply.

---

13. Read the entire feature at www.edge-online.co.uk/archives/2006/06/a_bugs_life.php.

DOES LEARNING JAPANESE HELP YOU?

Yes and no. Emmeline Dobson is fluent in Japanese, and says, "I studied Japanese in university, purposefully because I believe it is very attractive to companies that frequently negotiate with Japanese firms." However, unless you're going to a company for a specific skill such as Japanese translator, you won't have as many offers as you'd think. "No practical use for my language ability has occurred," says Emmeline, "although some 'near-miss' chances escaped me. Unfortunately, as my language is a 'bonus' rather than a 'core skill,' it seems to be impossible to negotiate improved pay, responsibilities, or job title based on having this education."

In short, knowing Japanese is great if you're going to work for a company who has dealings with Japan, and it could help if the developer needs someone with such a language skill, but otherwise, it's mainly useful for completing obscure Japanese RPGs before the American version is released and annoying your friends.

THE QA MIND-SET: MORTAL CONTACT

"Dude, I rock at *Halo 2!*" isn't the best way to bring your strengths to the table during an interview, or when applying for a job in QA. There's a specific set of qualifications employers are looking for. One of the most important is the ability to string a coherent explanation together. Christa Morse explains, "Good communication and being able to write good bug reports [are] the most important skill[s] a tester can have. When writing up reports as a professional tester, other people will be reading your reports to try and fix the bug and later verify it fixed. Bad bug reports are an enormous source of frustration for developers!" So polish up on those English classes; it isn't just about holding a joypad the right way.

One anonymous tester also mentions good communication skills but adds some additional skills you should have: "the ability to not get bored quickly, a positive and friendly attitude, scripting/programming experience, and the ability to learn quickly." Did we scare you with the "scripting/programming" bit? Don't worry—this pertains to people who want a more technical tester position; but if you're going into an interview and know a smattering of C++ or Java, you might have a better shot than someone without this knowledge.

Matt Ibbs offers some advice on what previous work experience looks good for a tester candidate: "Apparently, being a guild leader in *World of Warcraft* counts as management experience these days…so there you go." Anything that shows you can be organized within a team dynamic, even if this team mainly hails from Ironforge, is something to add to the résumé.

So, if you're thinking of heading down the programmer career path, consider entering as a part programmer, part tester: "If you've been playing games since you were younger, it'll help," says one anonymous source. "For this role, however, scripting and programming experience is a huge plus. Tinker with the likes of the *Unreal* and *Half-Life* series; learn how scripting works in those two engines. Use that knowledge and become part of a modding team. For college, choose something with a programming module, in a language such as C++ or Java." Again, these skills are in higher demand than the cattle farms of folks who are sometimes shoved into a project at the last minute.

At the end of the day, it's all about dealing with the monotony of this job. "Planning and self-motivation are needed to prevent testing that merely 'goes through the motions,'" Emmeline Dobson tells us, "rather than systematically and purposefully exploring the limitations of the game, or making a plan and thoroughly checking off correct functions from it."

REPETITIVE STRAIN INQUIRY

There are some people who are content to stay within a test department and who are just as valuable as the rest of the team. Good-quality, intelligent, and motivated testers are in short supply. Two of the authors have worked with over 100 QA departments in their slightly spotty careers, and on the whole, the embedded testers and QA managers have been nothing short of heroic. Imagine gathering hundreds of bugs in a day; liaising with the rest of development, who not only respect you, but also look to you for guidance; and work with them to produce the best possible game within the allotted time limit.

$90 PER HOUR! NO EXPERIENCE REQUIRED!

If you're dipping your toe into the ocean of video game testing, don't get it bitten off by the sharks. This section of the chapter is chock full of ideas on how to land your first tester job. Avoid doing a Google search and clicking through websites promising a gigantic hourly wage. If they promise you $70-plus an hour, they're likely scams.[14] If they want $40 for a booklet containing hiring companies, they're likely to be scams. You'll get a booklet. Possibly. With lists that are readily available online.

Final pieces of advice from our assembled testers? Go for it—once your expectations have been lowered. Nick Scurr says, "It's very hard to find a permanent place in testing, so look around for contract work. Even if it's only for three months, you may get that renewed. If not, the experience you gain will help you find another, better job in testing. Also do not look at testing as a quick way

---

14. In fact, look closer, and they'll amend the "$90 an hour!" to "between $9 and $90 an hour!" Guess which monetary figure is closer to your actual pay?

into becoming a designer, etc.; [it is] better to get an education in that field if that is what you wish to do." That's not to say it's impossible, but who's going to hire someone whose previous experience in design is "writing on the menu board at Chuck E. Cheese" rather than someone who has a design degree?

Indeed, Christa Morse thinks that even when you're inside a company, internal company jobs aren't a shoo-in, noting, "A lot of testing positions are very sweatshoplike. This job has an extremely high turnover rate at such places, so don't get too attached to it. You may see a job at the company you are presently testing at that you'd like to move up to. Be prepared to apply to that job as if you were an outsider."

We'll give the final word to one anonymous tester, who sums it all up for us: "Only become a tester if it is something you really want to do. It [can be] a great way to get into the industry, but it isn't as easy as it sounds. If you think all you have to do is sit down with your feet up and play games, think again."

Conclusion

If you're set on being a tester, and moving up the ranks to senior, lead, and manager, make sure you can cope with the monotonous nature of the job.

Good testers are hard to find, and great testers are in high demand; if you don't mention this job as being a stepping stone to another discipline, you might find getting the job easier.

If you *are* using a career in QA as a stepping stone, make sure the tiny amount of free time you have outside work is dedicated to building experience and/or a portfolio for that design/art/programming position you really want.

But don't expect to change careers once you become embroiled in a company's QA department; the boss wants and needs you to stay.

Get out there and network! Send off résumés to every recruiter you can! Doing volunteer work for organizations within the gaming industry helps, too.

Communications skills, some possible programming skills, database knowledge, and self-motivation are all useful.

Take your feet off the table. Sit up straight. You're not at home now.

PUSHING PIXELS: VISUAL ART

How to Get Paid to Play with Polygons and Texture Maps—Becoming a Video Game Artist

"Every child is an artist. The problem is how to remain an artist once he grows up."
—Pablo Picasso[1]

"Art is making something out of nothing and then selling it."
—Frank Zappa

IF YOU'RE THE SORT OF PERSON WHO CAN

take a vision from your mind and create it in reality—in any medium—you might be cut out for a job in visual design. There's a wide range of visual design jobs in the game industry, from environmental modeling to character animation, but they all come down to the same basic skill: using technology to bring a world or a character to life.

Being a visual artist in the video game industry means creating never-before-seen worlds for players to explore, or crafting characters who take on lives and personalities of their own. Of course, on the downside, you'll probably be asked to design *yet another* lava level for an action-adventure game,[2] or model a character who looks "kind of like Sonic the Hedgehog, but not so much that we'd get sued."

Everyone knows if they've got artistic talent or not. If you've never been able to progress beyond stick-figure drawing, this isn't the career for you.[3] But if you *have* creative ideas in your head, and if you can take those ideas and capture them in pen and ink, clay, watercolor, and so on, and if you're willing to learn the ins and outs of a few vital software tools, you might have a future in visual game art.

This chapter is chock-full of insights from a dozen visual artists, from 3-D modelers who are just starting out in the business to art directors who fight the never-ending battle to keep programmers and game designers from putting their grubby paws all over their team's vision.

A Day in the Life

Although many of our interviewees said that working from home as a video game visual artist was an option, none of them actually did so, unless they were taking work home with them. All of our respondents are full-time employees who work out of their respective companies' offices (see sidebar).

MY STUDIO OR YOURS?

Visual art seems to be the kind of job that could easily be done from home. After all, most artists work alone in their studios, right? So why wouldn't artists in the video game world be better off doing the same thing? Josh Staub, art and visual design director for Cyan Worlds,

---

1. Picasso obviously never met the man-children who make up the art departments of certain video game companies. How many action figures do you really need on your desk for "reference," anyway?
2. And if there's any justice in this world, there's a lava-level afterlife waiting for anyone who thinks *that* idea isn't played out.
3. Don't listen to the matchbook cover. Being able to draw Spanky the Rabbit doesn't qualify you for a career in art. It goes a long way toward a doctorate in Gullible, though.

MY STUDIO OR YOURS? (CONT.)

explains why that doesn't work in the real world: "Some of [the concept work] I could do at home, but I work closely with the artists in the art department and prefer to do that on site."

Video game art is a much more collaborative process than traditional art. Video game artists aren't creating entire works of art by themselves; they're each contributing parts of a game to the whole thing. For that reason, it's absolutely essential that the artists work as a collective and be on the same page at all times. And it's much quicker and easier to just invite someone over to your desk to look at something than it is to upload your latest character model to an FTP site, e-mail the other artists on the project, and wait for them to give you feedback on it.

"It is possible for art assets to be created from home, but there will always be a need for a few people to work in house," says Tim Appleby, a character artist at BioWare. "The art assets will always need implementation, art pipelines will need to be tested, and there are many benefits to being involved in development at a studio. As part of a studio team, you all work together to come up with inventive solutions to complex problems that face game developers. Having a pool of talent to understand and discuss solutions is invaluable and definitely an aspect of game development that working from home would hinder."

The art director (sometimes called the visual design director) heads the visual art team and is responsible for communicating with[4] the heads of the other departments to coordinate the art department's contributions to the game's development. Oliver Clarke, a lead animator at a game development company, compares being the head of a team to being "a glorified secretary. It's my job to make sure the other animators know what they're doing and when it should be done by."

At the start of the development process, the art director is heavily involved with helping define the game's look and style. During the design process, the director sets the goals for the art team and reviews the finished work. And because art directors almost exclusively rise up through the ranks of art teams, they're usually called upon to create or tweak art assets if the team is heading into crunch time, or if the director figures that it's easier to make the changes themselves.

The artists and animators are the grunts of the art department. Working as a team, they get assignments from the art director and create art assets according to the design documents and concept art provided to them.

In bigger companies with large art teams, artists tend to specialize in certain aspects of visual design. Tim Appleby, a character artist for BioWare, is charged

---

4. Sometimes with pointy sticks and heavy, blunt objects.

with the task of "translating a concept of a character and re-creating it as a fully functional 3-D character, within the limitations of the 3-D game engine."

But at smaller studios, the artists take on more general roles. James Kay, a designer at Marvelous Interactive, handles character model creation and "texturing and UV mapping and animation if needed." He also handles "other 2-D graphical tasks like front-end and GUI design and anything else other people don't want to do; this can include scripting and testing when my own tasks are done."

Alan Sawdon, an artist at Circle Studios, concurs. "'Artist' is a very loose term," he says as he lists his duties, which include 3-D modeling, texturing, lighting, rendering, editing, and compositing, "with the occasional audio task thrown in for good measure."

And like many jobs in the game industry, the day-to-day lives of artists and animators are often unpredictable: "The task list and schedule soon become very liquid during the project, due to unforeseen circumstances and in reaction to other team members' progress," says says an anonymous 15-year artist veteran. "I don't always know what I'll be doing when I get into work in the morning."

An often-overlooked visual art position is that of a level designer or mission designer. Straddling the line between visual art and game design, level and mission designers take existing art assets and create new ones in order to assemble a particular level or mission in a game. Mission designers, such as Val Miller of Flying Lab Software, "put together the missions and can build out the actual battles or goals within each mission, using variable settings to add different flavors to the gameplay. We also put together the assets used in the shared spaces like the towns and taverns to make the world feel more lively and vibrant."

A BUNCH OF OTHER ART JOBS WE'RE NOT COVERING

"But wait," you say. "My cousin Rodney designs cover art for video game packaging. How come his job isn't covered in this chapter?" Well, because Rodney's job isn't a video game job, per se. Yes, he works for a video game company, but designing packaging for video games isn't fundamentally any different than designing packaging for breakfast cereal.

But that does raise an interesting point. If you've got a background in graphic arts, there are plenty of jobs in the video game industry that you could move into without much additional training. If you've mastered 2-D design, you could get a job laying out video game magazines, instruction manuals, strategy guides, websites, and so on. Conventional 2-D artists might be able to land a gig creating concept art for games, which the 3-D artists then take and use as reference for their modeling.

A BUNCH OF OTHER ART JOBS WE'RE NOT COVERING

The bottom line: the video game business is so visually driven that anyone with any artistic ability and a good work ethic can find work if they keep at it. And the better they are and the harder they work, the more opportunities they'll have.

SUMMARY

Art directors lead the visual art team and are responsible for defining goals, reviewing newly created art assets, and communicating with the other department heads.

Artists and animators create the art assets according to the assignments given to them by the art director. In larger companies, they tend to specialize in a specific area, such as a character artist, while in smaller companies, they have more general responsibilities.

Level and mission designers take existing art assets and create additional ones in order to design levels and missions for the game. Their job is half visual artist, half game designer.[5]

The Good, the Bad, and the Ugly

Now that you have an idea of the types of visual art jobs available in the video game industry, it's our duty to hype how fantastically awesome they are before crushing your spirits with the harsher day-to-day realities of the jobs.

PAYMENT FOR PLAYMENT

Because visual art jobs require specialized technical skill, they tend to pay a little bit better than other jobs in the video game industry. Artists and level designers should expect to earn something around $40,000 to $60,000 per year as part of an art team. Experienced artists can pull in closer to $80,000.

Senior members of art teams can do even better than that. An art director's salary is comparable to that of any other department head at a development company. The actual paycheck varies, but the annual salary is usually in the high five figures or low sixes.

COLLABORATIVE CREATION AND UNPREDICTABILITY

For those with true artistic talent, not using it isn't an option. Most artists will say that they don't feel alive unless they have a chance to express their creativity,

---

5. But we put them here because the game designer chapter was getting too big.

and video game visual artists are no different. Richard Gray, better known to fans of his work as Levelord, is co-owner of Ritual Entertainment and a level designer for the company. He's one of those lucky few people who's managed to get paid to do something he'd spend his free time on anyway: "Because level designing is something I would do in my free time as a hobby, it is something I do all the time. I love all of it, from making the basic geometry, to texturing, to lighting, to placing the bad guys and pick-ups, to the final detailing and polishing...all of it!"

Chuck Eyler, art director for Maxis's *The Sims*, gets a similar rush from the creative process and gets his biggest kicks from "participating in creating something that never existed before. The moment when you get to see it realized."

Matt Kresige, a character modeler from Pandemic Studios, echoes the sentiment, saying, "I love it when I can see a character I have created coming to life in a game and knowing that people will be interacting with that character."

Josh Staub gets his greatest pleasure from "creating worlds and watching people explore them;" this should come as no surprise to fans of the *Myst* series, which he's worked on.

Visual art careers in the video game world also give artists the chance to work collaboratively, which is good news for artists who don't relish the idea of slaving away at a drawing board in total solitude. "The people I work with are the best part of my job," says Matt Kresige. "At its best, working on a video game makes you bond with your coworkers and gives the team a sense of pride in completing something that the world will enjoy playing."

THE FUTURE OF VIDEO GAME ART

BioWare's Tim Appleby is the perfect person to reflect on the future of video game visual art jobs, as he's part of the team working on the almost-photo-realistic graphics of *Mass Effect*: "Advancing technology drives the games industry. Games are now being created in higher resolutions than ever before, and the increase in rendering capability has led to an increase in the standards of the art in games. All of the elements that we now use in game development mean that creating cutting-edge art is far more difficult than it ever used to be.

"I believe the way the games industry is dealing with this is by having more specialized roles. It used to be the case that an artist would wear many hats, but modern development requires a higher degree of expertise to create the strongest artwork for a game.

"Many artists have crossover skills, and things will vary from project to project and company to company. But each aspect of art creation might potentially require a specialized employee to do that job, whether it's lighting levels or creating morph targets for a facial animation system."

Tim Appleby shares that sentiment; he says he's "constantly impressed and inspired by the talented and creative people that I work with."

Working as a visual artist in the video game business is never dull, either, and that's something our veteran artist is grateful for. "The best thing about this job is the variety of work," he says. "It's pretty rare to be doing the same thing over and over again week after week, month after month because a game needs so many different types of art assets."

James Kay concurs: "The work almost always presents a challenge of sorts, be it in new technology or creatively. This forces me to keep on learning and finding out new things."

AN OVERWORKED COG IN A GREAT BIG MACHINE

On the downside, visual artists in the video game world keep the same long hours as pretty much everyone else in the industry. Two-thirds of our respondents reported working, on average, 40- to 50-hour workweeks, with the rest saying they worked slightly more or slightly less. And that's just the baseline— workdays get longer and crazier just before the major trade shows when demos and promotional trailers have to be shown on the floor. Artists also report dramatically increased hours prior to milestones and "art lock" deadlines, when the game's art assets have to be finalized. "The hours can be long and brutal," says James Kay.

But even when artists' duties are complete, that doesn't mean their job is done. They've still got to fix animation glitches and other bugs found by QA, and sometimes they get drafted into helping test the game and find the bugs themselves.

And while being part of a team can be rewarding at times, it's also a constant reminder that you are just one small cog in a huge development machine. Chuck Eyler says, "The worst is when you are reminded this isn't really your own personal game. Art is vital, but not the driving component. It can't save a bad game design."

Artists are also slaves to the development schedule and sometimes have to stop at "good enough" when they'd rather go all the way to "perfect." Tim Appleby says, "Sometimes we all need to be reminded that we are not just creating fantastic art; we are creating assets for a game. I think it's a common desire to want to spend more time on the art assets than we can."

Sometimes, even the most artistic people hit a wall and just don't feel inspired. "It is a creative job," says Levelord, "and one of the most frustrating situations to be in is one in which you need to be creative and fresh and innovative, but you just don't have anything in you."

That can happen on any project, but it's especially dangerous for artists who are involved with projects they don't feel a personal attachment to. "It helps a lot if you believe in the product you are working on," says Matt Kresige. "But if you are stuck on a dud project, it can make it difficult to get up in the morning."

Even when you're excited about the project, there are monotonous elements to the job as well. Levelord laments the final testing phase, "because running through a level more than a hundred times can get tedious."

And as video game hardware improves and evolves, so do the tools required to make games. No one knows that better than a visual artist. "To survive the long haul, you need an ability to constantly learn new skills and keep up with the changes in the industry," says Matt Kresige. "Every five years, game artists have to learn a new set of tools and skills when the hardware changes."

Finally, if you're looking for a video game career in visual art because you think you'll get to spend your days playing video games, think again. When asked what the biggest misconception is about his job, James Kay says people think "that it's all fun and games. That we spend our days playing games, fooling around, driving around in Ferraris and attending lavish launch parties. It is none of these things."

Alan Sawdon doesn't get paid to play, either: "I play fewer games now than ever before. I don't have the time! I have no idea why it's so hard to explain to people that creating a game takes huge amounts of effort, and the last thing we have time for is putting our feet up and kicking each other around on *Tekken 5* for a few hours!"

SUMMARY

The good parts of being a visual artist in the video game industry include:

- the thrill of creation
- working with a team
- constant unpredictability that keeps things from getting boring

But it's not all fun and games. Some of the job's downsides are:

- long hours that only get longer near deadlines
- a lack of creative control over the project
- tedium, especially near deadline when the artists are focusing on fixing bugs instead of creating new assets
- constantly having to learn new software tools to keep up with technology
- working in the video game industry and not getting to play games

Take This Job and Love It

Still with us? We didn't manage to scare you off? Good. Now that you've decided the perks are worth the pains, it's time to find out how to stalk the job, learn its habits, and ambush it by its watering hole.[6]

---

6. These job-hunting strategies may be prohibited by state and federal law. Check with local law enforcement agencies, or just don't get caught.

EDUCATION

Nearly all the visual artists we interviewed had at least some college experience. Only one interviewee was able to break into the industry without it. Over half of them graduated with a bachelor's degree. Many of them studied the traditional arts. "I think traditional art courses can be hugely valuable," says Tim Appleby. "Having learned the foundations of art enables a person to take that knowledge and then apply it to 3-D work." (See sidebar.)

"OLD" ART MATTERS

Just because you young whipper-snappers want to be hotshot video game artists doesn't mean you can afford to skip out on a traditional artistic background. Tim Appleby says, "Traditional backgrounds are hugely important to anyone that wants to build or texture art assets. Students gain invaluable knowledge studying traditional art, color and shadow theory, the importance of form and silhouette, composition and lighting. A dedicated student who utilizes their time well can learn all the important artistic principles that will enable them to become strong digital artists. You can have equally strong artists that become experts with their 3-D software, but in addition to their expert knowledge of the program, they also need the knowledge of creating art.

"I believe a wise artist will utilize all tools that are available to them. Simply because an artist wants to create concept art does not mean they should ignore working in 3-D, just as a person who wants to model and texture should not ignore knowledge of anatomy or composition.

"Try everything and find your strengths, then focus your time and energy on putting together a portfolio that you feel best represents your talent. Some artistic jobs are more competitive to land than others, due to the number of people who want to fill those roles. Having production experience can help land you your ideal job, but it will also give you insight into what the work really entails, as the perception of a job can often be quite different from how it actually is."

If you have the option of attending a school that offers courses in 3-D art or animation, take advantage of this asset. "Level designers are still often self-taught," says Levelord. "This is changing, though, as great schools like the Guildhall at Southern Methodist University are offering degrees in level design and game design."

But whatever you study, remember that a diploma is just the beginning of your quest for a career in visual art. "School can teach you a foundation," says Matt Kresige, "but the development process is much different than the classroom experience. At the end of the day, it is sink or swim."

PRIOR EXPERIENCE

Obviously, having any prior experience in video game visual art is the best possible thing to have on your résumé. And if you're looking for an art director position, it's pretty much mandatory that you have several years of working on art teams and have provable management or leadership experience. But since every art job depends on landing that critical first gig, let's look at how to do that, exactly.

Experience with 3-D modeling or animation outside of the video game industry looks good on the résumé, including work at a Hollywood effects studio or a graphic design firm. That's how our veteran artist got his start: "Being part of a production team that was tasked with generating a whole TV episode every eight weeks really tightened up my 3-D skills. I was also exposed to a lot of talented people that I would never have met in the video game industry."

If you don't have any prior work experience, make sure you have an impressive portfolio of work you've done on your own time. "If you want to be an artist, you should have a huge portfolio already showing your lust," says Levelord. "Level designers should have directories stuffed with levels they have made for their favorite games."

James Kay says, "For my very first job, it was the artwork I had done in my spare time that convinced them to hire me, rather than any art college portfolio I had. It doesn't have to be specifically game related, but if you have the skill to make something look good, it can be enough."

And make sure your portfolio contains only the best of your best work. "Getting a job in the industry is incredibly hard," says Matt Kresige, "and you should do whatever you can to make your portfolio or demo reel shine. If it takes an extra three months to add something or polish it, do it. It will really pay off for you in the long run."

Many of our respondents also recommended independent mod work as a good way for aspiring game artists to get their feet in the door. "In some ways, working on a great mod can mean more than a lot of other work experience," says Matt Kresige. "It will teach you teamwork and deadline discipline that will really help in a professional environment."

NETWORKING

Networking might not seem as vital to visual artists as it is to other aspiring video game pros. Obviously a game designer has a much better shot at landing a job if someone can vouch for him or her, but a visual artist's portfolio should speak for itself, right? Well, yeah, but remember that most video game art jobs are never publicly advertised, and everyone with a copy of Photoshop applies for the ones that are.

"Never underestimate the value of networking with other people in the industry," says Tim Appleby. "It's something I have heard a lot, and I can definitely advocate that sentiment now." Tim heard about his current job from another character artist online. Half of our interviewees reported that a professional connection was at least partially responsible for landing them their current job.[7]

"It's amazing how effective [networking] is; people who know friends in the right places can give you that sliver of an edge over the competition," says Val Miller. But the sword cuts both ways: "Similarly, don't burn bridges; game companies hire away from one another, so often that word gets around."

SKILLS

Good visual artists are artists first and technicians second. Here's a quick way to tell which one you are: If you can use more than one medium to create an image, you're an artist. If you can work in only a single medium or with one program, you've probably technically mastered that medium but haven't developed your artistic sensibilities to the point where you have marketable skills. This is especially true in the video game industry, where the technology changes radically several times a decade. "Spend more time on the traditional art background and less on the technical," recommends Josh Staub. "Become an artist first, and then find a way to make great art using the computer, not the other way around."

TECHNOLOGY IS YOUR FRIEND

This sidebar will probably be hilariously out of date by the end of the decade, but right now these are the programs that aspiring video game artists should familiarize themselves with:

- Adobe Photoshop (www.adobe.com): 2-D image editor, used for creating textures
- Autodesk's 3D Studio MAX (www.autodesk.com): 3-D modeling
- Autodesk's Maya (www.autodesk.com): Animation
- Cosmigo's Pro Motion (www.cosmigo.com): 2-D painting
- Pixologic's ZBrush (www.pixologic.com): 2-D and 3-D modeling, texturing, and painting

Matt Kresige offers similar advice: "The most important skills I would recommend are a good drawing or sculpture background and the ability to learn new skills quickly. The drawing/sculpture background is important because it shows you know how to work in multiple media and will help your 3-D modeling abilities."

Of course, before you can be a video game artist, you must be familiar with the technology. James Kay recommends that you have "knowledge of the major

---

7. The other half attributed their success to pluck, gumption, and derring-do.

software packages in your field and technical knowledge of the limitations and strong points of the hardware you're working on."

If you're planning on moving into a managerial position on an art team, you must be familiar with everyone else's job and be able to represent them to the rest of the development team.[8] "I describe [being an art director] as being an art broker," says Chuck Eyler. "I finesse deals between art, engineering, and game design. Clear and comfortable communication is absolutely vital. Being an artist, I understand what an artist needs to do a good job, and I do my best to supply it."

OTHER ADVICE

The best way to become a video game visual artist is to just do it, whether there's a paycheck involved or not. Start off small. "Don't start by making that epic animation experience," says animator Oliver Clarke. "Make a simple humanoid character, rig it, skin it, and make a run or walk cycle for it. If you can do that, well done! It's a great start."

It's also important to show prospective employers the unique qualities you bring to the table: "Work on something you truly like doing in your spare time," says James Kay. "Don't try too much to create something you think people want or need, but create something you have a passion for and *finish it!* Nothing looks worse on a résumé or portfolio than a bunch of unfinished hobby projects." One of Valve Software's finest artists got his job this way, with a portfolio that consisted almost entirely of aliens with gigantic genitals. Don't believe us? Read the sidebar.

Never stop studying your art. For aspiring animators, Oliver Clarke recommends Richard Williams's *The Animator's Survival Kit* and the following exercise: "Take your favorite animation and go through it frame by frame—I can't stress the importance of doing this. Do the same with dancers, Buster Keaton DVDs, and so on."

This is vitally important in the video game world, where the technology changes so quickly. "A prospective employer will be impressed with an interviewee who has no previous industry experience, yet knows and can demonstrate some of the latest tricks and methods that are utilized today, especially in the whole next-gen area," says Alan Sawdon. Most of the major programs used to create visual art have personal learning editions (PLEs) that you can download for free and use to get a working knowledge of the software before making an investment in purchasing it.[9]

Even if you've already got a video game visual art job, don't stop learning on your own time. "Working in a production environment does not always give

---

8. Being able to break up slap fights between overworked and overstressed employees is also an advantage.
9. Note that this is different from stealing the full version of the program from a warez site. That's illegal, and we do NOT endorse it.

you enough time to experiment and learn during the creative process," says Tim Appleby. "Doing the same things [outside] of work can give you the time you need to experiment and push your skills, which then leads to improvements in the quality of your work."

The worst mistake you can make is resting on your laurels and not adding to your skill set. No matter how old of a dog you are, you absolutely must be able to learn new tricks. "Don't reach a certain level and think, 'I know enough to do this job; I don't need to learn anything else,'" advises our veteran artist, "because your peers will be developing their skills and you can be left behind, becoming slightly less employable than them."

And once you do land a job, keep in mind that you've been hired to create specific art assets for a specific game, and you must be able to accept criticism of your work. "Learn to swallow your pride and accept that there are many people out there with greater knowledge than you," says Tim Appleby. "Fresh eyes will always find errors in your work quicker than your own."

Remember, as great as the job might be, it's still a job. Develop a personal separation from your professional work. "There's a fine line between having professional pride in your work and being too 'precious' and 'protective' about it," says our veteran artist. "Don't try and make your professional artwork an extension of any personal art you might create as a hobby."

SUMMARY

- Practically every video game visual artist has at least some postsecondary education, often in an artistic field of study.
- Prior experience in 3-D art is the best thing to have on your résumé. If you haven't worked professionally in any related field, make sure you have a solid portfolio of amateur work.
- Develop your artistic ability in more than one medium and become familiar with the programs used to create video game art. Never stop studying your art, and maintain a personal separation from professional criticism.

Conclusion

If you're artistically inclined, willing, and able to master new technology quickly and like the idea of being part of a team that's working together to bring a video game to life, a career in visual art might be up your alley. If you want a job where you can work independently from home, or if you want to create without restrictions and retain strong personal ownership of your work, this might not be the job for you.

If you decide that you want to go for a career in this field, the two most important things you must do are constantly work to improve your artistic ability and research and become familiar with new technology as it becomes available. Most video game artists do this over the course of a postsecondary education as well as on their own time as a hobby. Just as in almost every other job in the video game industry, be prepared to commit yourself to it fully, because it's not a nine-to-five gig.

*Audio Director * Sound Designer/Developer * Audio*
*Manager * Soundtrack Composer * Voice Actor*

STICK IT IN THEIR EAR: AUDIO ARTIST

How to Get Paid to Play Music and Create Sound for
Video Games: Becoming an Audio Artist

"Everything in the world has a spirit which is released by its sound."
—*Oscar Fischinger*[1]

"This is a journey into sound."

—*Every crappy techno song ever*[2]

SOUND JUST MIGHT BE THE MOST UNDER-

rated aspect of video game production. Whenever the next generation of console or PC hardware hits the market, the emphasis is always placed on the graphics—the resolution, the polygon counts, the support for high-definition video—with the audio stats buried toward the bottom of the press release. But with home audio systems now sporting capabilities that you once could experience only at a movie theater[3], the ability of sound to enhance every aspect of the video game is greater than ever.

Good sound design is about more than whacking watermelons with a mallet to get the perfect "exploding head" sound.[4] It's about positioning the proper sounds in three-dimensional space to give the player the illusion that their avatar is in a living world. If the job is done properly, most gamers probably won't pick up on three-quarters of the audio artist's painstaking work, but the audio will subconsciously draw them into the game in ways that the best graphics never could.

And let's not forget about the power of a game's soundtrack and voice-overs. The right music and voice acting can make or break a game, either enhancing the gaming experience and taking it to the next level, or ruining the illusion through unintentional hilarity. In fact, many game soundtracks are now sold separately as legitimate album releases, a clear sign of video game music's coming of age.

If you've got a love of musical composition or a keen ear for sound, you might be cut out for a career as a video game audio artist. We've interviewed several audio artists, from soundtrack composers to voice actors, to hear what they have to say about the field.

A Day in the Life

At the top of the video game audio artist food chain is the **audio director**. Like other departmental directors, the audio director must deal with the heads of the other departments in order to ensure that enough resources are allocated for the game's audio component. And because a PC or console has only so much processing power, it can be difficult to get the programming and visual art teams to free up the necessary bandwidth for complex audio processing. After all, truly excellent 3-D audio doesn't show up in screenshots.

Tim Larkin is the audio director at Cyan Studios, home of the *Myst* series of games, which have won critical acclaim for their inventive use of sound and

---

1. German experimental filmmaker of the early twentieth century and inventor of the Lumigraph color organ, which as far as we know has never been used on a video game soundtrack.
2. The Coldcut remix of Erik B and Rakim's *Paid in Full* excepted.
3. A primitive communal cinematic viewing establishment. Ask your parents.
4. Sorry, Gallagher.

music.[5] In addition to his managerial duties, Tim spends his time "composing music, creating sound design, and overseeing audio implementation for [Cyan's] games."

Jason Page is an **audio manager** at Sony Computer Entertainment Europe, and his job is a great deal more technical than his job title implies: "Currently, I manage the team who is writing the MultiStream audio engine for PlayStation3," he says. "Day-to-day work involves managing of the team, creating many reports and presentations to show what we're planning to create (essential when working with non-English-speaking parts of Sony) and handling developer support for all audio-related PlayStation issues. I also try to keep designing and programming as much as possible, just so I don't get too rusty." His previous work experience includes sound design for *Gran Turismo* and other first-party Sony titles, and while he tries to keep a hand in that, "due to games just requiring more time in every area, it just isn't possible to juggle everything."

Sound developers (sometimes called *sound effects designers*) are an audio team's backbone. These are the artists who create and implement every piece of environmental audio, from the hollow click of an empty gun to the gentle whooshing of a windswept plain. Raison Varner, a contracted sound effects designer, says that the primary goal of someone in his position is to "create original and unique sounds that help a game achieve 'suspension of disbelief.' That means that a sound designer's goal is to make the game sound authentic. He has to support the intentions and interactions of gameplay elements to support a player's immersion in the 'reality' of a game's narrative and design."

Surprisingly, a sound designer's job has less to do with creating the sounds and more to do with making sure that they behave appropriately in the game. "This means many things, from making sure things fit into memory (not as easy as it might sound) to scripting interactivity for the music," says a sound designer for a prominent development studio. "To a lesser extent, I actually create sounds and music, but implementation is 80 percent of the work."

Yannis Brown, sound designer and director of GroovyAudio, a game audio studio, elaborates: "Game audio is an IT field. It requires technical knowledge about implementation, audio engines, audio file formats, memory constraints, and nonlinear audio. [Many people think] that all you do is compose, or make sounds—being a [sound designer] requires a lot more than just making noise."

The day-to-day job of a **soundtrack composer** is similar to that of any other musician or recording artist. According to Raison Varner, it's all about making music that creates an emotional backdrop for the game: "This means being comfortable revising your initial efforts to achieve the best score possible for a game. As you work, you will begin to understand what the development team needs and wants in the music for a game."

5. Including awards for "Best Sound" from *PC Gamer*, "Best Sound Effects" from Gamespot.com, and a Game Developer's Choice nomination for "Best Audio."

It's more common for a sound designer or sound-

RECORDING CONTRACTS

track composer to be an independent contractor than it is for them to hold an in-house position with a development studio. In fact, two-thirds of our respondents said that they were either partially or completely freelance.

There are several reasons for this, one of which is the prohibitive cost of the equipment needed for sound design. As opposed to a programmer or 3-D artist, who can get his or her job done with a relatively inexpensive state-of-the-art PC and site-licensed software, a sound designer or composer might need several keyboards, amplifiers, microphones, effects processors, and PCs or, more commonly, Macs; they also need a sound-proofed studio, a sound effects library, plenty of recording software, hundreds of yards of heavily shielded cables, and a high-end surround sound system. In a modest development studio that works on only one title at a time, it often makes more sense to subcontract the sound work to avoid laying out the cash for a studio, especially if the company is a small start-up.

It also often makes financial sense for audio artists to be freelance. For instance, depending on how quickly they write, some composers can work on multiple games in a single year and charge a respectable fee for each soundtrack from development houses that consider it a bargain, since they don't have to pony up the cash for an in-house soundtrack artist.

Voice actors are also becoming increasingly more prominent audio artists in the video game world. With the advent of high-capacity game media like DVD and Blu-Ray Disc, developers now have space for hours of audio that never would have fit on old-school game cartridges and first-generation game discs. And they're making good use of it: "Professional voice acting is becoming essential in video games as storylines and the characters themselves become more complex," says voice actor David Sobolov, whose credits include *EverQuest II*, *Spider-Man II*, and a slew of other games that don't end in a Roman numeral. "It's really the only element in the game that isn't simulated. Our job is to add an element that allows the characters to live truthfully under their given imaginary circumstances. Realistic, emotionally nuanced voice acting can be key to allowing the gamer to buy into the reality of what they're experiencing."

SUMMARY

Audio directors are the heads of their audio teams and work with other department heads to allot resources for the sound engine and all in-game audio. Depending on the company, they might also perform some sound developer or sound composer duties.

Audio managers deal with creating and refining a game's audio engine. Although it requires a background in sound development, it's much more technical than other audio jobs.

Sound developers create all the sound effects for a game and make them work within the game engine; the majority of their work is technical implementation. Soundtrack composers write and record the game's score. Voice actors make their living by performing lines that are then inserted into the sound engine, like any other sound effect.

The Good, the Bad, and the Ugly

If you've been paying attention so far, you know that this is the part of the chapter where we get the lowdown on the best and the worst parts of the career we're covering. And as usual, we'll lift your spirits with the good stuff before doing our level best to crush them with the bad. If you make it through this next section with any hopes or dreams intact, you might just be cut out for a career as a video game audio artist.

LIFE, LIBERTY, AND THE PURSUIT OF AWESOMENESS

There are many good things about being an audio artist, and one of the best ones is the work itself. That's what Yannis Brown gets a kick out of. He counts "having the satisfaction of being part of something cool, and having your work affecting the lives of other people in a positive way" as his favorite things about his job.

Because so much sound design is independently contracted freelance work, audio artists tend to have much greater latitude in the amount and type of work that they accept: "The variation from one project to another is great," says Scott Cairns of SCA Sound Studios, which has provided music and sound design for more than a dozen video games. "Writing music for a war title is completely different from creating sound effects for a horse racing game. I also have the freedom—to a certain extent—to work my own hours. Deadlines will always change that though!"[6]

Tim Larkin appreciates the freedom he's given in his chosen profession: "In my case, I enjoy my autonomy. I'm allowed quite a bit of freedom both as an employee where I work, and as a freelancer. I enjoy working on different projects with differing aesthetics and challenges. Each project helps to refresh your perspective for the next."

And voice actor David Sobolov has noticed that, as games have evolved, he's getting meatier roles: "The sheer variety of characters I'm asked to play always keeps things interesting. We're noticing that games have much more plot lately

6. Cairns also extols our personal favorite virtues of freelancing: "Not having to shave or dress for work is a big bonus too!" And here we thought we were the only freelancers who worked pantless.

and the characters are becoming increasing nuanced. This makes for a much more interesting experience than the 100 percent 'scream and die' characters we used to see in earlier games."

DEADLINE DOOM AND THE JOYS OF FREELANCING

But the life of an audio artist has its fair share of challenges as well. Like most creative people, it's hard for many audio artists to stop working once a project is "good enough," but the reality of tight deadlines and production schedules doesn't favor perfectionists. "The deadline that backs up against creativity sometimes inhibits the process," says Tim Larkin.

Scott Cairns notes that, while the job itself is enjoyable, deadlines can suck the fun out of it: "It's easy to write music generally; it's easy to create sound—in your own time and at your whim. It's much harder to create to a deadline, satisfying the needs of the project and the client all at the same time."

Like any job in video game development, you have to remember that it's just a job, even if you're producing work that you're passionate about: "If you like what you do as a job that much, it's not as easy to just forget about it after 5:30 p.m. each night," says Jason Page. "I learned a long time ago that you can't get too attached to your work, though. I've had many good ideas and have worked on many titles that have been canned, even though the whole team thought it would have been a AAA top seller. If you take this to heart, you're not going to last long."

If you're an in-house audio artist, particularly on the more technical side of things, or if you're a hard-working freelancer, the hours demanded by the job can be a killer. Most audio artists report longer hours in the spring and summer as they ready games for a fall release, but that's completely dependent on the production schedule for the particular game you're working on. There's no "off-season" for audio artists.

Then there are all the complications that come with being a freelancer or independent contractor. If you got into the sound design field, it was probably because you enjoyed working with sound, not because you had a driving passion for business. But as an independent contractor, you must be able to handle the business side of things: "You need good business management skills, negotiation skills, and [must] be able to keep it cool when things get hectic," says Asbjoern Andersen, sound composer and co-owner of Epic Sound ApS, which has handled sound design for several video games. "You also need a good network of people who can help you out with the business side of things."

Yannis Brown also laments how much time he has to spend away from the keyboard: "I'm an audio person; I would like to concentrate solely on the audio aspects of [the job], but being the owner of a business, I also need to do a lot of mundane non-audio-related activities."

One of those activities is simply keeping your (or your studio's) name out there. It's a fast-paced industry with short-term memory, so you must constantly remind people of who you are, as they probably won't do it on their own: "I think that a common misconception from other composers and sound guys in the industry is that once you are seen doing AAA titles, you've made it and that it's easy going from there," says Tim Larkin. "The truth is that it's a constant struggle and it takes constant marketing to keep in the top tier of composers. Ask any of the guys doing the high-profile games, and I think they'll tell you how much effort it takes to remain there. You'd be surprised at the percentage of time it takes to deal with the business and PR side."

Good luck if you're a voice actor who's just been hired to provide 200 takes of characters yelling in pain. "The 'scream and die' games are brutal on the voice," says David Sobolov. "To realistically portray extremes in horrific situations, we have to almost literally 'leave a lung on the glass' in the studio. This can lead to career-ending vocal injuries if we're not careful."

But surely, professional voice actors are extremely well-compensated for "leaving a lung on the glass," right? Wrong. "Often the general public believes that non-celebrity voice actors are paid tens of thousands of dollars to voice their roles in the game," says Sobolov. "While it's sometimes possible to negotiate more than minimum (union scale), generally professional union actors (as of 2006) are paid approximately $710 per [four-hour] session, with no additional payments even if the game makes millions in profits." That might seem like good money for four hours' of work, but most voice actors can't do more than a handful of those sessions in a week without seriously jeopardizing their ability to perform.

PAYMENT FOR PLAYMENT

Salaries for audio artists vary wildly, mainly due to the nature of contract work. A one-person studio that has established a reputation for itself over the course of many years and AAA titles obviously commands a much higher fee than several amateur audio artists scrambling for their first jobs. Our respondents reported annual salary ranges from a low of $25,000–40,000 to a high of $80,000–100,000.

The two major factors that determine how much you'll earn as an audio artist are your reputation and the amount of work you take on. Your reputation depends upon the length of time you've worked in the industry, the prestige of the games you've worked on, how well you were able to meet deadlines, the quality of the work you delivered, and your level of professionalism when dealing with your clients.

When deciding how much work to accept, be realistic about your ability to get it all done on deadline. It's a rookie mistake to accept more work than you can reasonably complete, which usually results in blown deadlines or half-assed work, or both. And if that's the first impression you make out of the gate, it's going to require a lot more work to reestablish your reputation going forward.

Finally—and we're probably starting to sound like a broken record[7] by now—the games industry isn't all fun and games. Many times it's neither, even for audio artists. Raison Varner says that the two most common misconceptions about his job are "you get to 'play' while you work…and how much discipline and expertise this industry requires for you to even have a shot."

SUMMARY

- The good: The work itself is a hoot, you get a greater degree of freedom than in most game development jobs, and there's a constant evolution of bigger and better roles for audio artists.
- The bad: Deadlines are an ever-present buzzkill, maintaining a personal separation from your professional work can be hard, and being a freelancer means you must spend a lot more time on business matters and self-promotion than you might like.
- The ugly: Many freelancers apparently do not wear pants.

Take This Job and Love It

If after reading the previous section you're still keen on becoming a video game audio artist, you're probably wondering how to go about doing that. In fact, that would be a marvelous idea for the next section of this chapter.

But before we get into that, let's give Raison Varner one more crack at scaring you off: "I believe that of all the disciplines involved in the video game industry, audio is the most difficult to break into, due to the low ratio of audio professionals to other disciplines. For example: In most cases, every 30- to 50-man studio you encounter will typically only have one audio guy. You can imagine the level of competition this introduces."

Still want to do this? Good. That's the attitude you need to have if you want to make this work.

EDUCATION

If there's one thing we found from our respondents, it's that there doesn't seem to be any magic formula for getting the perfect education that prepares you for being a video game audio artist. A couple of them had some college experience but no degree. One had a four-year degree in computer science. Two had a specialized arts education, and the other two ended their formal educations immediately after or during high school.

Studying composition is almost a must for soundtrack designers. If your school offers programs in electronic music or multitrack composition and

---

7. An archaic polycarbonate recording medium. Ask your grandparents.

recording, take them. Even if the software you use isn't the stuff that the video game pros use, the experience of mastering one set of tools will make it that much easier to learn a second set.

For sound designers, learn all you can about audio production. That's what Raison Varner did. "I spent about five years after high school (I did not attend university) perfect-

> **TIP** Check out the NON-profit organization G.A.N.G. (Game Audio Network Guild) at www.audiogang.org. Also, check out the book **The Complete Guide to Game Audio**, by Aaron Marks

ing my technical knowledge of audio production. That includes mic placement and mic selection for live recording, understanding audio production standards and quality expectations, learning the fine elements of mixing music and the tricks of the trade to produce professional-quality recordings, analyzing movie scores and sound design constantly, being proactive in discovering ways of reproducing intriguing sounds I heard and interesting music that captured my interest, training my ear to hear specific frequency ranges, and how to identify what an object should sound like from looking at it." If you're lucky enough to attend a school that offers specialized courses in sound design for games, take them.

No matter what job you're trying to land in the world of video game audio, it doesn't hurt to take a small business management course or two. Odds are, you'll work freelance at some point in your career, and knowing how to promote yourself, drum up work, and stick to a budget are vital skills to have.

Above all, constantly work to improve your skills on your own time, above and beyond your formal education: "Don't just settle for the workload of your course," says Raison Varner. "You have to work on side projects and build mods or work on indie games to understand how what you're learning in school applies to games. It's up to you to fill in the gaps of your college education with real-world experience."

PRIOR EXPERIENCE

As with every job in video games, your prior experience goes a long way toward landing you a job as an audio artist. "I was a working musician for years before working in the game industry," says composer Tim Larkin, "so obviously the experience gained from years of performing live and in the studio as well as producing and composing were a huge help." He also suggests that it might be beneficial if aspiring soundtrack composers have a commercial or studio background, or have worked in television or film.

And while that might be good advice for a soundtrack composer, it's a different story for an aspiring sound designer. The interactivity of video game audio makes video game sound design a completely different beast from sound design in any other medium. That means that the only experience that matters when trying to break into this highly technical and specialized field is other game audio experience, amateur or professional. "If it's nongame industry work, I don't think it's really worth mentioning," says Jason Page. "Or at least mention it just to show you've not been out of work for five years."

Sound designer Yannis Brown was "heavily involved in the audio side of the demo-scene," composing and designing sound for a number of amateur game projects. He also brought some serious technical skills to the table: "I worked as an IT professional for eight years and have a college degree in computing, so I had an extremely strong technical background." He encourages anyone who wants to do what he does to just do it: "An active participation in any sort of game development is key. Basically it shows that you give a damn about what you do and it's not for the money. We're talking about passion and determination here."

Having that kind of strong technical background sometimes pays unexpected dividends for a freelancer, as Scott Cairns found: "I run six computers in my studio, all networked." He says, "I saved a lot of money building them myself. My technical background helps me when talking to developers too."

Raison Varner got his start with an internship at Human Head Studios: "After having a really positive interview where I showed that I understood the technical aspects of creating games, I was brought on to the team," he remembers. "As I showed an ability to handle more responsibility and worked on more and more critical game assets, my internship turned into a full-time paid position. During the rest of my contract with Human Head, I worked on every area of sound design for *Prey* and took on the full responsibility of a sound designer."

Voice actor David Sobolov has a wealth of previous acting and performance experience to draw on when he gets into the recording booth: "I was a French horn player and singer for many years. There's music in every character rhythm—tone, pace, etc.—so it's been helpful to have a musical background. I also appeared in stage productions for many years prior to starting voice acting. You have to be unafraid to be 'big' at times doing game voices, so the stage experience was good to have as well." He also lists prior voice acting work (in animation, for example) as a valuable asset.

NETWORKING

For Yannis Brown, being a video game audio artist was a lifelong dream, and it was through perseverance, talent, and effective networking that he made it a reality: "I started talking to friends in the game industry once I knew I was good enough to be doing this professionally. I got my first break when asked to submit a demo for a game [that] was, audio-wise, technically challenging. Both personal and professional connections have gained me both in-house work and contracts alike. All I can say is, friends help friends. Watch who you become friends with."

When he was first starting out, Scott Cairns made good use of trade shows and other events to make his industry connections: "I attended every game-related seminar and conference I could, striking up relationships along the way."

MUSIC4GAMES.NET

If you're an aspiring audio artist and you ever meet Greg O'Connor-Read, you'll want to get down on your knees and kiss his feet for creating and maintaining a little site called www.Music4Games.net.

"Music4Games.Net was launched in 1999 to raise the awareness and profile of video game music," says O'Connor-Read. "[It] delivers an invaluable spotlight on today's video game soundtrack industry and is the leading provider of game music infotainment for dedicated gamers, game music fans, audiophiles, composers, developers, publishers, producers, audio directors, and music executives. Music4Games.Net is regularly consulted, quoted, referenced, and utilized as a reliable resource for media articles, conferences, seminars, and market studies on the art form and business of music for video games."

David Sobolov generally has to audition for each of his voice acting roles, but having positive experiences with a producer or a casting director sometimes puts him at the top of the list for additional projects later on. He also emphasizes the importance of having an agent do some of the heavy lifting for you: "When you're starting out as a voice performer, the first step is to convince an agent of your worth as an actor. You have to have professionally produced voice demos to present to an agent, and a personal recommendation is often essential."

But it's not all up to your agent: "The most valuable 'connections' you can make are through your work experiences," says Sobolov. "Work leads to more work if you're professional, creatively interesting, and pleasant to work with. I'm finding the longer I work doing voices in video games, the more work I get doing voices in video games!"

SKILLS

Obviously, to succeed at being an audio artist, you must have a knack for sound design. And since you'll probably wind up doing it on a freelance basis, you'll want to develop your business sense by learning to network and self-promote effectively. You'll also need some solid time-management skills: "Be organized and competent in managing your time," advises Raison Varner. "If you fall behind in your work, you're going to feel a lot of anxiety about it. It's really rare to encounter any disrespect, but you don't want to be the source of stress in an already stressful environment when crunch time comes around."

You also have to master the technical side of audio production: "Things have changed over the years that I've been in the industry," says Tim Larkin. "You not only need a great aesthetic sensibility, but [also] an understanding of the technical side that goes into audio implementation, as well as the tools that allow you to create."

One of those tools is the multitrack recording standard ProTools, which Larkin recommends being familiar with. However, another sound developer at a major development house complains about "the misconception that ProTools knowledge is required. It isn't."

And even though many audio artists prefer to work on Macs, this same sound developer recommends that aspiring sound artists develop a familiarity with PCs: "Game companies hate it when you say you want a Mac. Get Sonic Foundry products." He also emphasizes the fact that sound design and development is at least as technical as it is artistic, advising would-be audio artists to have "basic audio recording knowledge, strong familiarity with Windows-based computers, and the ability and willingness to deal with highly technical, nonartistic aspects of the work. One should be comfortable with working in a text editor and dealing with formal language scripting [such as] Python or Perl or something newer. Studying some actual computer programming would be even better."

And if you're a freelancer, work on those people skills: "It may sound cliché, but people skills are very important," says Scott Cairns. "Every e-mail and phone call must remain courteous and civil. It sounds like this would be obvious, but I've seen a few individuals lose their patience with the client and say something like, 'Come back to me when you've figured out what you want!'"

Jason Page puts it more bluntly: "Just don't be an arrogant dick. You *do* have to work well as part of the team."

OTHER ADVICE

Asbjoern Andersen advises aspiring audio artists against uniformity in their portfolios: "Spend time honing your primary skills by working with a diverse selection of projects. Compile a presentation that really shows off your skills."

Ultimately, it all comes down to what you know and how well you know it: "There's not many people in this industry nowadays who I don't think should be, unlike five or ten years ago," says Jason Page. "It's just not really possible to hide the fact you can't do your job anymore!"

No matter how good your presentation or portfolio is, it won't do you any good unless you get it into the hands of the right people. "Many people in the audio side of the industry tend to be the 'distant creative types,'" says Scott Cairns. "If you want to make a career out of this, you have to come out of your hole, down from the mountain and all that. I suggest going to as many conferences and game-related functions as you can. Meet as many people as you can. Sell yourself, but be nice about it! Don't be pushy."

And for aspiring voice actors, David Sobolov says that voice acting is more than just walking up to a mic and reading from a script: "Voice work in video games is probably the most creatively and physically demanding end of the voice-over business today. Expect a 'full body' experience and be ready to deliver far more than a surface performance. If you don't let yourself 'live truthfully under the given imaginary circumstances' of the character, the player won't believe it either. Few are skilled enough to do that without some past experience and/or training in acting. If you haven't had some serious acting training or extensive experience on stage, you probably aren't ready for this type of work."

We'll give Tim Larkin the last word, with a bit of advice that applies to just about every job in the video game industry: "Make sure you're ready for the job when you take it. It's not an easy industry to break into, so you definitely don't want to make a bad first impression. As large of an industry as it is, it's a small community as well."

SUMMARY

Audio artists' educations vary wildly. There's no definitive formal education path to a career in video game audio. Composers tend to study composition, while sound designers and developers usually have a background in programming.

Prior professional experience is valuable for a soundtrack composer or voice actor, no matter what medium it's in. But for a sound designer, the only experience that matters is other video game audio work.

People skills, self-management, and basic business smarts are vital for any freelance audio artist.

Conclusion

Video game audio often goes unappreciated by the vast majority of gamers (and even some developers), but outstanding sound work can take a good game to the next level. And for most audio artists, the work is its own reward.

It's important to note the difference between soundtrack composition (which is similar to soundtrack composition in any other medium) and sound design and development (which is a highly technical field and requires as much programming skill as audio knowledge).

Most audio artists work as freelancers or independent contractors for at least part of their career. That means that in addition to all of their audio and technical knowledge, they've got to develop the skills necessary to drum up work, build a client list, and deliver quality work reliably.

PRODUCTION VALUES: GAME MANAGEMENT

How to Get Paid to Plan: The Ups and Downs of Being a Manager, Boss, and Figurehead

"We must all hang together, or assuredly we shall all hang separately."

—*Benjamin Franklin*

"I have eight different bosses right now. Eight, Bob. So that means when I make a mistake, I have eight different people coming by to tell me about it. My only real motivation is not to be hassled; that, and the fear of losing my job. But you know, Bob, that will only make someone work just hard enough not to get fired."

—*Peter Gibbons, Office Space*[1]

DO YOU LOVE RISK AND THE FEELING OF

victory? Were you one of those children who meticulously positioned your GI Joes/Transformers into firing positions most advantageous to your living room's topography, and then barked orders to them? Do you enjoy multitasking? Or perhaps you have an awesome idea for a brand-new video game called *Zombie Town* (which melds the free-form gameplay of *Grand Theft Auto*, and the delicate zombie destruction of *Resident Evil*), but want to order a team around when you make it instead of doing the work yourself? Can you meet milestones in a game's development without a full-scale team mutiny? Are you ready to become the spokesperson of your company's latest franchise and get interviewed on extended basic cable TV? Then you might be ready to roll as a manager, producer, or visionary.

Producers often get a bad rap in the industry, and it's a job that's perceived to be the "easiest" and "most maligned" by many who don't know any better, and by some who do. Department heads fare a little better, but only certain personality types are cut out for being a boss and having the extra responsibility of managing teams.

As for the visionaries, you need that extra "X factor"—a mixture of chutzpah and charisma. If you can easily explain to a CNN coanchor exactly why everyone should buy the game you've spent the last three years slaving over, *and* hold your own in a technical conversation with a programmer about bloom lighting, then you might be the next John Romero.

In fact, John Romero is one of the people we were lucky enough to interview for this chapter, along with over a dozen producers, managers, and creative directors. Even an ex-president got in on the action. This chapter is bulging with anecdotes about team-building, running a team (preferably not into the ground), and what it takes to rein in developer types while keeping the project solvent, the eyes on the prize, and all action items and deliverables on the same page. Let's open a dialog,[2] shall we?

A Day in the Life

MIDLEVEL BOSS: PRODUCERS AND PROJECT MANAGERS

Organizing, scheduling, understanding the intricacies of Microsoft Outlook, and liaising with team leads—this is basically what you'll be in for when you enter the world of video game producing and managing. Of course, this being an industry where roles are notoriously difficult to pigeonhole, expect to be thrown into the deep end while wearing a large number of hats. Roles in this part of game development aren't cut-and-dry.

---

1. This is proof that there are far worse jobs out there than the ones we're covering. You won't usually encounter eight different bosses unless you're applying for a job at Gigantic Ego Studios, LLC.
2. Yes, you may have to speak like that, usually when dealing with marketing departments.

For Andrew Watt, a project manager at Circle Studios, his *raison d'etre* is the "day-to-day management of the development teams and scheduling of the product. It also involves the chasing and collating of assets from both internal and external sources."

The workday is similar for Erik Wujcik, a game design studio manager at Ubisoft Shanghai—"managing all game design resources for a variety of projects"—but his particular department also demands he lends "creative oversight" to his own, smaller team, as well as "recruiting and training junior game designers."

Emily Newton Dunn, a producer at Criterion Studios, breaks it down still further: "There are many stages to making a game and each demands different skills from a producer. In preproduction, I work with the production team to set the vision for the game and work with the design team to create the gameplay for that vision. I then work with the development managers to ensure that it is achievable in the time we have. Once we've set the vision, I have to communicate it to the rest of the team. I also work with the marketing team to ensure that they undestand our game and to help them create a great marketing campaign to promote the game. This means that, day to day, my job is extremely varied; some days I'm deep into detail and others I'm looking at the game from a bird's-eye view. An important part of my job is to make sure that we're not missing anything that might come and bite us when we can least afford it. Often this leads to side projects like working with an external company or internal team to create additional videos for the game."

Once the game is humming along nicely, Emily Newton Dunn's role becomes more about squeezing the last drop of awesomeness from the title in development: "How smart can we work? What could we tweak to make this even better, more spectacular? I take great pride in my job and want to push the team to as much success as we can—after all, we all work long hours and put our heart and soul into the game. If producers don't stay objective and stop striving for more, then you could end up with a mediocre game and all that hard work will have been for nothing."

Once the game's gestation period is finally nearing a working build, the producer explains to the marketing departments what they've got to pimp to the public. Emily explains, "At this point I'm working to create assets that will help promote the game; we want people to know about it as early as is feasibly possible so that they can get as excited about it as we are."

Then come the horrific milestones, countless meetings, and conniption-inducing bug fixing as the bundle of gaming joy is finally birthed. "One of the most fun parts of the job," says Emily, "is going out to meet the press and show off the game when it's done. Not only do I get to travel far and wide, but I [also] get to meet lots of people who (hopefully) enjoy the game as much as I do." That's one aspect of being a producer you might not have thought about: you'll get to actually leave the office. But this freedom is tempered by the fact that you've got 15 minutes to encapsulate your game to the most feared (and often reviled) specimen in all of gamedom—the *Lusororis Inlotus*,[3] or video game journalist.

Usually, these public demonstrations and galvanizing team pep-talks fall to those with previous experience in such matters, such as a senior producer with a string of successful titles under his or her belt.

For Kevin Mulhall, a senior producer at Neversoft whose job encompasses the work of both a midlevel and senior producer, he (along with a project lead) is "ultimately responsible for leading the entire development team on a product from conception to completion. A senior producer will also be tasked with leading a team of producers that make sure all aspects of the game (from internal development, to outsourcing needs, to marketing and publishing materials) are handled in a timely and efficient manner. The job of someone in production is to make sure that everyone else contributing to the product has the inspiration, information, and tools that they need to get the job done."

ON THE VERGE OF A BREAKDOWN: THE DEFINITION OF A PRODUCER

This nebulous, sometimes misunderstood creature is able to adapt to its environment, no matter what external forces are at work. We tracked down Andy Abramovici, senior producer at Amaze Entertainment, to break down what a producer's role is within a company: "Just about every company seems to have different definitions of what a 'producer' does. My favorite permutation, and the one I feel most comfortable with, looks something like this:

"The producer is responsible for ensuring that the design team and dev team are setting out to build a high-quality game, on time and on budget, and setting/meeting expectations both internally and externally.

"[They] co-create and maintain the creative vision of the products in development. Now, this does not necessarily mean that the producer is the 'creative genius,' as there are plenty of creative folks who focus solely on game design. What the producer is responsible for is making sure that everyone involved with product development is consistently aware of what is most important to the product.

"Along with a separate project manager, [the producer] is one of the linchpins of people/project management. [They] ensure that teammates are communicating and working together to manage dependencies. The most successful projects typically see the project manager manage team members and project schedules, with the producer focused more on managing

---

3. Roughly translated: an unwashed writer of satires.

ON THE VERGE OF A BREAKDOWN: THE DEFINITION OF A PRODUCER (CONT.)

the creative process and evangelizing the product both to external forces and internal team members.

"The producer should be the first line of high-level quality assurance. He/she is accountable for managing product quality vs. expectations at all times.

"Whew. There's a lot more, too, and most every day is different. That's why I love this job!"

OFFICE SPACE: STAYING HOME ISN'T AN OPTION

Working from home as a producer or team lead is unfathomable—after all, you've got to be the most amiable person in the office, and *actually be in the office*, to berate—whoops, we mean motivate—your team.[4] More seasoned producers, such as Andy Abramovici, have tried telecommuting, "but the difference is night and day. Working exclusively with external development teams, it is possible to work from home (when you're not away from home, working on-location with your external team). But for internal projects, where the producer should be leading teams and driving the creative process, working from home is pretty much not an option. It makes one pine for the days of garage game development!"[5]

TIME TO PAY, OR TIME TO PLAY?

Once you've nabbed that plum producer job, you'll be wondering whether to rent an apartment near the developer studio or just give in and set up a sleeping bag under your desk permanently. Every respondent stays at work at least 40–50 hours every week, with around two-thirds upping that to 50–60. For director-level positions, make sure you park that preowned Porsche in a covered parking lot; you won't be seeing it for the 60–70 hours you'll be at work. And as for the creative heads of companies? Hope that real-world technology catches up to *Star Trek*'s technology, so you can teleport directly from your mansion to your window

---

4. And know not to use the phrase "your team" when there are design, programming, QA leads, other team members...well, just about anyone except other producers about. The team doesn't see you as their leader; rather, they see you as a conduit.

5. If you're interested in making games using your own money, or a rich uncle's, and putting your livelihood on the line, working from a garage, shed, or remote outhouse, you might want to check out the chapter on DIY gaming.

TIME TO PAY, OR TIME TO PLAY? (CONT.)

office. There's well over 70 hours a week of workload to shoulder, leaving only a modicum of free time to pilot your helicopter to your gold-plated Viper.[6]

For Emily Newton Dunn, face-to-face time is much more valuable than working remotely: "I know that if something isn't right, I can just walk over to the person who creates that part of the game and we can talk through the problem and try something different. I couldn't do this if I was working from home."

So don't bet on becoming a freelance producer. Andy Abramovici says, "Because an important (and often underrated or overlooked) part of the job is to form relationships and trust with the talent who actually make the games, I can't see 'freelancing' working long-term." But then he ponders a little more, wondering what the ideal producer job would be. It seems to be a cross between Robert Evans and Mr. T: "That would be pretty badass. I mean, who wouldn't want to be so good and effective at their job that they could be air-dropped into any (crisis) situation and be able to shepherd a different team to success each time?"

PANTS NOT OPTIONAL: LITTLE CHANCE FOR FREELANCE

If you're hoping for a quiet life of working pantsless in the comfort of your own home, don't become a project lead. In fact, there's a good chance you'll be in the office, managing a team of (possibly) pantsless freelancers from your cubicle. David Hunt of Empire Interactive spends his days "running a number of simultaneous development projects undertaken by a special projects group in the company, [involving] day-to-day technical oversight of the projects." With these projects, "the majority of the people we employ are contractual employees who work from home."

BUSY, BUSY

Just as with their job descriptions, a producer or manager's busiest time varies from company to company. But there are similarities. Andrew Watt is "very busy toward the end of a product. Apart from that, it's a mixture of manic and very relaxed."[7]

---

6. Okay, so the Viper wasn't gold-plated, but Dave Perry did have his own helicopter. It was even used as the impetus for his game *R/C Stunt Copter*. Our "hooptie" is also the impetus for our other game idea—*R/C Pinto*.
7. This was the only one out of over a hundred respondents who mentioned that part of their job allowed them to be "very relaxed." The only time most video game industry folk are "very relaxed" is when they're on vacation after a product ship or have collapsed at their desks.

Brian Beuken, a freelance project manager, tries "to maintain a constant flow, but there is usually a bit of a rush before a delivery, especially if some change or new feature has been requested, and not yet seen."[8]

As producers are involved in every aspect of development, the pace, according to Emily Newton Dunn, "is unrelenting. There are always decisions that need to be made, something that needs to be reviewed or iterated. The list goes on. But at least you'll never be bored as a producer!"

CRUNCHED, OR CRUSHED? A HECTIC SCHEDULE

Andy Abramovici usually works around 45 hours a week, even on a slow week: "But then there's crunch-time. If we all were able to plan and scope correctly, there'd be no crunch time. My teams and projects strive to make this a reality. But realistically speaking, you're going to have weeks that are a lot longer (including weekends) around major miletones and the finalling process. In my opinion, the most successful teams create quality software, to spec, but minimize the overtime. No matter how much an employee gets paid, nobody deserves a death march. Life needs to be a balance—I love my job, but I love my personal time more."

If you're working for one of the bigger software companies, your schedule ramps up just at the time when you could be tanning. Soren Lund, a producer at the aptly titled Deadline Games, stares at his monitor most "during the summer months as we go through alpha, beta, and master periods in order to be ready for [a] Christmas release."

Kevin Mulhall, senior producer at Neversoft, works on the *Tony Hawk* franchise, "which has [had] a new game released every holiday season for the past seven years." He says production ramps up even earlier than summer: "The busiest time for me has been the spring through summer months of the year. This is the time when everything is coming together and we start cleaning up the game, tying the loose ends, and getting it ready to submit and ship. The least busy time has definitely been the latter part of the year, when we have just shipped a game and we are in the very early planning stages for the next game."

END-OF-LEVEL BOSS: DIRECTORS

Now you know what producers and managers do, but what changes at the director level? More responsibilities, that's what. For Richard Lemarchand, game director at Naughty Dog, it's "every aspect of the player's experience of their

---

8. Funny story: Certain elements, such as mini-games, collectibles, and other goodies, sometimes are implemented late into a game cycle. Case in point: a very minor fighter character was put into a "sandbox-style" game, but there wasn't time to thoroughly play-test him. He ended up being invincible in the final release. Whoops.

game; from the moment they plug it in to the time when they decide to stop playing. They're the person who holds the vision of the game project and leads the team toward making that vision a reality. It's their job to ensure that all aspects of the project get integrated into a great piece of game design."

Just as with producers and managers at development studios, directors often must wear multiple hats. At Naughty Dog, Richard also "plans the schedule and ensures that every last thing needed for the project is getting designed, documented, built, and implemented. [He] answers day-to-day questions about the direction of the project and [he's] the person who makes the-buck-stops-here-type decisions about the project when necessary."

GOING CABALS DEEP: VALVE SOFTWARE'S HIERARCHY

For Valve, superstars who bask in the media spotlight and become the focal point of the company instead of the game itself are useless. There aren't any grandiose titles on business cards at Valve, and although you technically know what your strengths are, teams are split into four five-man groups known as "Cabals," each responsible (for example) for a few of the levels in one of Valve's games. The Cabals frequently meet with one another, where larger decisions are made, delightfully free of ego, and testers play through created levels while Valve's crew furiously takes notes on bits of the game when the action was too slow, too difficult, or too hectic, based on a set of guidelines. The result? Borglike pods of people all working separately but without the bureaucracy that bogs down many other companies.

The word preceding your "director" title is also important. Richard's is "game," so he balances a third hat on his naughty noggin. This enables him to "generate original game design, whether that might be creating specifications for the creation of concept designs, generating level layout maps, placing enemies and power-ups in a level, or scripting the game's events."

Directors make thousands of decisions on a weekly basis, and these can range from the tiniest tweak, such as how big the brain explosions should be after each shotgun headshot in a first-person shooter to overseeing screenshots, cover art, attending stockholder or journalist meetings, and speaking at conferences, being real evangelists for their game titles.

Ryan Lockhart, creative director at 7 Studios, spends his days "working on game pitches, reviewing progress on our current games, and communicating with the various leads in order to gather ideas." The main difference between directors and managers is that directors oversee multiple projects at once and act almost like a producer for each of the team leads or for multiple teams.

Richard Lemarchand again: "Good leadership and communication skills are essential for a game director. The director not only helps facilitate communication within the team, but also acts as an interface between the development team and whoever is sponsoring the project." Directors have the added pressure of showing the business suits just how incredible their new game is, whether the Armani jackets are worn by CEOs of the software company itself, the publisher, or the stores selling the game.

Alex Ward, the creative director of Criterion Games and writer of this book's foreword, takes us even further into the day-to-day activities of a director: "I am happiest being in the office at Criterion working alongside the staff on our two-game series, *Burnout* and *Black*. I meet daily with the senior staff on both titles. We talk about anything and everything—from what happened on Xbox LIVE the previous night to talking about obscure home computer games from the 1980s. There is always some aspect of our games to look at, review, and give feedback on."

Currently,[9] Criterion is working on another *Burnout* game: "Every Wednesday afternoon we have a meeting known internally as 'show and tell.' This is an important meeting where the leads from each department on the team—from programming, audio, design, and art—present their latest progress on the software." This powwow allows for almost constant criticism, which Alex feels is essential: "We pride ourselves at Criterion in having a *very* open and honest culture of critique. It's all about making the best game possible. Sometimes it's tough, and there's no denying that it's extremely challenging at times, but we get stronger as a result. In my experience in this business so far, it has always amazed me how so few people are able to stop and say, 'Sorry, that's just not going to make it.'"

BECOMING TRULY SUCCESSFUL IN THE GAMING INDUSTRY: PART 1

When you're working in an environment you thoroughly enjoy, there's no need to stop thinking about gaming when you're off the clock. Alex Ward, Creative Director at Criterion says, "The games business takes place everywhere. I spend most time at the office, but I am always thinking about gaming—when I eat and when I sleep. It's hard to get away from. Even when I travel, I am always scouring for coin-op games and pin-tables, and then I have a PSP and a DS close by on all long-haul flights. What a freak, eh?" Hey, you said it, pal.

---

9. As of summer 2006.

BUSY, BUSY

As directors are juggling multiple projects, and possibly nursing multiple ulcers, they tend to work the same hours as producers and managers. But 40-hour weeks are at the *low* end of expectations, as Ryan Lockhart elaborates: "It depends on our current projects and needs—40-hour weeks are possible when everything is moving smoothly along in the middle of a project, but during trouble spots and at the start and end of projects, the hours could climb much higher (50–60 range)." If you're the most senior team member, like Richard Lamarchand, expect a weekly routine that's always above 60 hours.

"The busiest times of the project cycle are at the very beginning, during preproduction, when the plans for the project are laid, and toward the end, as the footprint of the game's design gets finalized and the game receives its final polish." For Dan Jevons, whose role as creative director for Union Entertainment has him working as a contractor for games without publishers, he's at his busiest in April and May "leading up to E^3," but also in September, which "is 'buying' season for most publishers."

BECOMING TRULY SUCCESSFUL IN THE GAMING INDUSTRY: PART 2

"I think to be truly successful in any industry requires passion, drive, and commitment. And those are hard things to be able to turn off. I truly love what I do. It's never felt like boring work to me; it's always been extremely vibrant, exciting, and creative. So I feel that if you're a sort of '9-to-5' type of person, then you'll end up producing a very '9-to-5' type of game," says Alex Ward, creative director at Criterion Studios.

As 80 percent of games are sold between Thanksgiving and Christmas, it's generally thought that games must be on the shelf by Thanksgiving. "This means the game needs to be completed during the summer, usually by the end of July," explains Alex Ward. "Working back from this date, this means that you would have shown a great version of the game at E^3 in May. This means that March and April would have been busy too. We're now looking at a minimum of 18 months to make a game. That said, some of our best work to date at Criterion has been done in very short time frames, and of our own choosing, too. We made *Burnout 2* in nine months and did *Black* from start to finish in less than twelve months." Alex knows this isn't ideal, but this is "what the business is all about, and we've put out a lot of software in one hardware generation. People know who we are and what we do, and that's part and parcel of being successful."

END-OF-GAME BOSS: HEAD HONCHOS

But what about guys in charge of almost everything? When you get to become the president of Shiny Entertainment, like Dave Perry did, you're spending upward of 65 hours a week "running the company, overseeing projects, presenting products, relationship management, game production…basically steering the ship!"

After some high-profile triumphs, John Romero now captains the game development portion of Slipgate Ironworks in his role as executive vice president. John wears enough hats to open up his own boutique: "I direct the development of our MMOG, which includes hiring the dev team in all areas (production, programming, art, design) in addition to other business-related activities such as raising capital, planning marketing and PR, etc. Day to day I work with the team to make sure we're all trying to meet our short-term goals. I work on recruiting, maintaining our internal website/wiki, do IT work, tons of e-mail…." In short, the higher you rise in a company, the more you'll be juggling. The trick is not to drop anything.

SUMMARY

Basically, producers and project leads are the hubs, conduits, or valves in a development studio's piping. They ensure milestones are met and explain the game to PR, marketing, and the press.

Of all the disciplines, producers are least likely to work from home, as their corralling abilities are needed in the office.

Directors have a similar role as producers, with an emphasis on the type of work they did before the promotion. However, senior producers, and to a greater extent directors, manage multiple projects and multiple teams within each project. Directors also make company-wide decisions that can impact development tremendously.

In the development part of a company, people in vice president positions and above basically run everything, collect a gigantic check, but take the heat if a game tanks.

VPs and presidents are the company's figureheads and go-to spokespersons, although directors and producers also fill these roles.

The Good, the Bad, and the Ugly

The stigma attached to being a producer hasn't lessened your enthusiasm? You're a big thinker, are you? Then prepare to be overwhelmed by the sheer elation of being a manager, director, or company overlord, then prepare to be underwhelmed by the crappy bits of the job no one else is going to tell you about.

PAYMENT FOR PLAYMENT

Just how much do producers, directors, and head honchos make? Although none of our respondents would go on the record, the general annual pay for a project manager, producer, and project lead is between $60,000–80,000. Senior producers make around the same, but if you've been around for a bit and have a couple of titles to your credit, expect to bump that up to between $80,000–100,000.

Almost all creative directors make between $80,000–100,000. More seasoned senior producers take home $100,000–150,000, while those at the highest positions in the companies gather up their cash in gigantic parachutes and deposit them in trucks: You're likely to be earning over $200,000 by then.

THE GOOD

What's so great about being a project manager? "Seeing the end product," says Andrew Watt. "It's great to see the games evolve from nothing to a product on the shelves in-store." The majority of our respondents agreed, and one anonymous respondent added that "working with the most talented game designers on Earth, as well as junior game designers with enormous potential," is another bonus; and the same is true for other project leads. David Hunt still can't get over the fact he's "paid to do what I consider a hobby. Additionally, the industry is very dynamic and forward moving; it is nearly impossible to get stuck doing the same thing for very long. Work is always mentally stimulating and challenging, and even apparently simple and mundane tasks can disguise a wealth of detail and possibilities."

Producers also enjoy seeing people snapping up games they've helped create. Before store release, when the early copies of the final game arrive, Kevin Mulhall tells us, "I usually am most pleased with my job when I can walk around to each person on the team and hand them some copies of the final product. That is the best feeling and worth every bit of work that went into developing the title."

For Soren Lund, though, his favorite part of the job is "the day-to-day challenges of the different groups and coming up with creative solutions and suggestions to everyday problems. Specifically, the 'creative' period of prototyping and preproduction holds a dear place in my heart."

When someone said "variety is the spice of life",[10] he was also talking about Andy Abramovici's Seattle-based journey to work: "Each day as I negotiate the morning commute, I go over what situations I expect to encounter or tasks I expect to be working on that day. The first great thing is, almost every day, the list is different. Now sometimes, the list in my head is exactly what happens. Other times, I find that due to circumstances out of our control, an entirely new 'to-do' list gen-

---

10. Actually, William Cowper (1731–1800) said this.

erates itself based on what is going on that day. Although we try to stay as proactive as possible, this job is ofttimes quite a reactionary experience. Although this can also be frustrating, it's this 'predictable unpredictability' that keeps this job a fresh experience every day. Until we get free pretzels and energy drinks in the lunchroom,[11] that is by far my favorite part of the job."

"PRODUCER" ISN'T A DIRTY WORD

Producers have received a bad rap in the past. Andy Abramovici sets the record straight on what a true producer is, soapbox style: "Yes, some producers are…um…worthless. I've met some of them. But then, I've met some worthless artists, engineers, project managers, QA, marketing reps, etc. But then, I've met some elite ones, too. Producers often get a bad rap because their contributions to a project can differ based on the makeup of the dev team. Long ago, one of my mentors, who is an extremely successful VP/EP for a major publisher, explained to me that he never expects to see his day-to-day contributions evident in [the] game. After all, he is not creating any art nor writing any code. Yet at the same time he can see his fingerprints on every aspect of the game. To me, one of the unsung traits of an effective producer is that he is able to bring the best out of his team, which in turn will be reflected in the quality of the product. A great producer touches all areas of a game by helping the talent 'produce' in the most effective ways."

The reward for Alex Ward is more basic: "You just can't beat getting free games, and anyone in this business who no longer gets excited getting a free game is probably dead already or a PC developer! By making a career in this business, I've got to meet my heroes, see the world, and work with some truly talented people. I look back to 2001 as being a particularly special time. Making *Burnout 2* was a great experience. There was a real sense of collaboration and teamwork in the company, and we strove to be the best in the world."

Ryan Lockhart loves to see ideas take on form and function, and go from thoughts bouncing inside his head to realities bounding around in a game. "Just making small suggestions that have a large impact are also great—often games are the sum of many, many, many pieces, and certain ones can really help or hurt, even if they seem 'insignificant' at the time. I also love helping give energy to ideas, to push people into thinking in slightly different ways, and then seeing their faces light up when they take my suggestion and make it into something even cooler in their head."

---

11. In general, most video game software development companies provide snacks, drinks, and food during crunch time, and for the biggest companies, valet parking, basketball courts, laundry services, bunk beds, and no reason to visit your apartment except to see if your cat/goldfish/girlfriend is still alive.

It also seems that the more senior your position, the greater the array of enjoyment you can experience. For Dave Perry, his contentment comes from creativity at a meta level: "We are paid to think. It's also competitive and it's fun (every now and again) to get a hit!" For Richard Lemarchand, "it's a job that offers an incredible variety of challenges and a huge amount of creative satisfaction." In fact, this could be Richard's perfect career: "I'm incredibly lucky. I really can't name a worse part of the job!"

We'll let some other folks think up a few downsides to a managerial role, then.

THE BAD

Stress is pretty much the worst aspect of being part of management. Andrew Watt says, "Knowing that you're ultimately responsible for delivering the product on time and to a high quality does have its scary moments, especially when things start to go wrong." Kevin Mulhall agrees: "You really have to take responsibility for the entire project into your hands. This can become very stressful at times, especially when you are racing to meet a deadline at the end of development, and you have to make and keep priorities in your head every second of the day." John Romero's worst days are spent "dealing with a demoralized or overworked team if something bad happens during development."

But this pales in comparison to dealing with the inexperienced. There's "the increasing number of unqualified idiots you have to deal with. We've all bumped into [an] 18-year-old ex-tester who's been promoted to ass prod[12] and wants to show his bosses he can get the project in on time," says Brian Beuken, speaking from a programming and project management background.

For Andy Abramovici, "the worst parts of this job are not learning (or putting into practice) project scoping and scheduling lessons we've learned on previous games. Seeing or experiencing the same mistakes repeatedly is extremely maddening."

But there's a much more terrifying exterior force to contend with: the dreaded publisher.

Not every publisher follows a strict hierarchy, especially if you're an autonomous game studio holding all the cards. But publishers frequently clash with development teams more often than you'd think. With Soren Lund, "it's the 'bureaucracy' involved when dealing with publishers and their tendency to want to micromanage."

Then there's the clash between the creatives and the suits. Ryan Lockhart says, "Working in a creative industry that's also driven by needed goals can be frustrating at times—we (and the people we're working with/for) want to add in so much, but we're also bound to release dates and contractual obligations and limitations of current technology."

Alex Ward is a little less diplomatic: "Personally speaking, the worst parts of the job tend to involve having to spend time with people who simply don't

---

12. What associate or assistant producers are affectionately called by the rest of the industry.

love video games, don't follow video gaming, and have little or no interest in gaming. I once sat in a meeting where someone said, 'We don't sell what's in the box. We sell what's on the box'—which is a pretty bad place to be."

There's also the doom-and-gloom scenario, when a publisher ignores or limits the potential of a game. "We're constantly battling for originality and quality against deadline and marketing pressure," an anonymous manager tells us. Andy Abramovici explains, "I hate to see dev teams become frustrated because they feel that their project is doomed to fail at the publisher level. I've worked for some pretty large publishers, and there are always projects [that] are somewhat of the also-rans. This doesn't mean that folks aren't working as hard on these games, but it's natural for morale to take a hit when a team knows that in the long run, due to forces they cannot control (for example marketing support, distribution, release date, etc.), there is a glass ceiling on their potential for success. Nobody wants to impede success, but sometimes it's difficult to get your teammate's head around these factors as they give their heart and soul to ensure that their contribution to the game is the best it can possibly be."

THE UGLY

Pretty much half of our respondents stated that people often think people in the video game industry sit around and play video games all day.[13] Kevin Mulhall states, "Granted, I do play-test the game that we are developing on a daily basis, but I think the idea that I get to just play any game I want and that I am not working is pretty funny to me." But wait. At least Kevin is actually playing *a game* during part of his job. That's got to be at least partially exhilarating, right? Well, even the most pant-soilingly exciting software gets a little tedious when you're wandering around a half-finished game world, colliding with half-finished obstacles, with placeholder textures. And remember: you'll be wandering around the same, finished world 18 months later, hoping all those bugs get fixed.

DON'T HATE THE GAME; HATE THE PLAYERS

Gaming nirvana or America's sweatshops? Anonymous contacts throughout the industry tell us a few of the worst parts of management, and game development in general:

- Overtime that's not only excessive, but also without reward.
- A lower salary with the promise of royalties to bolster that salary that isn't forthcoming.

---

13. It's as if the authors of this book had some kind of nefarious plan to coax readers to buy it with promises that a video game career would be all about, say, being "paid to play," but in reality, it's a series of cautionary tales to weed out those with only a passing interest.

DON'T HATE THE GAME; HATE THE PLAYERS

- Unrealstic deadlines for projects that "must make the holiday season."
- Maintaining a balance between management and development.
- Dealing with incompetent simpletons, especially those in senior positions for reasons that aren't entirely clear.

Other misconceptions about being a producer or manager? "That you're a millionaire living in a massive house. Oh yeah, and the fact that when you tell people you make computer games, they all of a sudden start telling you about a problem they're having where their version of Windows XP keeps crashing. I'm a project manager, not Bill Gates," says project manager Andrew Watt.

Other respondents definitely get confused stares when the general public sees them step into a midrange sedan. For most development teams, this job doesn't come with gigantic paychecks, "but people associate big games sales with lots of money, and reality is a long way from that," says Brian Beuken. Those going from DIY development are in for a shock, too, says David Hunt: "Many people outside the industry fail to appreciate that informal home-brew working practices don't scale very well to full-scale commercial development. They expect large teams to be as agile as their one-man basement experience." Yes, modders, you won't hit milestones as fast, but you will get paid. Just not to play more than one game.

For directors, another couple of fallacies need clearing up: "The business sucks—it's rough for employees; big corporate 'evil' empires rule the roost and creativity is dead," says Alex Ward. "I simply do not agree. This is the most exciting time for gaming and game creators ever."

According to Richard Lemarchand, "a good game director is actually the busiest person on the project, living and breathing the game for as long as they work on it, constantly playing the game and making lists of things to improve, and pitching in to help build things whenever and wherever they're needed. Everything that the game director does is geared toward improving the game, and there's never any shortage of things to do."

Ryan Lockhart points out that there are "many creative people here that help in the process. I just make sure everything is put together and 'works.' Often, though, people think I 'hold the creative candle' or can 'make all the final decisions,' and that's certainly not the case at all."

And when you reach the top of the development hierarchy, to vice president and president, it isn't any easier. According to John Romero: "It's hard work, especially if you plan on being great at something and not just okay. The money you get for the amount of hours you put in is less than other industries, but the balance is that the work is more fun. Way more fun."

Dave Perry says that during his tenure at Shiny, he lived by the mantra, "'This is big business; every minute counts.' The challenge, as the Game

Developers Conference used to explain it, is 'making games on time, on budget, and with an audience.'"

SUMMARY

The Good

- Producing and managing are two of the most varied of all the jobs in the gaming industry.
- There are constant challenges to overcome and a feeling of satisfaction when problems are solved by a team you'd take a bullet for. Or at least, take a soda to.
- But this pales in comparison to the whooping and hollering you'll do when you hold in your sweaty mitts the game you've helped steer toward completion. Which can then be traded in for "kudos" for the next couple of years.
- You can look back on the time when you launched a successful franchise in the same way Hunter S. Thompson looked back on "that time" in Las Vegas, but usually with smaller quantities of narcotics.

The Bad

- Do you like your blood pressure extra high? Then you've come to the right job. You'll be counting milestones and the veins popping in your forehead.
- You need to juggle gigantic amounts of information and fight battles between the team and marketing or publishing. With this in mind, you're occasionally seen as "one of the suits" rather than "one of the boys." Or girls.
- You're bound to clash heads with the unqualified (which is probably likely in any job), or a marketing or publishing department made up of people you'd love to Taser.

The Ugly

- Testers may fare worse, but producers have the lowest perceived prestige in terms of how everyone else in the industry perceives their job.
- You'll be paid to play, but it'll be that lava level where the collision detection hasn't quite been finished yet, and you're noting hundreds of bugs over a period of months.
- These jobs are much more difficult than you'd imagine. Have we stressed that enough?

Take This Job and Love It

So I'm guaranteed an entry-level producer job, with the possibilty of scaling the game industry development job ladder if I follow the advice to come in this section of the chapter? Yes, this is guaranteed.[14] What about if you cut a *God of War* logo into your arm with a bowie knife? Not so much.

---

14. Guarantee not valid in the lower 48 states. Or the other two. Or the rest of the world.

LANDING THE JOB

Our respondents were all over the map in terms of how they achieved success in obtaining a managerial job. Andrew Watt "started off working in a warehouse picking and packing games. I then moved into PR because I got on well with one of the girls in there. I then did customer support working on games helplines, then eventually moved into PR and marketing; [I] did this for a few years, then was offered the chance to become a producer on *Tomb Raider*.... It was nearer home and the money was better." He didn't need any schooling, but he hung around long enough to get his foot in the door.

Andy Abramovici's career was helped by a four-year business management degree, or at least that's what he was told when he landed his first job; however, he credits "my years of sitting in front of the TV playing games (much to the chagrin of my parents, of course) as my most valueable asset [in getting a job]." Veteran project manager Brian Beuken takes a quick stock of his career and life: "I started 25 years ago and have basically moved up and down the ranks as circumstances changed. This is all I've ever done...sad, eh?" Actually, we'd consider a career you hate to be sad. Mr. Beuken's living the dream here.

Emily Newton Dunn "started off writing game reviews for a small London-based magazine. I loved games but just couldn't afford to buy them, so a friend of mine who was editing the mag at the time offered to give me a gaming column. This allowed me to blag[15] consoles and games, and I was set as a journo! Shortly after that, I started PRing computer games, which meant I met a lot of people in the industry. I was very lucky because some of these industry insiders recommended me for a job presenting a show about games on Channel 4. I did that for a couple of years, while still writing about games and doing a million other jobs." These jobs entailed more PR, running websites: "I was obviously cut out for the role of multitasking producer! I did this for six years before deciding that I wanted to make games, rather than just talk about other people's."

Yes, it seems a great way to become a manager or director is to simply fall into it after a variety of other opportunities have come your way. Dan Jevons was a "a game journalist, game designer, business acquisitions manager, producer, and executive producer." He got his position when the boss of the company he worked for during previous jobs offered him a role. Working freelance and getting snapped up once you prove you're not a gibbering imbecile is a great way to get an interview.

Ryan Lockhart followed a similar path: "I worked in magazines and strategy guides for years before 'following my dream' and moving to Los Angeles. I actually gave my two weeks before securing a job and blasted out dozens of résumés and cover letters. I was able to start at 7 [Studios] as a designer and worked as hard as I could, and after four years, [I] made it to the position I currently hold." In fact, Ryan's extensive game reviews actually helped more than a college degree "because it gave the impression that I could carefully analyze

---

15. Blag: to appropriate, or steal, but without the negative connotations.

games and vocalize their strong and weak points. These types of communication skills are very important in a designer, and even more so in a creative director."

Another way you can land a managerial role is to work your way up from within, usually holding a directoral position in the discipline in which you're most well versed. For Richard Lemarchand, "I got my job as a game director by working for many years as a game designer and lead game designer. Over time, I've done almost every kind of game design task that a character-action game project could require and worked side by side with people from every discipline. Doing this gave me the experience I needed to be able to talk intelligently with my teammates about whatever we're working on, to be able to analyze a game design and make course adjustments when necessary, and to be able to make sensible decisions at the right times." Soren Lund took a similar path, learning the ropes, then striking out on his own: "I come from a technical background and started with programming, doing graphics and game design. I then started a development studio and by that route became more of a planner and supervisor. I have now been producing games for 13 years."

And for anyone currently hawking preowned software at a game store but secretly longing to work on a game involving skateboards, your dreams can come true! Well, if you're Kevin Mulhall, that is: "I got a job the day I turned 16 working at Babbages as a sales associate in the local mall. From that job, a coworker of mine became friendly with some frequent shoppers that happened to be working at a nearby game developer [Malibu Interactive]. My coworker got a job testing games, and within a couple months got me in there to test games as well. My job with Babbages definitely opened the door to video games as a career, since I met the right people at the right time.

"They made a lot of SNES/Genesis games back in the early to mid-1990s. I met a lot of really cool and talented people at Malibu Interactive." After taking a break for college, Kevin parlayed his testing experience to land another test role working for Paradox Development: "I quickly found that there was more to do than test games for them, as they didn't have a producer.[16] Before I knew it, I was placed as the official producer for a project we had with Virgin Interactive. I worked with Paradox Development for four years before accepting an offer to come over and join Neversoft Entertainment. The three founders of Neversoft had also been employees at Malibu Interactive, and that is how they knew of me.... I've been with Neversoft now for more than six and a half years."

ALEX WARD: A CAREER RETROSPECTIVE

Alex Ward didn't become one of the visionaries behind *Burnout* overnight. He (and many others in a directorial position) began with humble origins:

---

16. Back then, producers weren't always needed for smaller teams, as the lead programmer or artist would sometimes act as the producer as well.

ALEX WARD: A CAREER RETROSPECTIVE (CONT.)

"I have been following the business since 1982 when my parents purchased a Commodore VIC-20.[17] I studied psychology for my degree. I went overdrawn at the bank to buy a Super Nintendo. I nearly starved for four years, but I had **Super Tennis**, **Sim City**, and **UN Squadron** to play! I wrote my final-year thesis on video gaming—any excuse to bring the SNES into work!

"After I left university, I took a job writing about cell phones and fax machines. It was my first taste of office work. I HATED it with a passion and used to read **Edge** magazine under the desk.

"I wrote off for every job advertised in the back of that magazine. I eventually got a job as games tester at US Gold software in Birmingham.

"I was a terrible games tester; [I] hated it and tried to enter video game journalism instead. I did not succeed and subsequently was fired from my testing job.

"I was unemployed for a few months, and it was a pretty rough time for me. I nearly gave up on the gaming business. I wasn't sure if there was a career for me or whether or not I could earn decent money anywhere.

"I then landed a job at Acclaim Entertainment in Knightsbridge, London. I used to answer the 'consumer hotline' and give out cheats over the phone. It paid next to nothing, was as entry-level as you could get, and was literally starting at the bottom. But Acclaim was an exciting place to work, and the people there were fantastic. I learned so much every single day. I believed in myself and set out to be the hardest-working employee in the company. On my first day, I washed the dishes in the small kitchen, not knowing there were office cleaners who came to do that sort of thing!

"After a few months, I was promoted into a marketing position, and then I started to work with a wider group of people in the company. I got to travel a little and gained incredibly valuable experience from smart people in areas such as sales, marketing, operations, coin-op, and distribution.

"The European boss of Acclaim, Rod Cousens, was an industry veteran who I had followed for years. We got on really well, and he took me under his wing and always had time for me. Everyone needs a mentor in life, and Rod gave me lots of opportunities.

"I worked there for five years and enjoyed every moment. In 2000, I visited an incredibly talented UK developer called Eurocom. These guys were amazing, and after spending the afternoon with Matt

17. A contraption that loaded games from tape cassette. Ask your parents.

ALEX WARD: A CAREER RETROSPECTIVE (CONT.)

and Hugh—the directors of the company—I drove home determined to move from games publishing to games development. I had never made a game before, but I had sure played enough hits."

Alex then landed a job at Criterion, initially partnering with Acclaim on the *Burnout* series.

STAY IN SCHOOL!

Around half of our respondents have bachelor degrees, and all of them have finished high school; a good portion of them attended college until the game industry bug bit them. Even though you don't need a college degree to get your foot in the door, if you want to wiggle that foot a little bit, get most of your leg in, and actually look through the door at the prize your future career will bring, it's a good idea to get some form of degree, even if it isn't in business and management.

Andy Abramovici completed a bachelor's degree in business management and a minor in philosophy: "While not closely related, I do think that they have both helped to form (what I can only hope is acceptable) day-to-day behavior and perspective for my duties as a senior producer."

For Emily Newton Dunn, it was a seemingly irrelevant French degree: "It has absolutely no bearing on the job I do today, [but] it has come in handy—I have been interviewed by several French journalists! The discipline of being able to organize thoughts coherently also helps immensely."

THE PERFECT PRODUCER

Andy Abramovici runs down the psychological traits needed to be an effective manager, without turning into some crazy tyrant with a Napoleon complex and an office full of Totoro toys:

- Patience
- Compassion
- Organization
- Communication (written, oral, psychic)
- Attention to detail
- Ability to inspire others
- Ability to collaborate with others
- Ability to control one's ego
- Abililty to shepherd large and diverse groups of people to share one vision
- Game knowledge and history

What *is* useful in this business, particularly in a job that you can reach in many different ways, are industry contacts. You'll probably be forming these during the time before you interview for a producer or manager role. The best piece of advice Andy Abramovici can give is "treat people right and DON'T BURN BRIDGES. To that end, my motto is, 'Don't piss anyone off, unless you REALLY mean it.' This industry is growing but [is] still very small. I live in Seattle and recently interviewed in a few offices in the area. You will inevitably see people who know you from previous work experiences. If your interviewer sees these people come up and hug you or shake your hand, it doesn't take a rocket scientist to know this is a better sign than people coming at you with a machete or flying guillotine."

And try your hand at being a tester, as recommended by Kevin Mulhall: "Any hands-on production work at a game developer is good experience. The more the better. I believe that all producers should be involved in the quality assurance department at one point or another, because you learn a lot as a tester."

But with a job that's so social, in an industry stereotypically seen as full of misfits, communication is the best asset you can bring to a role like this. Alex Ward says, "If you are a wallflower, this is not the business for you. I remember reading the website of one of my favorite developers, Liverpool-based Bizarre Creations, where MD Sarah Chudley wrote about this. It has always stayed with me. It went something like, 'While it might sound easy working as part of a team, it's actually pretty damn hard and not everyone is up to it.' Reading that really hit home [with] me; it really isn't for everyone, and it is damn hard work.

"Personally, I'm not a big believer in early work experience as a way in— magazines often advise people to made mods for *Quake* or something. That doesn't do it for me. I am looking for passion, enthusiasm, a willingness to learn, and people who want to really do this."

Conclusion

- A real passion for games should drive you. Play lots of them, but understand them, too.
- Get a job in the following ways: Land an entry-level position at a company, either in the QA department or, if you want to manage a team with the same skill set, in the programming, technical, or design departments. Or, prove you have an eye for detail and enter via game journalism.
- Production work in other fields, such as television, can allow you to move between industries.
- A college degree isn't vital (unless you're taking the road to becoming a manager that involves another discipline), but it is recommended.
- Try a degree with courses that involve abstract thinking, breaking problems down into minute detail, and patience. Then fall back on this degree if you burn out; the attrition rate can be high.
- You're only as good (and eligible for hire) as your last project, but a really great game can hide a couple of turkeys you subsequently made.
- Expect to rise up through the ranks for a period of around 10 years to achieve a senior position.

Public Relations * Marketing * Business Development

PUBLISH OR PERISH: GAME PUBLISHING

How to Get Paid to Play Nice with Game Journalists and Development Studios: Publishing Video Games

"You needed a cool name to put on a T-shirt, and you needed a T-shirt to give to people. It was part of getting people excited enough to work 70 hours a week."

—*former Apple engineer Erich Ringewald*[1]

PUBLISHERS ARE TO VIDEO GAMES WHAT

record labels are to recording artists. They're the people who shepherd a game's development, slap their name on the finished product, and market it to the teeming masses of humanity eager for their next interactive fix. They're also the ones who—fairly or unfairly—take the heat when an unpopular business decision has to be made, from enforcing a release date to canceling the development of a title altogether. A few development studios are also their own publishers, but as game development becomes more and more complicated—and therefore more expensive—it's become good business to leave the marketing and distribution in the hands of those who specialize in it.

Good publishers are some of the most valuable commodities in the video game industry. They secure the funding that allows a studio to spend months or years creating a game without being distracted by financial concerns. They ensure that the project remains on schedule for a properly timed release, and is accompanied by a promotional blitz that would put a presidential campaign to shame. They also make sure that distribution agreements are in place so that the game gets maximum placement in as many retail outlets as possible. That way, no one who wants it has to be told that it's out of stock.

Although there are many facets to video game publishing (see the "More than Marketing" sidebar), most of them overlap with jobs we've already covered in this book. This chapter focuses mainly on marketing and public relations, and we rounded up a handful of some of the top PR pros in the business to give us the skinny on their jobs and how they got them.

MORE THAN MARKETING

The degree of publisher involvement in a game's development varies wildly from publisher to publisher. Although public relations and marketing are the primary jobs of a publisher, with some just taking the finished product and selling it, most publishers have at least some hand in their games' development—from game design to the writing of the manual.

Producers and project managers keep an eye on the game's development, setting development milestones to keep it on track and coordinating efforts between the developers, the marketing department, and everyone else who's involved in the game's production. These jobs (and jobs similar to them) are covered in the "Game Management" chapter.

Some publishers have internal quality assurance (QA) teams of testers. This is especially common with larger publishers that ship several titles,

---

1. It was also (quite unintentionally) part of getting on the bad side of Apple Corps, the multimedia company founded by the Beatles.

---

as it's more cost-effective for them

MORE THAN MARKETING (CONT.)

to retain a staff of testers than to have their developers go through the trouble and expense of hiring their own QA teams. It's also a good way for American publishers that work with overseas developers to catch translation errors or other language glitches. (We covered these jobs earlier in the "Technical Jobs" section. Hope you were paying attention.)

A Day in the Life

Most folks in the marketing and public relations areas of video game publishing are full-time employees and work on-site at the publisher's offices. Occasionally publishers contract a third-party PR firm to handle their press, but again, it's usually a full-time office job.

Alison Beasley fits into the latter category. As the managing director and president of Lincoln Beasley PR, she represents a diverse array of video game and software developers, among them Blitz Games, Frontier, Relentless, and FreeStyle Games. In addition to managing her own business, she also handles a variety of duties for her clients, including "writing and distributing press releases, meeting/talking with journalists to obtain coverage in magazines and websites, research for clients, attending and arranging for clients to talk at various conferences and events around the world, and liaising with publishers on behalf of clients."

Ken Berry handles marketing and business development for XSEED Games, developers of *Wild ARMS 4* and *Shadow Hearts: From the New World*. Berry's day-to-day schedule is never dull or predictable: "Since we are such a small operation, it encompasses just about all aspects of being a publisher, in addition to marketing and biz dev duties; localization and QA, evaluating new titles for publishing consideration, even customer service functions by answering fan inquiries into our general e-mail account."

On the other end of the spectrum, a senior public relations specialist for a major international video game publisher has considerably more specialized responsibilities. As the public face of the publisher, she has to "maintain media relationships as the representative of a video game publisher; proactively outreach to media to pitch for coverage of games; be the primary contact for media requests; write PR coverage plans for print, online, and broadcast media; and work with European PR counterparts on global communication plans."

SUMMARY

Public relations and marketing specialists are usually full-time employees who work from the publisher's office. Some are employees of contracted PR firms.

Their responsibilities are many, but they generally revolve around communicating with the press to hype their games and coordinating communication between the developers and the outside world.

The Good, the Bad, and the Ugly

There's a lot to love about working in PR and marketing for a video game publisher. But, not surprisingly, there's a lot of stuff that keeps the job from being 100 percent fun. And despite the fact that PR types are paid to spin negatives into positives for a living, we still managed to get some of them to cough up a few details that might cause you to reconsider whether this really is the career for you. Hey, don't thank us. It's our job.

MEET INTERESTING PEOPLE

To be effective at public relations in any field, you need to like dealing with people. This isn't a career for misanthropists, although dealing with enough greedy man-child video game "journalists" might turn you into one. The video game industry is filled with, shall we say, "unique" personalities, and fortunately, our respondents all seem to enjoy dealing with them. Alison Beasley gets a kick out of working with her clients and the journalists who cover them. "[My clients] are all interesting and unique in their own ways," she says. "Their personalities, products, ambitions, and creativity are always surprising and inspiring. My criteria for taking on a client is that they have to have at least one of the following: be known to me and be someone I like and respect; be recommended to me by someone I like and respect; have a genuinely interesting product/service to offer. Being part of a company's success and seeing them grow is hugely rewarding."

Our anonymous senior public relations specialist seems to have had mostly positive experiences with the video game press. Or at least that's her story, and she's sticking to it. "Working within a close-knit industry allows for working with editors who are also friends," she says. "With the video game industry growing as an entertainment industry as well, it also is growing in popularity with mainstream media and audiences, so it allows for more professional growth and exposure to different industries and relationships."

Ken Berry likes what he calls the "unique atmosphere" of the industry.[2] "Though the sales numbers may indicate otherwise, it's still a fairly small industry in terms of everyone knowing each other and being genuinely friendly," he says. "And though technically we're competitors, we all realize that our industry is in its infancy and still has a lot of room for growth, so we all root for each other and hope that each and every new title succeeds and expands the marketplace for all of us. We are all working together to expand the pie rather than fighting for the same slice."

---

2. And we're pretty sure he's not talking about the aromatic aura exuded by frantic, unwashed editors or developers on a deadline.

If you're cut out for PR work, much of your job can seem a lot like fun. "As with all PR jobs, there's a huge amount of socializing to be done if you want to—a certain amount is actually essential," says Alison Beasley. "So depending on who you work for, you can get to go to movie premieres, gigs, exclusive shows, lots of foreign travel, great restaurants, and various other fun events." And, of course, it's all on your clients' tab!

However, Beasley also emphasizes that the job isn't one big party. "Newbies are almost always shocked at the amount of preparation and planning that goes into PR. Even when out at parties, PR reps have to be aware of who they're talking to and how they're perceived—falling over drunk and being picked up out of the trash in an alley ain't always the best way to make a good impression!"[3]

And although the hours can be long (more on this in a second), the job's busiest times are fairly predictable. "The weeks preceding events where clients are speaking (i.e., [the Game Developers Conference] in March) are always the busiest," says Alison Beasley.

April and May were always very busy times, as was the case with most of the industry as everyone tries to wow the press at our industry's largest trade show." And, of course, the weeks and months leading up to a game's release[4] are incredibly intense, the marketing equivalent of Rocky Balboa running up snowy hills carrying logs on his shoulders before the big fight with Ivan Drago.

A (CHRISTMAS) RUSH AND A PUSH AND THE LAND IS OURS

Around the turn of the millennium, right about the time that you started seeing all of those hyperbolic headlines claiming "OMG!!! Video Games R Totally teh Biggest Business teh World Has Evar Seen!!! LOL!!", it was common for most publishers to release their biggest titles almost exclusively in the fourth fiscal quarter (Q4).[5] This strategy was obviously geared toward taking advantage of the most lucrative retail season in the Western world. Nondenominational types refer to it diplomatically as "the holiday season," even though we all know it's actually a three-month-long celebration of the miraculous night when Rudolph the Red-Nosed Reindeer braved a blinding snowstorm to deliver baby Jesus to Santa and Mrs. Claus.

However, as Pat Garratt of video game media behemoth Eurogamer Network explains, the ship-everything-for-Christmas attitude is one that's

---

3. Unless you're doing an impression of a hopeless drunk, in which case, nice work!
4. Which used to be almost exclusively September through December, although as our nearby sidebar informs us, this is a changing aspect of the video game industry.
5. October to December to those not versed in corporate-speak. Which is to your credit, unless you're going for a job in game publishing.

A (CHRISTMAS) RUSH AND A PUSH AND THE LAND IS OURS (CONT.)

changing in the industry. "Publishers became acutely aware around two years ago that the traditional idea of 'releasing everything in Q4' was not only short-sighted, [but] it was also incredibly dangerous from a business perspective. Games are notoriously prone to slipping, meaning that a huge amount of product would traditionally become bunched in the second or third week of November." If you're one of the big boys, that's not a problem. You can make deals with video game retailers to showcase your product, forcing smaller and poorer publishers' wares into the corner with little or no signage to alert gamers (and more importantly, their parents) to their presence. But even then, if you and a rival publisher have each sunk $50 million into the development of your blockbuster titles, nobody's going to come out of that fight unbloodied.

As a result, smaller publishers are starting to move away from the all-or-nothing Christmas gamble, and even the larger publishers are spreading out their releases a bit more evenly. A February blockbuster might not put up the numbers of an October blockbuster, but it beats having a quality product swept under the rug because it wasn't one of the five hottest titles of the holiday season. "The first and second quarters are now full of big-selling releases," says Garratt, citing *Fight Night 3*, *Ghost Recon Advanced Warfighter*, *Elder Scrolls 4: Oblivion*, *Shadow of the Colossus*, *ICO*, and *Ridge Racer 6* as big European releases in the first half of 2006.

"The insane November scrum still exists," says Garratt, referencing a rugby term that will go right over the heads of our American readers, "but companies have really had to smarten up in terms of release planning. The annual cycle of bunched releases has largely had its back snapped by the physical realities of high street retail, and it's reasonable to assume that the unstoppable growth of online retail and digital distribution for next gen consoles as well as PCs will break this cycle almost completely in the next five years."

GRINNING AND BEARING IT

If you thought that working in the publishing arm of the video game industry was going to be your ticket to escaping the long hours that wear down and crush the spirits of most other folks who toil in the digital fields, think again. Most of our respondents claim that they work 60–70 hours a week. The lightest workload any of our interviewees reported was in the 40- to 50-hour range. If you think that's unrealistically inflated, consider that a single two-day press junket already puts you well over the 40-hour workweek.[6] Not to mention the fact that, if you work for an international company (or one with strong international ties), you have to deal with a dozen time zones' worth of requests. Even if you're just in charge of North American operations, the demands start pouring in from the East Coast at 6:00 a.m. Pacific Standard time, and if a PR contact gets a reputation for being slow to respond, it can negatively impact the game and the publisher in the eyes of the gaming media.

"Long hours would definitely be the worst part about this job," says Ken Berry. "When you're trying to stick to a release schedule, you just have to do the best you can to meet deadlines no matter how impossible they sound, because moving a product's release date is the absolute last thing that you want to do." The reason being, the marketing push for a game's release begins months in advance of its planned ship date. Advertising must be bought, magazine covers must be negotiated for, and exclusive "first looks" are scheduled, all in the name of ensuring that the game comes out just as the buzz reaches a fever pitch. Delaying the release by even a week or two makes it hard to sustain consumer interest, which leads to a sharp decline in sales. And when money is left on the table, the grumbling begins and job security is in doubt.

Also, you must be obliging and work within everyone else's schedule. Nothing ever moves at your pace. "We have to work around magazine deadlines—sometimes months or a year in advance—and compete for the space," says Alison Beasley. "Equally, we have to be ready to respond at a minute's notice, especially for radio or TV. We have to think up ideas and constantly pitch them to journalists—not all get accepted and sometimes persistence pays off…. But there's a fine balance between being persistent and being a pain!"

Our senior public relations specialist tells us that her biggest gripes with her job are the "misunderstanding and misconceptions of the role of public relations representatives." Journalists know that it is the PR rep's job to—how to say this delicately—blow smoke up their asses. No one in charge of PR for a crappy game is ever going to sit down with a reviewer and say, "You know what? I'm not going to lie to you. This is a turd of a game." Instead, they'll emphasize whatever positives they can—like the fact that Fingerhate 30's new song is exclusive to the soundtrack or that the polygon count for the main character model has increased 50 percent since the last game—while trying to avoid discussing the fact that, in the retail version of the game, you can glitch through the street while walking down it and fall out of the game world.

As a result, marketing types who have had to go to bat one too many times for a disaster of a game might find they've started to lose credibility with their professional acquaintances in the video game media.

Our senior public relations specialist has been on both sides of the equation. As someone who worked in an editorial capacity for a video game publication

---

6. Of course, on the bright side, how many people can claim three (okay, six) hours of drinking and eight (okay, four) hours of sleep as "work time?"

prior to moving into PR, she knows how she and her peers are seen by the press. "Often when you are an editor, you question whether or not a PR representative is being honest or just protecting the company for whatever reason when something can't be discussed or delivered," she says. "For example, when a PR person is unable to provide an asset or build, the first instinct of an editor is often to ask, 'How is this possible? They must be hiding something.' Or 'maybe they're lazy.'

"Now having been working on the video game PR side, I understand the role that PR representatives have. We are the liaison between the development/production teams and the media. I think it's hard for some in the media to comprehend the complexity of developing a video game. For example, while it seems easy for one to grab a screen, because media can often do that with builds in their office, these builds are...in a more complete form, and thus much easier to capture screens. But in the early stages of a game's development, it's a lot harder to do because the game is still being built. Because of disconnects such as this, PR reps sometimes get the bad rap of being ineffective or being held personally responsible for something not being able to happen."

Finally, and this bears repeating, public relations and marketing are fields for people who really, *really* like dealing with people. It's not enough to just put in the long hours and work hard. You have to do it with a smile on your face. When you've courted a game reviewer for weeks with exclusive first looks and free swag, only to have them savage the title they seemed so enthusiastic about when you showed it to them last week, you must resist the urge to scratch their eyes out when next you meet. When a developer who you've shed blood, sweat, and tears for slags you in the press and blames the publisher for their substandard game's poor sales, you can't respond in kind. And at the end of a 12-hour day, you'd better sound as cheerful on the phone as you did at the start of it.

SAY HELLO TO THE BAD GUY

We've said it before, and we'll say it again: If you want to get involved in video game publishing, be prepared to be seen as the bad guy. The publisher is the one who holds the checkbook, and any time business decisions conflict with creativity—and they usually do—tempers flare and feelings get hurt. And don't expect too many sympathetic ears to turn in your direction. You're a representative of the big, bad corporation who's trying to exploit the creative geniuses of the earnest young development studio...even if the studio's full of overrated slackers who haven't produced anything of value since the fluke hit they stumbled onto by accident five years ago, which led to the talented half of their team cashing out their stock and going to work for other companies.

You've got to have a thick skin to work in publishing. You have to accept that it's your job to make the hard decisions that are best for business.

SAY HELLO TO THE BAD GUY (CONT.)

what's good for business is good for the product and all of the people who worked on it.

Of course, it's equally possible that you'll find yourself working for a publisher who really is out to screw over upstart dev studios and suck them dry. They're out there, and accepting paychecks from these people can have seriously negative effects on your karma.

And—do we even need to say this?—you won't be paid to kick back and play games all day. It's a frickin' job. "The business functions such as marketing are no different than the same functions in another industry," says Ken Berry. "You have to evaluate the strengths and weaknesses of your product and create your marketing strategy accordingly." So not only will you not have time to get your warlock up to level 60, but you'll also be fired if that's how you spend your workday.

SUMMARY

PR and marketing are fields for "people people." The people who last longest in these jobs are the ones who like the people they interact with in the industry. It's also a job for people who like to socialize.

The hours are long, but the schedule is predictable—as long as the game's development sticks to the timetable.

Working for a publishing company means you get blamed for a lot of other people's screwups, even if you had nothing to do with them. And you're not allowed to hit back.

Take This Job and Love It

We use that header in all our career chapters, but in this case, it's even more appropriate than usual. All our interviewees seem to genuinely love their jobs and couldn't think of anything they'd rather be doing. Of course, that could just be good marketing. Either way, let's take a look at how one goes about getting a job like theirs.

EDUCATION AND SKILLS

All of our respondents had at least some college experience. Most graduated with a four-year degree. "A public relations/related communication major definitely helps," says our anonymous senior public relations specialist. Alison Beasley agrees: "There are tons of media courses that have all sorts of relevant modules [to public relations and marketing]."

Both of them emphasize a need for great communication skills, both written and verbal, which only makes sense given how much time you'll spend on the phone, hosting events, responding to e-mails, and writing press releases. Multitasking and time-management skills are a must in this high-pressure job, as is the ability to handle sensitive information. Beasley also counts "a liking of people, creativity, sense of humor, and reliability" as important qualities for a PR representative.

PAYMENT FOR PLAYMENT

The salaries for PR folks in the video game industry are in line with PR salaries in other fields. Obviously, the bigger the company and the more high-profile the titles that you promote, the healthier your bank balance will probably be.

If you go into a career in PR, expect to make somewhere between $40,000 and $60,000 a year. Obviously, this can fluctuate, but it's not a job that'll have you eating beans and rice six days a week. Unless you really, really like beans and rice.

PRIOR EXPERIENCE

Obviously, if you're going for a public relations gig, it helps if it's not the first one you've had. "Marketing or project management experience definitely helps in any business-related job in our industry," says Ken Berry.

In addition to that, our senior public relations specialist advocates having journalism experience or any job that allows you to establish relationships with game enthusiast or mainstream consumer media. Alison Beasley recommends anything that "involves working with people and working [with] schedules, [with experience ranging from] event organization to student parties to fundraising for charity."

Sometimes seemingly unrelated jobs put you in a better position for a shot at a PR or marketing slot. "My first job out of college was at an import/export firm that specialized in trade with Japan," says Ken Berry. "It helped me learn more about the Japanese working culture and environment, something that became important when dealing with development teams in Japan after joining the video game industry."

And sometimes it's just a matter of being in the right place at the right time. "I started working for a publisher—now known as Codemasters—many years ago as an office junior," says Beasley. "They teamed up with another publisher, and I noticed that they didn't have anyone doing their PR, so I asked if I could have a go. They agreed and gave me free [rein] to do what I thought was right whilst at the same time providing a lot of support, advice, and a good expense account to pay for all the lunches!"

NETWORKING

In a job that depends upon forming and maintaining relationships with a diverse array of other people, networking is a key component to success, but it's not the whole enchilada. "Having a friend already in the industry definitely helps in getting your foot in the door," says Ken Berry. But that's not how he got his start. "I originally got into the industry completely by coincidence through a headhunter. Like most headhunters, they didn't tell me much about the company I was going to interview at.[7] When I got there, I saw all the artwork and toys lying around the office as well as a group of motivated young people that had significant roles within the company and I was sold."

When our senior public relations specialist worked as an editor, she made contacts that paid off when she began looking for a new job. "I heard about the opening while I was unemployed after our magazine was closed," she says. "I contacted my previous PR contact while I was an editor, and I went through the entire interview process as other candidates did…. It may have helped to have an inside line, but I don't think it necessarily helped me get hired. I think that my previous editorial experience was the bigger advantage, that and the fact that my mom owned an arcade when I was growing up."

But she doesn't discount the value of networking, either. "I think in any industry, more often than not, who you know is a huge advantage. Having come from the video game editorial side and having personal relationships with most of the journalists within the industry, I believe it helped make me an attractive candidate for the PR position I currently have. I personally knew several of the PR representatives at my current company, and I think having had a good rapport and professional relationships and friendships with them made it much easier to get my foot in the door. But in the end, it's really what you can bring to the table in terms of your skills and experience."

Alison Beasley credits her early associations in the video game industry (including Jim, Richard, and David Darling of what is now Codemasters, and Martin Alper, Alan Sharam, and Frank Herman of Mastertronic) with her current success. "These guys were my guiding lights, a huge inspiration, and [they] remain friends to this day," she says. "[Those] were the wild days of games where no rules existed and all sorts of crazy things happened, but it was a hell of a lot of fun."

OTHER ADVICE

Our senior public relations specialist lays out all the things you need to know about her job in one concise paragraph. "Be prepared to work hard in PR," she says. "People tend to think all you do is send out screens and take editors to lunch.

---

7. But unlike other headhunters, they didn't wear bones through their noses or lower a buxom blonde into a pot of boiling water.

This job has proven to be much harder work than I ever imagined it to be, especially coming from the editorial side. Know how to write and be able to express yourself verbally. Enjoy interacting with people in all departments and across all types of audiences because that is a major tenet of this job. Understand that this is very much a service-oriented field, but also know that it will also be tremendously rewarding and [that it] provides a great opportunity to grow as a professional as you will be exposed to and will be managing all types of relationships."

To this, Alison Beasley adds: "Take the long view and believe in karma. Help wherever and whenever you can. A young webzine/fansite [employee] could end up as the next editor, and a tester could end up running his own company. Everyone has to start somewhere. Respect confidentiality. Sometimes one of the most frustrating aspects of being a PR is *not* telling the press something that is due to happen, but until you've got full approval, you almost always have to keep quiet. Oh, and like people. You'll spend a lot of time with them, sometimes in large groups, and on long trips and you'll be expected to look after their every need."

SUMMARY

College experience is a huge plus for a job in PR or marketing, especially if you study communications, public relations, or media.

Prior marketing and PR experience is a big plus, even if it's not in the video game industry. Having held a game industry job where you formed relationships with other pros also looks good.

If you love people, are outgoing, have great communication skills, can manage your time well, and can keep several balls in the air at once, you're well-qualified for this job. If not, learn how to manage your time.

Conclusion

Public relations and marketing people are only one aspect of video game publishing. Their job is to get excited about whatever it is that they're selling and to transfer that enthusiasm to whoever they're trying to sell it to, usually journalists. They're hardworking, friendly, extroverted types who bust their asses to make sure their product is featured in the best possible light and make it look easy while they're doing it.

People who work in publishing also get beaten up pretty badly by people who don't know how their jobs work (or by those who know way too much about the evil companies that some of them work for). They are the holders of the purse strings, the negotiators of distribution arrangements, the promoters of the product, and the enforcers of milestones, all of which can rub the developers they work with the wrong way. They also don't get much time to play games, but the best ones are at least very familiar with their own titles.

WRITE ANGLES: WRITING FOR GAMES

How to Get Paid to Play with a Game's Story and Help Gamers: Becoming a Writer for Video Games

"Writing gives you the illusion of control, and then you realize it's just an illusion, that people are going to bring their own stuff into it."

—David Sedaris

"Nobody ever committed suicide while reading a good book, but many have while trying to write one."

—Robert Byrne[1]

SO YOU'VE GOT SOME WRITING CHOPS,

and you want to break into writing for video games, huh? Well, the good news is that there are more opportunities for writers in the video game industry than ever before, including a few you might not have thought of. As the industry grows and matures, game companies won't have any shortage of work for those who can tell a video game story that's as compelling as anything read between two covers or seen on a screen. And with games becoming more and more complex, there's a need for writers who can help gamers get through a game and enjoy every facet of it.[2]

And this is just the first of two chapters on jobs for writers in the game industry. This chapter deals with writing *for* games. If you want to write *about* games, you want the next chapter on journalism. These two fields aren't as separate as the chapter division implies, so all of you aspiring wordsmiths should check 'em both out.

A Day in the Life

We've broken down the category of writing for games into three categories: script writer, support writer (translator and manual writer), and strategy guide author. That doesn't mean that writers pick one of these and stick to it exclusively. It's just the easiest way to organize the jobs and avoid confusion, and we're very easily confused.

FEEDING THEM LINES

Having a scriptwriter for a video game is a relatively new concept. The earliest games were so technologically primitive that it simply wasn't possible to inject anything but the simplest story elements into them: "You're a space ship trapped inside of an infinite asteroid field—try not to die." As games evolved, some started to add basic narrative structure, but the technology still prevented creators from trying anything too ambitious.[3] The Japanese RPGs of the mid-1980s were among the first games to include relatively sophisticated story lines, but it wasn't until the late '90s that production values had improved to the point where virtually every game that had a beginning, middle, and end also needed a scriptwriter.

Because video game script writing essentially evolved out of game design, the scriptwriter or writers work very closely with the design team to figure out what kind of story they want to tell, what sorts of characters they want to include in it, and how the story and gameplay will be integrated. In fact, it's not uncommon

---

1. Why, yes, this is the chapter where we talk about being a strategy guide author. How did you know?
2. Or help keep an eight-year-old's parents sane by making sure the kid doesn't get stuck in the game they just bought him and start wailing his head off.
3. For example, the entire story of the original *Legend of Zelda* fits on two pages in the game's instruction manual. And that thing was *epic* back in the day.

for a scriptwriter to also handle some game design duties, especially anything that involves implementing the story line in the game. Some studios have on-site staff scriptwriters who work on one or more games per year, but it's not uncommon for a studio to contract freelance scriptwriters, who work from home offices.

Video game script writing is much different than script writing for any other medium. On the surface, it might seem like writing a game script would be pretty similar to writing a screenplay. And if you're talking about an extremely linear game with no branching story pathways and only one ending, you'd be right. But video games are interactive by nature, and any halfway decent video game story will involve some element of user choice and several potential outcomes, if only to enhance its value to the gamer by showing them something new every time they play through it.

Even games that don't seem to have a narrative often have a need for a scriptwriter. For instance, you don't need to write up a story line for a football season, because the act of playing toward the Super Bowl is the story in and of itself. But if you've got a commentary engine in the game that simulates announcer play-by-play, someone's got to write all of those lines for John Madden to slur through in the recording booth.

WRITING BEHIND THE SCENES

One essential but often overlooked video game writing job is the translator or localization specialist. If you're releasing a game in a foreign country, you'd better make sure you've got a good localization specialist, because nothing kills a game's mood faster than an unintentionally hilarious translation of the game's text and voice-over script. A good localization specialist will manage to preserve the tone and subtleties of the script in its journey across the language barrier. A bad one will have your game's villain proclaiming, "All your base are belong to us." Publishers who regularly import games to America often have their own localization department, while smaller publishers or developers contract the work out to freelancers on a per-assignment basis.

Video games aren't the only things that need localizing. Elizabeth Ellis is a localization specialist for DoubleJump Publishing, Off Base Productions, and *Hardcore Gamer* magazine. "The biggest part of my job is translating Japanese instruction manuals into English," she says, but she also translates strategy guides as well. "In addition to these things, I often try to remain on call for smaller jobs, like giving a quick translation of a designer's note, or searching Japanese Web pages for information on an upcoming release. I've also had to do brief English-to-Japanese translations and conduct communications with Japanese representatives, but these jobs are much rarer."

Don't forget that practically every game needs a manual writer as well. Those little booklets don't write themselves, you know. Greg Off, president of Off Base Productions, handles a great many responsibilities, including creating website content, authoring strategy guides, writing articles for *Hardcore Gamer*, consulting for video game publishers and developers, and managing an editorial staff. Somewhere in between all of that, he also writes game manuals as an independent contractor. Game publishers who don't contract out their manual work either have a staff manual writer or assign that duty to the design team.

The skills required to write a game manual are similar to those required to write a strategy guide. So without further ado...

WRITING UP A GAME PLAN

Another career option for video game writers is that of the strategy guide author. Why is this writing "for" games rather than writing "about" them? Because official strategy guides are licensed products that tie into the game's release and are approved by the game's publisher. Strategy guide publishers pay money to a game's publisher (the "licensor") for the rights to create and sell the guide for the game, which includes getting pre-release builds of the game in the weeks prior to the game's retail release. They then pay money to an author or two to write the thing, usually from a home office, but occasionally from the developer or publisher's studio.

Two of your humble authors have way too much experience toiling in the strategy guide mines, having authored about 100 game guides between them, from AAA titles like Nintendo's *Legend of Zelda: The Wind Waker* and Konami's *Metal Gear Solid*, all the way down to a bunch of little titles most people won't remember. So trust us: if there's one career on which we have lots of advice, this is the one.

The first question everyone asks when they find out what we do for a living is, "Aren't your mothers ashamed of you?"[4] The second question is, "So do you have to figure out everything in the game on your own, or does the game company tell you all of the secrets?" And the answer to that question is, it depends entirely on the licensor. Some are incredibly cooperative, providing tester-developed walkthroughs of the entire game, memory cards with fully unlocked game saves, regular updated builds, 3-D map renders, and so on. Others, well, are not so cooperative.

Most of what you see in a strategy guide is the work of the author, including all the text and screenshots. The licensor creates spot illustrations and concept art, which they provide to the guide publisher to jazz up the layout.[5] Some authors and author studios handle the book layout and design themselves. However, it's much more common for the author's text and screens to be passed along to a separate designer, who uses the author's technical coding as reference for how to lay out the book.

---

4. And the answer is, no, they're not, but our college professors might be if we didn't send regular updates to the alumni magazine boasting of our achievements in the fields of molecular biology and international espionage.

5. In fact, it's a major no-no for a guide publisher to include non-official game art in their guides.

If you're a guide author, you have to be good at games, and you have to work quickly. "To make great guides, I need to quickly develop a thorough understanding of a game's core mechanics so I can create a logical outline for its guide," says Prima strategy guide author Stephen Stratton.[6] "Once the guide's organization is in place, the rest is just work—I tear through the game and put in long hours in an effort to meet my manuscript deadline, keeping in constant contact with my project managers and editors."

STRATTON'S STRATEGIES: BEING A FREELANCE WRITER

Although we've separated these writing jobs into their own categories, many writers are freelancers who move between these jobs on a regular basis, and they all require some similar skills. Stephen Stratton has been a freelance writer since before he could legally drink alcohol. He's spent the last six years authoring more than 30 strategy guides for Prima Games and writing for video game websites. He shares the following advice on freelancing:

"Freelance writing is a great way to dip your toes into the industry without having to commit to it full-time," he says. "I'd advise anyone who's looking to transition to the industry to start small and try to land easy freelance gigs, like writing reviews and previews for one of the many gaming websites out there. Keep your day job and just write some articles on the side for a while. Once you've made enough contacts and built up your résumé, your knowledge and experiences will help you land a steady job or continue to work full-time on a freelance basis."

SUMMARY

Most games have scriptwriters who work with the design team to create the game's story and dialogue. Some are independent contractors or freelancers, while others are full-time employees of the development studio.

Games, manuals, and strategy guides created in foreign countries need localization experts to translate them for English-speaking audiences. Writers are also required for drafting game manuals. Like scriptwriters, localization experts and manual writers can be freelancers or employees.

Strategy guide authors play a game a month or two from its release and write the guide with varying degrees of assistance from the developer and publisher. They are almost always freelancers.

---

6. No relation to one of the authors of this book, except for the fact that they were both born to the same mother and father.

The Good, the Bad, and the Ugly

Hopefully one of the jobs you just read about looks like the sort of thing you'd like to get paid for doing. If not, consider moving along, because this section is where we mention a few perks of each job and then brutally remind you that there are plenty of reasons these things are considered "work."

THE GOOD

Everyone we talked to about writing for video games seemed to like their jobs. Here's why.

Old Dog, New Tricks

The best scriptwriters are natural-born storytellers. For them, the best part of the job is just telling a story. And when they're given a chance to invest themselves personally in the story, it brings with it the satisfaction that only comes with doing the thing that you love and getting paid to do it. As mentioned previously, video game scripting is a relatively new career path available to writers, and each game requires its own unique style of scripting. If you're a writer who loves taking on structural challenges you'll probably get a kick out of trying to figure out how to write a script for a game that has multiple branching pathways.

If your game has voice acting in it and your studio is willing to come up with the scratch, you might also find yourself writing for some well-known actors. Hearing your words come out of their mouths can be a rush, and if you're looking to cross over into writing for TV or movies, it doesn't hurt to be able to boast that you've written for some big names.

Finally, being a video game scriptwriter puts you on the ground floor of a completely new storytelling medium. Prose fiction, movies, and TV have all been around long enough that most of the interesting structural challenges have been solved. Unless you're some kind of supergenius storyteller, you probably won't come up with a storytelling device that will turn the literary or cinematic worlds on their ears. But video games are uncharted territory, with unlimited potential for the kinds of stories you can tell and ways that you can tell them. Video games are also more interactive and immersive than any other storytelling medium in history. It's one thing to watch an unarmed character descend into the unlit basement during a horror movie. It's a completely different experience to *be* that character and know that you have to go down those rickety stairs if you want to advance the story.

Flexibility and Variety

One of the chief perks of being a freelance localization specialist or manual writer is that you can often work from home. "The lack of commute and flexible hours that come from working at home are definitely a major plus," says Elizabeth Ellis. It's also work that's broken up neatly into project-sized morsels, which gives you a great deal of latitude over how you want to arrange your schedule and how much work you want to accept.[7] You're also constantly moving from one assignment to the next, so even if you wind up having to work on a really difficult project, you can always see the light at the end of the tunnel.

Greg Off says that some of the chief perks of his job are "getting to play and see the games as they are being developed and having direct input on their creation, traveling all over the world to meet developers and talking to them about their games, being on the inside track of next generation hardware and software, and establishing long-lasting relationships with many friends and colleagues in the gaming industry."

And, of course, the best test of whether or not you're in the right job is how much you enjoy your work. And fortunately for Elizabeth Ellis, she seems to have chosen her career path well: "There's also the fact that I'm doing something in a field I and my friends enjoy, and that my work is highly appreciated by my bosses and coworkers."

A Good Strategy

There are many perks to being a strategy guide author. For one, it's one of the only jobs in the video game industry where you actually get to spend a lot of time playing games, and playing them before anyone else. Of course, there are downsides to this as well (as we'll see a bit later), but for the moment, let's stay on the sunny side of things.

Most of the time, the licensor sends the game to the author so that the author can play it and work from home (another perk!). Some licensors require that the author travel to the licensor's studio and work from there, due to fears that unfinished game code might be leaked to the public weeks before the game's release. Spending two or three weeks on the road at a time can wear on you, but it can also be a tremendous upside for true game fans. "I can't even begin to describe the incredible feeling I had the first time I visited Nintendo's offices to write a guide for one of their games," says Stephen Stratton. "It was like a dream come true."

It's also a great career if you want to establish connections with producers and developers, because you'll be in near-constant contact with them over the course of the project. If you impress them with your dedication and the quality of your work on their game, you might wind up creating new job opportunities for yourself. That's how one of your authors transitioned away from being a strategy guide author and into script writing and game design. After spending several years writing the strategy guides for a certain game franchise, he was approached by the licensor to write the manuals, and then to assist with the story script writing, and finally to help design the next games in the series.

---

7. Of course, drumming up the work in the first place is an ever-present concern for any freelancer, but if you're not skilled at networking or building up a client list, you probably won't last for long as a freelancer anyway.

Finally, if you're the sort of person who gets bored easily, strategy guide writing might be for you. Most projects take between three and six weeks to complete, start to finish. If you make it your primary career, you'll probably write between six and twelve guides per year. And because the pace of the work is so intense, the time goes quickly.[8]

THE BAD AND THE UGLY

You didn't really think that you would just be handed checks without having to earn them, did you? Here are a few reasons why these jobs might not be for you.

What Do You *Mean* "We Can't Do That?!"

The deadline is the natural enemy of the professional storyteller,[9] and video game script writing is no exception. There's always some part of your script you wish you could do another draft of or polish some more, but when you're just one cog in the development machine, it's unlikely that you can persuade everyone to grind their gears to a halt so that you can tweak a scene or two. This is especially true when it's a scene that's already in production. If the studio has already motion-captured the actors and started on the animation, you probably can't convince them to let you change things all that much, even if you've just come up with an infinitely better way to tell the story.

In fact, video game storytellers are often at odds with the technical aspects of game production. For instance, if you've written this brilliant scene that requires eight characters to be on-screen but the programming team says it's impossible to have more than five at a time, you must find a way to write three characters out of the scene without compromising the story. If all of the cutscenes in a game are rendered in real-time, it might take a few seconds to cut to a different location within the same scene as the new environment loads. And sometimes the development team runs out of time and can't do everything that you wanted, which means that certain scenes must get dropped from the script if the game is going to hit its release date; in that case, you must find a creative way to make sure the story doesn't suffer as a result.

Finally, you can't afford to be too precious with the things that you create, and that's a rule that applies to the game industry as a whole. Maybe you've written a scene that perfectly captures the characters' personalities and advances the story in an original and compelling way, but if you're overruled by higher-ups on the design team, you must rewrite it with a minimum of grumbling. Remember, game development is a collaborative effort, so expect a great deal of feedback on your ideas, for better or worse. And that goes double if you're writing for a game based on a

---

8. Well, in retrospect it does. Every guide author has had a project where they reach the halfway point and wonder how they're ever going to make it through the next 10 days.

9. Although, ironically, a lot of us have a hard time getting anything done unless we're running smack up against one.

TV show, movie, or other license, because your script has to be approved by that licensor as well. Sometimes you actually wind up getting a better scene out of the process. And sometimes…well, at least you got a paycheck out of it.

Deadline Pressure and Instability

If you're a freelance localization specialist like Elizabeth Ellis, you might never be exactly sure when your next paycheck will show up. "I'm basically at the mercy of the industry for when I have jobs and when I don't," she says, "so I don't have a steady stream of money coming in at all times." Like a lot of video game jobs, her summers and falls are extremely busy as she works on games and other products that will be released in the holiday season, but the work tends to dry up in winter and spring. Manual writing falls into the same feast-and-famine patterns, so these are both careers where you need to either have a robust client list or another job that you can do on the side when things slow down.

Greg Off laments the tight time limits that he has to work under. "Grueling deadlines are probably the worst part of this job," he says. "You really have to be organized and have structure to your work in order to be able to stay on time and on deadline."

Greg is also the 87th interviewee who reminded us that there's more to working in the video game industry than just playing games. "As I'm sure most everyone else in this book has answered, our jobs are not 'just sitting around and playing games all day,'" he says. "In fact, it's seldom that I have the time to actually sit back and enjoy a game without having to write about it, dissect it, or look at it clinically."

Strategic Withdrawal (From Ever Enjoying Games Again)

While it's true that strategy guide authors spend a lot of time playing games, they have little to no control over which games they play. In fact, the extent of their control is limited to, "yes, I'd love to write the guide for that game" or "no, I don't need to eat this month."

And strategy guide authors don't get to play games in the ways that most normal gamers would play them.[10] First of all, they have to play unfinished versions of the games that are usually a month or two away from completion, which means that they're full of glitches. Authors also have to play the games to completion, which can be tricky when the games are in their bug-ridden beta forms. A lot of gamers loved playing *Grand Theft Auto: Vice City*, but how many of them meticulously tracked down every hidden package and completed every single mission to perfection, no matter how long it took or how frustrating it got? And *Vice City* is widely regarded as one of the best video games of all time.

Unless you're one of the most experienced and proven strategy guide authors out there, you'll be lucky to get even one of those in your entire career. Most of the

---

10. Yes, we are well aware of the oxymoron in this sentence.

time, you'll be stuck playing a game that you probably would never play for fun, and you've got to play it so thoroughly that you see every last facet of it at least once. Multiple playthroughs are often required in order to write a complete guide.

It's also a technical writing job, and your avenues for personal expression are extremely limited. You're basically writing a glorified instruction manual, in a style dictated by the publisher and licensor.[11]

If you haven't figured it out by now, writing strategy guides is extremely high-stress, high-pressure work, especially when you consider how inflexible the deadlines are. The vast majority of a guide's sales come during the first week of the game's release. If you blow your deadline, you've also blown most of the income that the publisher could have made from the guide—and probably your chance at getting offered another book from that publisher. Most author contracts also contain stipulations that allow them to withhold some or all of an author's payment if the author misses their deadline.

Strategy guide work is also seasonal and completely dependent upon the release dates for the games that the guides are based on. That means that August through November is the traditionally hot time for a guide author, while December through March is very lean. Authors have to budget their autumn windfall very carefully, because by the time Christmas rolls around, they might not get much in the way of work for the next three months. To make matters worse, release dates for games are prone to slipping around the holidays, which means that the project that was supposed to wrap up around October 1 now won't be done until the 15th. And you usually don't get paid for the work until you're done (not by the hour), so your next paycheck has moved out two weeks as well. And being freelance, with no guarantee of future work, can be a squeeze on other financial facets of your life.

It's not the kind of job that most authors can do part-time, either. If you pass up too much work from a publisher because you're doing another job, your name will slowly slip down to the bottom of their call list as more versatile and available authors get the work. There aren't many full-time jobs that will allow you to take three or four weeks off at a time so that you can write a strategy guide. And as you might have guessed, guide writing isn't something you can do in the evenings and on the weekends. Although some freelance writers are able to have a thriving career outside of strategy guide work, it can be very tough to swing that arrangement, and the guide writing usually has to come first.

Oh, and strategy guide authors also need to make a pretty significant investment in hardware as well. Although your publisher will usually loan you the debug consoles required to play beta code, you must provide your own computer to write the text on and grab the screenshots with. If you want to be on the list for PC game titles, your PC had better be top-of-the-line and capable of playing unoptimized code for cutting-edge games. You might also need a digital video

---

11. For example, licensors for kid-friendly games don't want you to refer to the main character "dying" if their health bar is depleted. But they also don't want you talking about "extra lives," since that implies that the character has a life that can be lost, which implies death.

camera or other equipment to capture screenshots and game footage with, and if you're hoping to take on books that require travel, you'd better have a laptop.

Finally, putting too many of your eggs in the strategy guide basket can be very risky. Programmers have literally thousands of potential employers inside and outside of the game industry. Game designers have hundreds of places they can work. Dozens of websites and magazines publish game reviews and previews. But the two biggest North American strategy guide publishers are BradyGames and Prima Games.[12] So it's a tight market.

PAYMENT FOR PLAYMENT

Video game script writing salaries vary drastically due to several factors, including whether or not the scriptwriter also handles game design duties and whether they're full-time employees who handle scripts for multiple games or freelancers who script one game. The game script's length and complexity is a factor, as is the depth of the developer/publisher's commitment to a more-than-mediocre script. And, of course, if you're a big-name writer who can be used as a selling point for the game, you can expect a much larger check than an inexperienced writer who brings nothing to the table but raw talent. Generally speaking, writing for TV pays better than writing for games, but again, that all depends on who you're working for and how much work you're doing.

Translators and localizers should expect to make something in the low- to mid-five figures for an annual salary, depending on whether or not they're full-time employees. And obviously, if you're a freelancer, your income is completely dependent on how much work you take on.

No one's going to get rich from writing game manuals. Writing manuals on a freelance basis generally pays between $500 to $750 for a 16- to 32-page console game manual, with larger or more elaborate manuals paying more. This is a part-time job that's best supplemented with a better-paying gig.

Strategy guide authors are paid per project, which means that their annual income is solely dependent on how much work they are willing and able to do in a calendar year. On the low end, an author might make $2,000 as a coauthor on a low-profile title, while more experienced authors can earn as much as $9,000–$10,000 per book, provided that it's a major release.

---

12. Nintendo could be considered a third publisher, as they publish their own Nintendo Power guides, but we're not including them because they don't fit the mold of a typical strategy guide publisher. Their authors are all salaried staff members, and you have to live in or near their offices in Redmond, Washington if you want a shot at working for them.

SUMMARY

Video game script writing is a new and uncharted territory, which makes it an interesting challenge for storytellers. It also has its own creative limitations, due to technological constraints and having a bunch of other people fussing around with your script.

Localization and manual writing might not be the most steady or creatively fulfilling of jobs, but the work's bite-size nature makes it perfect for supplementing another career.

Strategy guide writing is stressful, labor-intensive work with little stability and few employment options. It's practically guaranteed to kill your desire to play games for fun, or at least the games you work on. On the bright side, it pays pretty well, it's a great way to network with producers who can get you a better job, and you can work from home.

Take This Job and Love It

Wait, you're still reading this? Didn't you see the bit about how large chunks of your script can be axed for technical reasons or the part where strategy guide authors have to exist on cabbage soup from January to April? Well, if that didn't scare you off, the only way to dissuade you might be by telling you how to get these jobs, and then you can experience the horrors for yourself.

SCRIPTWRITER

The best way to land a job as a video game scriptwriter is to be a writer in another field first. The video game industry has seen a recent influx of TV and movie writers making the jump across the digital divide. Comic book writers are also getting a piece of the action. Fan-favorite comics writer Garth Ennis wrote the script for THQ's *Punisher* video game, which was spun off from the comics series he's written for the last several years. Eisner–award winner Brian Michael Bendis is the writer for Marvel's *Ultimate Spider-Man*, and he cowrote the script for the Activision game of the same name. But even if you don't have fiction or narrative writing experience, any previous writing experience helps, especially if you can demonstrate a familiarity with the source material you'll be working with.

Networking is essential. No developer or publisher is going to read your unsolicited script for their game franchise. This would leave them open to legal hassles if you try to claim they stole elements of your pitch, and they usually have in mind a direction they want to take the series. They frequently go to writers they've worked with in the past or try to recruit journalists and other writers who have written about or worked with their products before subjecting themselves to the deluge of insanity that comes from an open job posting.

If you've got an agent, point them in the direction of the games industry. If you don't, try and get face time with a game's producer, either as a journalist or strategy guide author or a guy with a fedora that has a little card in the brim with "PRESS" written on it.

And this probably goes without saying, but before you try landing a writing job, make sure you can actually do the job.

LOCALIZATION SPECIALIST

If you're going to be a localization specialist or translator, you obviously need to be fluent in at least two languages. And Elizabeth Ellis reminds us that *fluent* is the key word here. Someone who wants to do what she does should have "a strong knowledge of Japanese grammar (at least a four-year degree or equivalent through immersion), a strong grasp of English, and [an] ability to render coherently and faithfully from one to the other. General knowledge of Japanese culture, mythology, and other points of reference can also be useful."

She also emphasizes that teaching yourself Japanese by playing tutorial CDs during your morning commute probably isn't enough to do her job. "I think a lot of people underestimate the amount of Japanese knowledge you need to be a translator," she says. "For any job in the games industry, people seem to think that a love of games is enough. Unfortunately, it's like any job; you really need to have the qualifications or you won't last very long.

"You also need a good grasp of English. People (even people in the industry) seem to have the misconception that you need to be native Japanese to be a good translator, but I think it's just as important to be able to express what you've translated in English. Many of the writers I work with have told horror stories about translations that they themselves have to 'translate' out of broken English before they're useful at all."

Because localization and translation is a career that requires a specific skill, it's much more common to find open job postings for these careers. Frequent developer and publisher websites and look for relevant online game job postings. And when applying for that first localization job, be sure that you can prove you have the necessary skills. Ellis says that valuable work experience includes "just about anything in the field of translation; qualifications about your general experience with the language is a must. Also, any job that shows proof of your ability to dedicate yourself to a project."

If you're a freelancer who earns a reputation for doing a quality job, you'll find that more gigs will be offered to you by previous clients, provided that you maintain your high standard of work. "I got my first job, the one with DoubleJump, basically because of an acquaintance with one of its writers," says Ellis. "He came up to me out of nowhere one day to confirm that I knew Japanese and asked me if I might help them with a guide, because the translator they were using kept flaking out and wasn't getting any work done. They sent me a sample piece of writing to translate, and I returned it much faster than they expected; after that, the job was mine, and my bosses in that job have since referred me to a number of other jobs."

MANUAL WRITER

Some companies will put up open job postings for manual writers, but because getting the manual written falls fairly low on the to-do list, it'll likely be forgotten until it absolutely must get done, at which point it'll get passed on to some unlucky junior design team member.

If you can network with producers, it never hurts to send out general inquiries to them and ask if they need a manual writer. Because strategy guide author and manual writer jobs require the same skill set, some guide authors supplement their book rate by also writing the manual for the licensor.

STRATEGY GUIDE AUTHOR

Taking on a new strategy guide author is a risky proposition for any publisher. Usually a single author is assigned to each project, and if that author drops the ball, there probably isn't enough time to hire another one and get the book out the door in time for the game's release. Therefore, landing a job as a strategy guide author is all about finding ways to set the publisher's mind at ease and prove that you can do the job and not embarrass them in front of the licensor.

The best way to get started is to know someone who's already a strategy guide author and work with them as a coauthor on a project that is too large for a single author to handle. That's how Stephen Stratton got his start as a freelance writer, which led to his career as a Prima author. "My brother, Bryan,[13] got me a gig working as an intern for a San Francisco–based video game website called incite.com," he says. "When the company went out of business, we eventually became freelance writers."[14] But what if you don't know any strategy guide authors? How do you convince a publisher to take a chance on you? Well, as with so many jobs in the games industry, doing the job for free on an amateur basis is a good way to start. Pick up a game that you're interested in on the day of its release, write a complete walkthrough for it as fast as possible, and submit it to a site like GameFAQs.com. Include the link to the FAQ in your cover letter to Prima or Brady, and be sure to point out how close the uploaded date is to the game's release date. If you can turn out a complete walkthrough within seven days of the game's release, you might impress them enough to give you a tryout book.

Your first solo guide from a publisher is not going to be a AAA title. It's going to be a low-priority guide for a game that no one will care about. If you screw up the project, the publisher won't lose much money, and they'll know to never hire you again. But if they see that you're willing to go above and beyond on a smaller title and that you're prompt, professional, and easy to work with, expect more regular assignments to come your way.

---

13. 1999 winner of the Best Brother Ever Award.
14. And in the name of full disclosure, it should be noted that while Bryan got Steve his Prima job by taking him on as a coauthor, David Hodgson gave Bryan his start the same way. Now you're starting to see just how tightly knit this industry is.

The best time to inquire about a strategy guide author job is in June or July, when guide publishers are ramping up for their busy season, which begins in August. If you can get yourself into any industry trade shows, you might get a few minutes of face time with the people who you hope to work for; this is a good opportunity to make a positive first impression. Follow up with an e-mail after the show.

And before you try to get a job as a strategy guide author, make sure that you're proficient in the skills you'll need in order to excel at the job. "Full-time freelance authors need to be completely self-reliant," Stratton says. "They need to be well-organized and responsible, able to juggle multiple tasks at once, and budget their money wisely during the slow season. They also need solid communication skills, as most freelance work is done from home. Previous writing experience is a huge plus. Experience working in the industry is also a great advantage."

SUMMARY

Practically all jobs that involve writing for games require some degree of networking in order to land them. You must also be able to demonstrate strong writing skills; the more published writing you've done, the better.

Translators also have to be fluent in the languages they're translating to and from, which you probably already knew.

When you land your first job, work hard, write well, be professional, and don't just beat the deadline, beat it like a dusty rag.

Conclusion

This is a golden age for writers in the video game industry. With most games requiring a movie-style script, the concept of a scriptwriter has become a legitimate position in its own right. With production values at an all-time high, good translation and localization of foreign video games is a must. Every game needs a manual, which means every game needs a manual writer. And strategy guide authoring is a good way to work from home, earn a decent living, and network with a number of publishers and developers all at the same time.

Of course, all of these jobs require hard work and strong writing skills. No one will take a chance on you unless you've got proven writing experience. You need to work quickly, be adaptable, and constantly hustle to drum up your next gig if you're a freelancer. And if none of these jobs appeal to your writerly interests, continue to the next chapter on video game journalism.

*Fansite Owner/Writer * Magazine Writer * Website Editor*
*Freelance Writer * Industry Analyst * Humorist * Video Journalist*

THE WRITE STUFF: JOURNALIST

How to get paid to play around with games and words:
Becoming a video games writer or journalist

"The newest computer can merely compound, at speed, the oldest problem in the relations between human beings, and in the end the communicator will be confronted with the old problem of what to say and how to say it."

—*Edward R. Murrow*[1]

THE VIDEO GAME JOURNALIST: A RARE

breed of writer with the ability to string a cohesive sentence together *and* demonstrate superior gameplay skills. The concept of a "video game journalist" might seem like an oxymoron to some, but the Web and magazine stands prove that there are many outlets for intelligent debate, hard-hitting reviews, entertaining features, and other examples of this growing trend in popular culture.

Naturally, there's an amateurish side to this emerging form of reporting, such as free-for-all fanboy forums featuring the half-cocked ramblings of the disaffected youth and some pretentious, egocentric fansites full of self-important waffle, but if you cleverly avoid these garbage-conduits, you'll find hard-hitting editorial in the gaming world.

If you're set to become the next Cameron Crowe or Hunter S. Thompson but find Hideo Kojima more of a maverick than Neil Young, or if you prefer the Tetsuya Mizuguchi–influenced mind-altering head trips of Rez over a truckload of acid tabs, game journalism might be your bag. If your life's ambition is to write about games instead of making them,[2] your career path is clear: Become the most entertaining writer possible.

For this chapter's selection of industry interviews, we rounded up a dozen writers with varying degrees of experience, from the recently hired to veterans with over 20 years in the business. We included the self-employed, fly-by-the-seat-of-your-pants types; three experts in charge of all editorial at their workplace; a few editors in the trenches of big video game media organizations; and a couple of humorists to show what can happen when your wit surpasses your encyclopedic knowledge of obscure NES or ZX Spectrum[3] titles.

A Day in the Life

Our respondents can be categorized into one of three editorial camps:

Camp A: The Freelancer

Camp B: The Full-Time Journalist

Camp C: The Overseeing Editor

There are variations within these camps (such as those working online or for a magazine), but this was the most proficient way to pinpoint our interviewees' jobs without pigeonholing them.

---

1. One of the most well-respected journalists of the twentieth century, Murrow never saw the invention of *Pong*, but his thoughts about how journalists should conduct themselves are just as relevant today.

2. Writing about games can springboard you into the wacky world of video game development as a game designer, script writer, or producer.

3. The ZX Spectrum was part doorstop, part UK computer that was like a British Commodore 64, with a keyboard full of keys you could pry out and use as erasers. This computer was popular in Europe, and some of the best platforming games you've never heard of (*Manic Miner*, *Saberwulf*) debuted on the system. The software company Rare cut their teeth on Spectrum titles.

WILL GAME FOR FOOD: THE FREELANCER

First, there are the freelancers, a ragtag band of individualists who sacrifice a steady paycheck for a greater degree of freedom in their day-to-day work schedules. If the prospect of having no commute, making your own hours, and not having to put on pants before starting your workday appeals to you—and if isolation and financial instability don't freak you out—you might be cut out for the freelance lifestyle.

Getting started as a freelance game journalist is tricky. Most editors won't hire you until you've proven you can write something publishable, and you can't write something publishable until you're hired by an editor. Instead of packing it all in and making a horrific, unplanned, knee-jerk career decision, pull yourself up by your bootstraps and get yourself noticed.

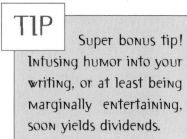

TIP

Super bonus tip! Infusing humor into your writing, or at least being marginally entertaining, soon yields dividends.

Freelancer and self-titled Outrageous Funnyman Seanbaby did it. When asked how, he replied, "My website, Seanbaby.com, rules." Years of making a name for himself with free and hilarious content led to the offer of a regular column for *Electronic Gaming Monthly*. "Once the devil himself conceptualizes a game and hands it off to disinterested game developers, magazine editors give it to me and I hate it," he explains. "The job also requires typing."

If you're planning on using a website as a means to an end, make sure that end is something more ambitious than creating a life-size replica of the Mushroom Kingdom out of empty Ramen Noodle cups in your parents' basement. The end goal, as with any career, is to make a living at what you're doing. If your site isn't generating money from page views, use it as pure promotion—pimp it on those forums you'd usually avoid. If you're the next Seanbaby, expect a gaming mag to come calling. If not, keep trying. It's the only way you'll get better. Eventually, you'll hopefully drum up enough interest to land a freelance gig or, like Jane Pinckard[4] (webmistress of gamegirladvance.com), a full-time position at 1UP.com.

Another tried-and-true method for getting noticed in the video game industry is to focus on entertaining or informing a niche gaming market, as did Uncle Clive of UncleClive.co.uk. His site initially catered almost exclusively to fans of the ZX Spectrum (a popular 1980s British computer, see previous footnote) and its inventor, Sir Clive Sinclair. Says Uncle Clive, "[I'm] mourning the passing of an era with a dwindling number of thirtysomething ZX Spectrum nostalgics who want to be 12 years old again, whilst simultaneously commenting on the state of current video game culture through the medium of Adobe Photoshop and low-quality Flash animation."

4. We'll get back to her in a moment.

Specifically, Uncle Clive's day is spent "trying to distill the ever-changing landscape of the medium into a single image, or a few paragraphs. But mainly it's about arguing via e-mail with a glut of Hotmail users who've taken offense to something negative written about their console of choice."

Persistence pays off, and the jack-of-all-trades mentality is central to freelancing. After you gather enough experience, you can strike out on your own more easily and take your career in several directions.

The venerable Bill Kunkel started out as one of the first-ever video game journalists (his first column ran in 1978), and he has seen it all[5] in the video game industry. In addition to being a regular full-time editor during his almost 30-year career, Kunkel (through his company, Kunkel Enterprises) has managed to parlay his experience into consulting work for various high-profile companies. On any particular day, his job responsibilities are now so varied, he says "it would take too long to say," but most consulting jobs involve going to a company, telling them how to improve their game, and not leaving until a big check is presented to you. Not a bad way to pass your days.

FULL-ON GAME ON: THE FULL-TIME JOURNALIST

Over in Camp B, those working as bona fide video game editors for one of the big publishing companies don't have time to worry about where to find work; it's already piling up. Those in entry-level editorial positions get to spend more time on a single game—for better or worse—playing it until their thumbs twitch uncontrollably and their eyes lose focus. It's around this point that writing a preview or review occurs. It's a great gig if you're asked to review the new *Half-Life* or *Resident Evil*, but if you're at the bottom of the totem pole, expect to get stuck with a lower priority title.[6]

As you gain experience and seniority in the world of staff editorial, and if you can keep yourself from breathing heavily through your mouth, you will probably be promoted to a midlevel editorial position. A sharp mind, a strong work ethic, and acceptable standards of hygiene earned Demian Linn a recently wrapped-up run as *EGM's* reviews editor. According to Linn, "Early in the monthly production cycle, day-to-day tasks include liasing with game publishers to determine what games will be in that particular issue, assigning three reviewers per title, and organizing multiplayer sessions. In the latter half of the cycle, the reviews editor edits all incoming text and makes sure screenshots are in and shepherds each review page through the production process, working with designers, copyeditors, and top editors."

As if that's not enough, there are bigger-picture duties, too, such as deciding "which games will get coverage and how much, recruiting and managing freelancers, creating and maintaining review templates, and ensuring that all

---

5. At least, that's what Bill Kunkel appears to have witnessed in his autobiography, *Confessions of the Game Doctor*.

6. Title deleted due to fear of lawyers.

reviewers meet the magazine's standards for thoroughness and fairness. The reviews editor is also a reviewer himself, so a lot of time outside of work is spent playing review games." And one of the perks of being the one who assigns the reviews is you get to keep the best ones for yourself.

Another midlevel editorial position common to most video game magazines is the features editor. Gary Cutlack, who holds that position on the UK's *Official Xbox 360 Magazine*, offers a sampling of his daily routine, which includes "writing features, reviews, news, and general copy for the magazine." He's also adept at "dealing with PR people and the readers."

Meanwhile, Ricardo Torres, who works as a senior previews editor at GameSpot.com, spends his week organizing rather than playing: His bullet-point list of activities includes:

- Talking to companies
- Coordinating departments
- Overseeing console previews
- Negotiating exclusives
- Visiting developers
- Organizing event coverage

With the advent of broadband, online publishers such as 1UP.com have an additional need: quality video content to supplement text pieces. Jane Pinckard,[7] a video producer, is at the forefront of this new editorial development, utilizing her talents as a writer and filmmaker. "Daily, we work on a weekly Internet show called *The 1UP Show*," says Pinckard. "We plan it, shoot it, edit it, arrange interviews or off-site shoots where necessary, capture the appropriate game footage, and publish it online. I split on-camera hosting duties with my colleagues. I also work with some other people on scheduling the show and coming up with ideas for narratives or other segments."

Actual video game playing takes a backseat to this routine and to more long-term planning, where Pinckard "thinks about other projects we'd like to work [on], whether it's other shows (like *Br0ken Pixel*, a spin-off that features really bad games) or a single longer project, say, a documentary on a specific game or studio. We also think about the direction we want *The 1UP Show* to take in the future."

If you're opting for the editorial lifestyle, expect to bring your work home with you. Around 10 to 20 percent of an editor's weekly workload occurs when they could be watching their TiVoed *Adult Swim* marathons.

The work that editors take home varies, but usually it involves playing a brand-new game for a preview, review, or feature. Thus, the line between job and hobby is blurred forever, as the pile of reviewable content takes precedence over the editor's *World of Warcraft* characters.

---

7. Told you.

If you're working on a print publication, kiss the weekend before your deadline good-bye, and if you're tied to an online pub, it's even worse. Says Pinckard, "A lot of us have worked on the weekends on editing projects, or late at night. Once in a while someone will not come into work because he is working at home on a big project and it's easier to do it without the distractions of other people milling about. And believe me, it can get distracting! We have a fun-loving team here...."

HAIL TO THE EDITOR IN CHIEF

For the feared and sometimes respected editor in chief, responsibilities are even more varied and hectic and leave even less time for actual game-playing. Dan Hsu holds the future of *EGM* in his hands every month. "I am responsible for the overall magazine, from cover choices to design to editorial direction to individual stories. I also manage a staff of editors and art directors who do most of the day-to-day work in putting the magazine together."

Dave Halverson—another editor in chief and veteran publisher responsible for the creation of *DieHard GameFan* magazine and now in charge of *Play*—has similar responsibilities: "securing covers, content, assets, planning coverage, assigning coverage, writing editorial, managing staff, helping with new revenue streams, and marketing."

John Keefer, the editorial director at GameSpy.com, offers up his personal on-the-job routine, consisting of "budgets, hiring, the editorial calendar, front page updates, long-range and event planning, site design vision, and implementation." Basically, the more senior your position as an editor, the more meetings you attend, the more people you manage, and the less time you have for actual game-playing. And the smaller the company, the more hats you wear.

The upper echelons of game journalism resemble a real-time strategy game, requiring editors in chief (EIC) to carefully manage resources and minions in a frenzied attempt to survive the publish-or-perish peril. It's not a 40-hour a week job, and it's not one you can phone in, figuratively or literally. Both Dan Hsu and John Keefer spend less than five percent of their job kicking back in their palacial mansions, sifting through the thousands of complimentary titles they receive from software companies. "The times I have to work from home," Keefer says, "I keep in touch via phone, conference call, and e-mail. Not ideal since face-to-face dealings are really essential to doing the job properly." Hsu echoes this sentiment. "I can take the occassional 'work from home' day when nothing pressing's waiting for me at the office. That's just to do game reviewing, e-mails, or writing. Ninety-nine percent of the time, however, I'm in the office."

IN SUMMARY

Freelancers work at home or are sent to press junkets. They spend their time chasing work from a pool of editors they know, are pals with, or of whom they have incriminating photos.

Full-time journalists have a host of duties to perform, and sometimes game time is with a title you'd rather not play. The workload bleeds into your weekend and home time, too.

Overseers have the weight of their magazines or websites hanging on their shoulders, and they delegate dozens of duties, grab exclusives, and pimp out their publications. They are never more than five feet from a bottle of antacids.

The Good, the Bad, and the Ugly

Attempting to wring out witticisms about the latest lackluster *Grand Theft Auto* rip off, or interviewing Michael Madsen about his voice-over work in the latest lackluster *Grand Theft Auto* rip off, demands more of your time than an average nine-to-five job. There are benefits to having one of the coolest jobs in the world, but an excess of free time isn't one of them. Here's what parts of your social life you'll lose if you launch into a writing career in the video game industry.

WHERE THE WORK IS

With the exception of Game Informer's Minnesota headquarters, most of the video game journalists with full-time jobs work on the West Coast. GameSpy is near Irvine, California. IGN, Ziff Davis, GameSpot, Future Publishing, and almost everyone else are in the San Francisco Bay Area, so adjust your standard of living accordingly. A $70,000 salary in the Bay is worth about the same as a $50,000 salary in the Midwest, so don't expect your gaming pennies to go as far.

PAYMENT FOR PLAYMENT

If you're a freelancer, expect to receive around $100 for a review. That's before taxes. For larger-scale features, this can balloon to $500, or even more if you're a recognized name. For full-time employed journalists, expect compensation in the realm of $50,000 per year, higher if you're ensconced in the laughably expensive San Francisco. For editors in chief, the blood-pressure medicine and 70-hour weeks certainly pay; these guys can earn between $80,000 to $120,000, sometimes up to $150,000, a year. Not that you'll have time to spend it, mind.

THE FREEWHEELING FREELANCER

Welcome to the secret world of the video game freelancer, where work schedules and workload depend on what you have lined up for the week. Uncle Clive has a "real" job away from the gaming industry and spends less than 10 hours a week on his website. Bill Kunkel, meanwhile, reckons he works close to 50 hours a week in his full-time but self-employed operation.

No one's going to check your time card to make sure you punched in on time, but the later you sleep in, the less time you'll have to visit a software company that the regular staff of a magazine are too busy to visit. Seanbaby, who reviews gaming detritus for a living, says it all depends: "Some games are nice enough to suck hilariously, so that's easy. Others are terrible in boring, uninteresting ways and I have to spend 20 damn hours coming up with a single sentence anyone would want to read about *Barbie Horse Adventure*."

Freelancers are busiest in the runup to the holiday season. With a deluge of titles starting to arrive around Halloween, freelancers can expect an IM or e-mail from their editors in the latter part of the year.

As for the lean periods of winter and summer, you'll need to become more creative in your writing, like Uncle Clive. "The summer gaming drought causes apathy, but there's always the safe and secure 8-bit past to mine for inspiration." Reviews and previews might be out during the slow months, but if you're a versatile enough writer, you should be able to pitch more general ideas and avoid having to take a second job flipping burgers. And if you're a gaming veteran like Bill Kunkel who's in demand from companies, the well of opportunity never dries up. Most consultants do brisk business during summer, when all the holiday season games are nearing completion. "Sometimes I'd rather play outside or watch TV than type jokes," remarks Seanbaby, echoing many of the problems also associated with freelancers who adopt a humor-free writing style: You're either bashing a keyboard furiously or sweating profusely at your lack of gigs.

There's that slightly sickening feeling when you realize that your game review was overly harsh or overly edited by a magazine more concerned with placating sales and marketing than sticking it to "the Man." Uncle Clive takes no prisoners, as he has no bottom line to keep buoyant. "I do occasionally [feel] guilty about ripping into a game, only to feel slightly sorry for the poor guys who've spent the past three years working 20-hour days trying to bring it to us."

But a bigger fear for the freelancer is pulverizing a game or company and waking up to find a virtual horse's head in your bed. Uncle Clive says, "When the Xbox first launched, I mocked up a spoof campaign [that] suggested they didn't have a clue about the market they were attempting to break into. I checked my Web stats the next day only to find over a thousand hits originating from Microsoft HQ in the space of 24 hours. Within four seconds I threw together a legal disclaimer and spent the rest of the day nervously reading up on fair use and satire legislation."

FREELANCE RAGE: A CAUTIONARY TALE

The freelancers interviewed for this chapter know better than to launch personal attacks on people within the gaming industry; the cardinal sin is never to lambaste a person or group you might end up working with at a later date. However, one freelancer who started up a "bold but not brash" website began to make comments about other journalists, mocking and questioning their ethics. Long story short, everything got out of hand, and the freelancer was blackballed. He did use his own name in the title of his website, though, which wasn't perhaps the most cunning of plans.

If you're intent on lampooning a major software company, make sure your country's laws allow you to. A final, major bummer for freelancers is the company they keep: According to Kunkel, "the best and worst aspect of any collaborative venture are the people you work with—whether it's designing games or working in the comic book or movie fields." As a freelancer, expect to deal with PR folks threatening to cut all ties after you described their latest big-budget title as less a "riveting roller-coaster ride." And expect to grin and bear it after a website's copy-editor replaces what you thought was a devastatingly biting satire about John Romero with a run-on sentence. You're a mercenary. Unless you're your own boss, you work for a paycheck, not personal writing freedom.

PAID IN PLAYOLA

Be careful if you become a freelancer and want to treat your career with a smidgeon of integrity; the PR folks at software companies know what you need—a free trip to the Bahamas to experience the latest first-person shooter. And you must be put on the list to receive all those free games, right? Not if the general public finds out, as you're then seen as a shill for the software company, and your review scores are questioned. Large magazines and websites have specific ways of refusing such displays of playola, but for the struggling freelancer there's always temptation, and careers have been ruined because of it. Buy your own games.

The public misconception of the freelancer is difficult to shake: There's a mixture of resentment and awe that "you're being paid to do something that millions would volunteer to do for free," says Uncle Clive. "Of course, when it's your bread and butter, a job is a job. It's hard work, busting your shoes at three in the morning (which is when, it happens, I'm [answering] this) because things have *got* to be done and there's often a lot of money at stake." So, there's pressure to meet deadlines, your hobby becomes just another job, and your footwear is at risk.

Seanbaby also wants to clear up a few points. "I think most people can wrap their heads around what it'd be like to play a bad game and then write about it. If anyone thinks that involves something completely crazy, then let me clear up the misconceptions right now: All those things you're thinking are nuts."

SIXTY-HOURS-A-WEEK SENIOR EDITORS

For those writing about video games with the luxury of actual health care benefits, the workload is generally in the 50-hour-a-week ballpark, although some folks work as little as 30, and others hit 60 hours when a massive game arrives hours before a deadline and needs intense coverage. These hours expand to hilarious sweatshop-style routines at the times of year you'd expect, too. For Jane Pinckard the holiday season is longer. A lot of companies release tons of stuff for the fall, so there is a lot to keep track of." With a site like GameSpot, Ricardo Torres has an even busier time of it: "It's pretty consistent year-round these days. It used to be slow January through February and post-E^3, but that's slowly gone away."

The year-round daily grind only applies to websites, though; print magazines have a monthly cycle in which articles are written, designed, and sent off to the printer (occasionally with hilariously offensive prose still left undetected) before the process begins all over again. "The last week in the magazine's production cycle is pretty hellish for the reviews editor," remarks Demian Linn. "And the October/November/December/January/February issues are the busiest, because of all the holiday releases coming out. In a slow month, the reviews editor might only have to oversee 13 to 15 pages of reviews, but in the holiday issues, the reviews section can balloon to 30-plus pages."

Magazines also have additional ways to make a buck, which cause headaches for everyone who doesn't have the words "VP of" before their title. Gary Cutlack explains: "Deadline week before printing [is bad], as we're usually pretty slack at doing things on time, plus Christmas is always hectic due to there usually being an extra Christmas issue." Is there any time to spend *not* worrying about deadlines? According to Pinckard, it's "just after E^3 and before Tokyo Game Show—the summer months, about June to late August. Ah, it's nice then!"

Grimly facing an eternity of incoming deadlines isn't the worst part of the job for a midlevel journalist, either. For Gary Cutlack, it's the "increasing levels of publisher pressure to 'sell' magazine covers based on positive coverage and advertising spending"—a dirty little secret no one else in the magazine industry wants to talk about.[8]

---

8. Yes, covers are bartered for. Large companies are constantly pressuring magazines and websites for positive reviews, especially of games that don't quite live up to expectations. Coverage on weak titles are used to barter exclusives on "must-have" games, and sometimes editors fall for it. Watch your step.

HOW IT REALLY WORKS

In the grand scheme of things, editorial doesn't matter to those with sharp suits gathering the company moola; it's advertising that powers magazines (and websites). That *Need for Speed* double-pager can cost Electronic Arts around $16,000 or more, and the rates depend on the subscribers, which is why you're constantly showered with small postcards telling you to commit. Your $24 a year goes some way to keeping the magazine staff in Twinkies and flat-panel TVs, but the real benefit is that the magazine's sales department can use its readers to leverage more money. Which makes the world go round, apparently.

For Linn the worst part is the offensiveness of mediocre software. "When you work all day and then have to go home and play a game you hate for four hours instead of having some free time like everybody else, that sucks. When playing a game becomes work, it's just wrong on all levels."

Torres doesn't deem any part of his job to be unpleasant; it's more the challenging aspects that can be vexing: "The one that stands to mind is having to reconcile deadlines with the reality of some of the situations my team and I find ourselves in. The assumption is 'Oh, you play games all day; that must be so cool!' But that's not always the case, and the game-playing doesn't happen in the most ideal conditions. For example, trade shows like E3 or the Tokyo Game Show [TGS] require us to write games up based on a limited amount of play-time. In the case of TGS, we're often dealing with games that are totally in Japanese with no English information readily available. On top of that, you're also having to deal with having to write quickly and, in some cases, on little sleep. While some may view this as the worst part of the job, you take the good with the bad and deal because it's all still great fun."

Whether you're conveying a game through text or video, the problems are universal. "It takes a *lot* of time, and when you're working with people who don't understand that, it can be frustrating," says Pinckard. "Say you shoot a 30-minute interview; then your boss says, 'When can you get it up online?' You're aiming for a 10-minute clip, so first you need to capture the footage in a digital format (at least 30 minutes), then edit it down to 10 minutes (about an hour, or less if the same person who shot it can edit it); then you have to render it and compress it out in all the formats your website requires (which for us would take about three hours, depending on the source file of the clip and how long it is). So a 10-minute piece actually represents about five hours of work for the video team—invisible work, since you don't necessarily see the results in the clip itself."

When this work applies to a trade show, there's rarely time to socialize. But sometimes this can be advantageous. Ms. Pinckard states, "Another potentially bad aspect—but this can also fit under 'good' things—is that you're highly visible if you're the on-camera talent, and people will feel free to either love you or hate you based solely on what they see coming out of their little screens. So you have to be prepared for that."

MEETING OF THE MAN-CHILDREN

Perhaps one of the most frightening experiences in a freelancer's life is being sent on a press junket to some far-flung corporate headquarters to watch long presentations about a game that isn't quite ready to be shown yet, while a self-absorbed game designer drones on about how his new game is the Second Coming of *Grand Theft Auto*. You need to grin and bear these events, and use them to cultivate friendships among your fellow writers and PR folk. Ignore the sweat-stained pits, the halitosis, and general malaise emanating from your fellow man, and embrace them. But not too tightly.

With all this goal-oriented content to produce, is there any actual fun to be had as a journo? There certainly is. How about having an all-access pass to all of the video game industry's most anticipated talents and titles? Mr. Torres explains: "The best part of the job is seeing games and hardware early. Some of the recent highlights [are] probably seeing a demo of the console formerly known as the Revolution given by Shigeru Miyamoto in Japan. Having one of the icons of this industry, and one of my heroes, personally show off this crazy new thing was surreal and impossibly cool."

Then there was late Game Developers' Conference Pinckard went to. "I noticed Fumito Ueda (*ICO*, *Shadow of the Collossus*) and Keita Takahashi (*Katamari Damacy*) chatting together, so I asked them to do an interview together. It was completely impromptu, but they were very game and gracious, and it turned into one of the best interviews I've done so far. It ended by their asking me out to lunch!" Which she promptly refused, as she had to cut, edit, package, narrate, and generally fiddle with the video footage she'd captured. But them's the breaks.

Despite her agonizing refusal to chow down with two video game luminaries, Pinckard still finds the job "vastly satisfying. When you do a good job, you *know* it; and other people know it, too, and get a lot of pleasure from your work."

Demian Linn's perks are more psychological: "It's not soul-destroying. It nice to play games early, or deliver a critique on a big game, or find one that's likely to be overlooked and give it its due."

Whereas Gary Cutlack's raison d'etre includes "going to L.A. for free, [which] is pretty cool when you're usually based in London or some other small town in England. And free games, at least, once a year when one you genuinely like comes out!"

TIME ACTUALLY PLAYING

50 percent (freelancer)
15 percent (editor)
10 percent (editor in chief)

But isn't this job really all about playing video games all day? "I wish, but unfortunately, no," Demian Linn counters. "I get to actually play games at work for maybe 10 percent of the time; it's not all sitting around with my feet up on the desk."

Ricardo Torres elaborates: "The fact of the matter is, while playing games certainly goes on, it's just part of our day-to-day experience. Obviously if we have an assignment due, we'll be playing something but we're also having to balance our time with taking screens, capturing video, filming video previews, travelling to see games, calling companies, etc. There's certainly fun to be had, and there are aspects that are certainly unlike any other nine-to-five job, but it is still a job."

For those tasked with creating compelling video content, the job takes even longer than you'd think. Jane Pinckard says, "It's definitely fulfilling and gratifying, but it ain't easy. I think about all the times I thought *writing* for online was tough! That's a piece of cake compared to making videos for online. In the end, though, it comes down to talent, plain and simple. You really, really do have to be able to write, [or] else you'll be shunted aside and forgotten about pretty damn quickly."

THE OVERWORKED OVERSEERS

Aside from a gigantic paycheck and the ability to fire people at will while hoarding a vast collection of free games (if your corporation doesn't consider it "play-ola"), the editor in chief's schedule hikes up the stress to embolism-inducing levels. Dan Hsu is most busy "right before and right after our annual video game trade show, the E^3, and in the fall, when we're working on our holiday issues (which traditionally hold more content and have more pages)."

For John Keefer, the additional Game Developers' Conference (GDC) (which websites traditionally cover more thoroughly) is also a key time. Being at the helm of an operation also means there are some broader problems to take in your stride. "The worst part of the job," reveals John Keefer, "is long hours, not being able to write as much as I used to, and not getting site projects implemented as quickly as I would like because we have to wait for other departments." Red tape, scheduling, and the meeting-based daily grind impede on what was once all about the writing.

Dave Halverson also has some pet peeves he has to deal with, such as "working with embargoes, as [I] feel they are detrimental to a game's well-being. Also PR people who don't understand our job and therefore misrepresent products that cost millions of dollars to develop"—a problem developers seem to have similar gripes about.

Dan Hsu seems less concerned: "I love my job. Well, maybe the hours can get a little bit long at times, especially during deadline. I've had to overnight it in the office before, because I just didn't have enough hours in the day to finish what I needed to. But I'm not complaining. The people who had to smell me the next day might, however." This "real work" often impedes on what everyone thinks a game journalist is doing—playing games. For Hsu, "most of my work-related game-playing (such as when I'm reviewing a product) happens after hours or on weekends, on my own free time."

But for all the flatplans, meeting with the sales and marketing departments, and appearances on CNN to placate the latest deranged diatribe against video game violence by some grandstanding politician, even the editors in chief know why they're still in the business. "The people, both in-house and in the industry, and of course the games, anime, etc., that we critique. Gaming is like a big family, and it's a wonderful thing to be a part of," Dave Halverson comments. Dan Hsu agrees: "I consider myself to be extremely fortunate to be able to work in a field that's also a lifelong hobby. Yes, I get paid to play video games, but not only that, I [also] get paid to learn about video games...to write commentary about them...to see them before they come out.... I'm a lucky, lucky man."

IN SUMMARY

Freelancers have more free time for actual gaming and can say what they like about software. They just have to put up with possible legal threats or overzealous editors.

Full-time journalists play games less than you'd expect, sometimes seethe as sales and marketing dictate editorial decisions, but feel good championing sleeper-hit games.

Overseers love the people, the games, and the industry. They consider it an honor to be "the faces" of gaming. They're less content with incompetent PR folk, red tape, and long hours at the office.

Take This Job and Love It

So, you're undeterred about the long hours playing an uninspiring fighting game starring a flavor-of-the-month rapper and attempting to lampoon it without offending the entire hip-hop community, are you? Then you'll want to know how the people whose stories you just read got their start in the industry. As usual, the responses are varied.

HOW DID THEY GET THIS JOB?

Bill Kunkel "started the first video/computer game review column in *Video* magazine in 1978 and the first magazine, *Electronic Games*, in 1981. Sort of made my own niche." Of course, nowadays it's a bit more difficult to start your own magazine and become a powerhouse consultant in the ensuing 30 years. Therefore, consider creating a website. "My website, Seanbaby.com, rules," remarks Seanbaby (for the second time). Uncle Clive did the old "viral marketing" technique. "Uncle Clive was my Internet name on the Edge forum (a UK video game magazine). I used my webspace to put up a few daft captions under some images from a 1970s Atari catalogue [that] I linked to from my signature. People seemed to dig what I was doing and started linking to it from across the Internet."

Gary Cutlack, the man responsible for the legendary humor site Ukresistance.co.uk, spent years cultivating a following of Sega fans lamenting the passing of the Dreamcast. He was then "spotted by a mag editor with a keen eye, thanks to my blog. But that was in 1997, before *everyone* had a blog."

Demian Linn, meanwhile, had just been laid off: "I heard about [the gig] through a previous coworker, interviewed for it, and sent in samples. After I was hired, my boss told me that I didn't interview very well, but that he loved my writing samples. What really sealed the deal, though, was a recommendation from someone who had worked with both me and my prospective boss." Ricardo Torres's journey to GameSpot ended under similar circumstances: "I was picked up by GameSpot in 2001 after having been laid off at CNET Networks during the CNET merger with ZDNET."

Jane Pinckard got where she is today with a mixture of chutzpah and editing equipment. She made up her job title and waited for the top brass to get with the program. "I was originally hired as news editor, but I knew that wasn't what I really wanted to do, deep down. So along with my friend we started making video segments in our free time. At first management wasn't into it, or didn't get it, which was fine since I'm not sure we knew what we were doing either, although we had a very clear vision of where we wanted to go. We basically worked on the show as if it were an independent, minicompany within Ziff Davis. Eventually the show drew enough of an audience that our corporate overlords approved of our work, and I got moved into a different department, and now the 1UP Show is considered a flagship product for the online group."

Dave Halverson's reasons for why he currently helms *Play* magazine are less specific, but no less compelling: "Passion. Pure passion and drive, and a genuine enthusiasm for games that is unrelenting."

Dan Hsu's ascension started with a career change a decade ago. "I didn't end up liking what I studied in college (statistics, of all things), and no immediate career paths looked appealing to me. [My girlfriend and now wife] suggested that I send out my résumés to companies for whom I'd like to work, regardless of whether they're hiring or not, regardless of whether it's in a field that I specialized in. Seemed like the longest of longshots, but hell, what did I have to lose? I knew I loved video games, so I sent out résumés and cover letters to about 30 game-related companies, from publishers to magazines, just hoping for something to stick…anything. I didn't get a single response, so I quickly gave up on that idea. But then, nine months later, the editorial director of *Electronic Gaming Monthly* gave me a call to see if I'd be interested in writing for the magazine."

John Keefer's rise to the top was due in part to the opposite: a 20-year "journalism and newspaper background. GameSpy invited me out for an interview, and they hired me as managing editor in January 2000. I've been running the editorial side ever since."

DID THEY HAVE A PREVIOUS JOB THAT HELPED?

Bill Kunkel did, as he eloquently explains: "I worked as a musician, which taught me that teamwork is more important than dysfunctional virtuosity. I wrote comic books, which taught me storytelling and dialogue. And I covered pro wrestling, which taught me that entertainment can be most enthralling when we're being fooled and we dig it."

Wait, wrestling is fake?

Dan Hsu had a brief stint as an Electronics Boutique employee, "but that didn't really help or hinder my chances of working for *Electronic Gaming Monthly*."

Dave Halverson's formative years were spent enduring "every crappy job I ever had that wasn't rewarding or made any difference." His current gig is completely different.

John Keefer, meanwhile, comes highly qualified. "I have a law degree and was in the newspaper business for more than 20 years as a writer, editor, designer, and jack-of-all-trades."

John brings up an interesting point; he landed a job as a high-ranking journalist on a large-scale website with *no* gaming connections. In fact, he says it helped. "GameSpy was looking for credibility; it wanted a professional who knew journalism and had professionalism to help get [their] name out there. I think the biggest thing going for me was that I wasn't a gaming guy. I built all my connections once I came in. What I did bring was how to run a news organization, how to train writers, copyediting, and ethics, despite what some of the jaded readers may think."

Demian Linn came to *EGM* with "two and a half years on staff at a car magazine, experience as a game tester and freelance game reviewer, and experience as a staffer at another game magazine."

Ricardo Torres used the infamous "it's who you know" adage: "I worked for a brief time at Rocket Science Games and made two great friends there. Once I left Rocket Science and went back to college, I kept in touch with them. I was still in contact after I graduated and was dealing with the standard 'What do I do now?' thing that all English majors specializing in creative writing do postgraduation. As it happens, my friend was working at CNET and knew about a job opening in the company's games division GameCenter. He got me an interview, and I landed the gig."

Jane Pinckard used more savory tactics: "I do know a lot of folks from hanging around the games industry for a while. The most important thing I think is that you must be willing to meet everyone; and if you are personable and professional, more people will want to deal with you." So wipe the Cheez-It crumbs from your chin, go to your mother's for a strategic shave and washing, then go out and entertain Cliffy B after he's read your blog and found it hilarious.

NEW SCHOOL JOURNALISM

An increasing number of blogs from freelance game journalists can be described as "new school journalism," a craze sweeping the nation where the journalist attempts to become part of the story. Sometimes the results are hard-hitting revelations about racism on Xbox Live or the life of a gold collector working for MMO players without free time on their hands. But most are self-important journalists with a flare for obscure references to existentialist poets. If you're going down this road, balance your personal style with prose that everyone will want to read...not just your mom.

HOW DO *YOU* GET THIS JOB?

You may have mad skillz when it comes to *Halo 3* or investigating every single particle of *Final Fantasy XI*'s *Valkrum Dunes*, but you'll need other, less gimpy skills to cut it in the world of video game journalism. Bill Kunkel offers his own X factor: "Communication skills, the ability to intuitively understand what gamers want. You have to *be* a gamer; you have to love it. You have to be a problem-solver." But when you're starting off, say at the helm of your own website devoted to the world of early British computers? You'll need "Photoshop, Flash, Dreamweaver, and a complete lack of a social life," says Uncle Clive. If you're more of a "name" writer, like Seanbaby, your wit must be gestated over more months than a baby elephant. "To be a comedy writer, you need good observational skills and a strong sense of lame. If you're unfunny and trying to train yourself into a comedy writer, God help us all. That being said, by deconstructing existing jokes and understanding what makes things funny, maybe years of practice could turn your brain into an engine of hilarity."

If you're not prepared for that kind of commitment, there's a skill set of a different kind. According to Demian Linn, you need "very good editing and writing skills. Strong organizational skills. Good interpersonal skills, knowledge about games.

By the time you've reached the upper echelons of game hackery, your skill set must be further honed. Dave Halverson's character chart includes "great gaming skills, good vocabulary, [a] broad knowledge of pop culture and entertainment, ability to write in such a way that readers feel they can trust what you are saying for better or worse. Humility, thick skin, sense of humor, self-confidence, balance, mental toughness, honesty."

Then add a sprinkling of what makes Ricardo Torres one of the best in the business: "There's a lot of multitasking because my group has to keep an eye across the current and next gen platforms from Sony, Nintendo, and Microsoft. You have to be organized, detail oriented, able to manage multiple projects at the same time, keep an eye on the import market, and have a good understanding of games." John Keefer's list includes "being friendly and knowing how to schmooze, without being phony. And above all, maintain integrity by keeping your promises and being true to yourself, the readers, and your publication." Finally, Dan Hsu's "anal retentiveness, an eye for details, [and a] vision for what the audience is looking for" should transform you into the most powerful video game journalist in the galaxy.

WHAT LOOKS GOOD ON THE RÉSUMÉ?

If you're preparing for a career in game punditry, it isn't like the old days;[9] you'll actually need "previous magazine experience" (according to Dave Halverson) or "actual experience on a print title" (Gary Cutlack). Naturally, you can't get this until you've worked on a magazine or print title. So what's a fledgling reporter with a penchant for *Super Smash Bros.* to do? Well, becoming the games reviewer for your college paper is a start. Or any kind of reviewer. Or reporter. Or a guy who hangs around reporters. The main point is to get some kind of an education. John Keefer says, "In my experience, I look for journalism first, then gaming. You can learn about gaming; you can't learn about how to write (at least not on the job). Being able to present your thoughts clearly and concisely while checking your facts is paramount. Keep the fanboyism to the fansites, not a professional site." "Obviously," says Seanbaby, "the more places you've been published, the better."

To train properly for this type of job, you'll need to sacrifice. Dave Halverson needs you to spend "lots and lots of gameplay time [and have a] vivid imagination. Watching loads of TV/DVD/and anime and listening to music." Reckon you can handle this chore? Dan Hsu also has some college courses you could try: "English, journalism, and to a much lesser extent, Japanese, are all good backgrounds to have when working for a game magazine." Demian echoes this advice: "Study journalism and creative writing in college, then demonstrate your skills writing for other outlets." If your plan is to craft video as well as text, Jane Pinckard reckons "a degree in broadcast journalism wouldn't hurt, but no one whom I work with has anything like that."

Ricardo requests you become personable, too: "For a job like mine, you want to have a strong gaming and writing background, but you also need good people skills as well. Besides the fact that I'm a manager and have a team of people to look after, I need to interact with companies on a daily basis and go to visit developers. Being able to establish a rapport with people is important because it helps me get access and information that helps me do my job."

As always, Seanbaby's advice is golden: "Creative writing or journalism would be good things to focus on, but for any creative art, college is better used as a fun four-year transition from childhood into alcoholism. If a writer is being prolific and getting nonretarded feedback from his or her readers, their skills will raise infinitely faster than if they were sitting through lectures in academia. And with the Internet, there's no reason for any writer to not be self-publishing." Any parting advice, Mr. Baby? "Has anyone already taken 'Believe in yourself and try your best!'? If not, I want that one."

9. "Old days" actually means the early to mid-1990s, where any old chimp with a *Street Fighter 2* tournament under his belt got a high five-figure salary and an office by the window and spent his days taking pictures of Sagat's high and low fireball attacks.

IN SUMMARY

Get a job as a writer by attempting one or more of the following:

- Send out résumés to anyone in the website or magazine business, and don't stop.
- Construct your own website or blog that's too entertaining not to be visited by millions of gamers on a daily basis.
- Tell people about your journalistic prowess by sowing virtual seeds on gaming forums.
- Spend years in a related journalism field, playing games on the side, then make your move.

To get qualified as a writer, try the following:

- An English or creative writing degree, or a degree in journalism.
- Learn a valuable second skill, such as Japanese for import game translations; you'll be more hirable.
- Try a minor in college in a semirelated field that websites are requiring help with, such as video production; it helps immeasurably. Watch for these trends.
- Interested in sports games? Writers with an encyclopedic knowledge of football or baseball are in high demand, too.

To get qualified as a gamer, try the following:

- Immerse yourself in popular culture from the 1980s onward, so your witticisms can be related to movies, television, or the latest dysfunctional celebrity.
- Polish your gaming knowledge to a particular genre, but have a good, well-rounded history of game-playing. You must be able to reference obscure PS1 titles like *Tail of the Su* as easily as the latest Ubisoft first-person shooter.

Conclusion

The career routes to take are fourfold:

1. Write for a website or magazine you (or a small band of entrepreneurs) own.[10]
2. Write for a website or magazine a gigantic faceless corporation owns.[11]
3. Go freelance and write for someone who pays you. Usually, these people work at the place in point 2.
4. Combine your writing ability with a relevant second skill to become twice as powerful and 74 times as awesome.

---

10. You'll have complete freedom to write anything you want. And no money to pay anyone for months at a time.
11. You'll have less freedom to write nasty articles.

*Cyberathlete * Sponsored Gamer * Game Trainer*

ACTUALLY PAID TO ACTUALLY PLAY: PROFESSIONAL GAMER

How to Get Paid to Play Video Games Better than Anyone Else: Being a Professional Video Gamer

"If you watch a game, it's fun. If you play at it, it's recreation. If you work at it, it's professional video gaming."

—Bob Hope[1]

"Dad, I won $4,000 playing a video game. What's this world coming to?"

—Jonathan "Fatality" Wendel[2]

WE WERE ACTUALLY ALL SET TO WRAP UP

the video game job descriptions with the Retail chapter, but we didn't want to call this book *Paid to Play* without including at least one way to earn a living by actually playing video games—not testing, not reviewing, not designing, but flat-out playing them. So we added this chapter on professional gamers, if only to raise your hopes of making an easy fortune in video games one last time before crushing them with the cold, hard reality of how hard it is to actually pull it off. It's what we live for.

A Day in the Life

Dennis "Thresh" Fong is widely viewed as the world's first professional gamer, or cyberathlete, who competitively plays video games for money. "The first major tournament I won was in 1995 with roughly $10,000 worth of prizes," says Thresh, but it was another couple of years before he achieved what was perhaps his most famous accomplishment: winning *Quake* creator John Carmack's Ferrari.

"In 1997, John Carmack donated his red and tan 328 GTS Ferrari as the grand prize for the biggest *Quake* tournament ever, called 'Red Annihilation,'" says Thresh. "Thousands of players competed via an online gaming service called Mplayer. The field was eventually whittled down to the top 16 players, who were flown to the E^3 (which was held in Atlanta that year) to compete on a LAN. We were broken up into groups of four and played round-robin, with the top two players advancing from each group. I ended up winning that tournament with an undefeated record and took home the Ferrari as the prize."

CYBERATHLETE SPOTLIGHT: FATAL1TY

If you know only one professional gamer—besides our good friend Thresh, of course—odds are it's Jonathan "Fatal1ty" Wendel of Kansas City, Missouri, arguably the most successful professional gamer of all time. Shortly after his 18th birthday, he began a pro-gaming career that has reduced his opponents to steaming piles of giblets and earned him hundreds of thousands of dollars in prize and endorsement money.

Fatal1ty has won tournaments in *Aliens vs. Predator 2*, *Doom 3*, *Painkiller*, and *Quake III Arena* and was placed in *Quake IV* tourneys, making him the most decorated pro gamer of all time. And he's put his fame to

---

1. Okay, he actually said "golf," but "professional video gaming" is more relevant and requires about as much physical activity.

2. We don't know, but Fatal1ty's gone on to earn a whole lot more since turning pro. We stole this quote from a *60 Minutes* story that you can read online at www.cbsnews.com/stories/2006/01/19/60minutes/main1220146.shtml.

CYBERATHLETE SPOTLIGHT: FATAL1TY (CONT.)

good use, signing lucrative endorsements with a number of sponsors. You'll see his moniker on all sorts of gaming hardware, from sound cards to his own custom gaming mouse, as well as his own branded line of apparel.

And just as other professional competitors make considerably more money if they're good enough to attract the attention of sponsors, pro gamers also boost their income through endorsements. "Generally speaking, the real money in any professional sport is in endorsements—not the prize money from tournaments," says Thresh, who signed a lucrative endorsement deal with Microsoft during his pro-gaming days. "It is a constant, recurring form of income and allows a pro gamer to focus entirely on practicing and competing rather than worrying about how he's going to make this month's rent." Thresh estimates that he probably made five to seven times as much cash from endorsements as he did from prize money during his competitive years.

Savvy pro athletes know that they've only got a few good years in them before others come along to knock them from their perch. If they're smart, they invest their fame and money into the next phase of their career, and any pro gamers worth their ergonomic mouse pads will do the same. For instance, Thresh had more than superhuman hand-eye coordination going for him. He also had a head for business.

"Along with being a 'professional gamer,' I was also an entrepreneur," he says. "I started my first company, a portal for gaming information called Gamers.com, in 1996 with my brother. We used some of my winnings and endorsements from pro gaming to fund the initial startup phase of the company. I was the CEO and my brother was the CTO. We eventually grew that company to about 40 employees, raised a bunch of money in venture financing, and grew the company to over 100 employees before having to downsize when the dot-com crash happened. At one point we were one of the top three gaming sites in terms of traffic and visitors and were ranked the number one gaming portal on the Internet. We eventually spun off two companies, Firingsquad.com and Lithium.com, from the original company, and all three companies are still in existence and relatively successful today."

But he didn't stop there. "After Gamers.com, I started Xfire,[3] an instant messenger and social networking site for gamers, with Mike Cassidy. I am the chief gaming officer and Mike Cassidy [is] the CEO. Xfire has grown to almost 5 million registered users in less than three years." Thresh has come a long way since that first 10-grand tournament prize. In April of this year, MTV Networks acquired Xfire for $102 million dollars, thus ensuring that Thresh will never be Ferrariless.

3. http://www.xfire.com

SUMMARY

Professional gamers are really good at games. Really, really good at games. In the future, when wars are fought by computer-controlled robot drones, countries will clone pro gamers' brains in vats to gain a tactical edge on the battlefield.

Most pro gamers make their names and initial money from competing in (and winning) tournaments. But the big money is in endorsements and parlaying your fame as a pro gamer into future opportunities. Imagine where George Foreman would be if he was still getting punched in the face for a living instead of shilling bachelor-friendly grills?

The Good, the Bad, and the Ugly

Playing games for a living...how can that possibly be work? If you're actually thinking that, this is the first paragraph you've read in this entire book, read on and weep.

CYBERATHLETE SPOTLIGHT: THE OGRE TWINS

Yes, Dan "OGRE1" Ryan and Tom "OGRE2" Ryan are actually twins, and at 19 years old, they are two of the most feared *Halo 2* competitors in the world. Hailing from Pickering, Ohio, the brothers started playing *Halo* online through GameSpy Arcade and quickly dominated the scene, picking up top honors with their clan, StK, at Major League Gaming's D.C. 2005 tournament and the World Cyber Games 2005 Grand Final in Singapore.

The OGRE Twins currently attend Ohio University, but they're not letting their academic lives get in the way of their pro-gaming careers. In fact, the brothers skipped their final exam in freshman economics to attend the WCG Grand Final. They were reportedly not too upset at taking the zero on the test after walking away with $20K in prize money.

A LEVEL PLAYING FIELD

Dave "Walshy" Walsh is a pro gamer who recently signed a contract with Major League Gaming. He sums up the biggest and most obvious upside of professional video gaming: "I get to play video games for a living! I get to do what I love to do and get paid."

Besides the fact that you can make money from playing games, the biggest perk of pro gaming is its low barrier to entry. "One of the advantages of the pro gaming circuit is that you can compete in the same tournaments the 'pros' compete in and have an equal shot of winning," says Thresh. "My suggestion to aspiring pro gamers is to compete in a couple of those tournaments first, and if they are successful, then to take a more serious look at dedicating themselves to it full-time."

Professional gaming is also slowly starting to earn some mainstream credibility. For a time, "professional gamer" was neck-and-neck with "compassionate conservatism" as the most ridiculous oxymoron of the twenty-first century. But as that smelly old hippie said, the times, they are a-changin'. "There used to be misconceptions about gamers—they are lonely basement types—but now everyone games," says Dave Walsh. "Really, everyone. My friends' mothers game, and I never thought that would happen."

JUST HOW GOOD AT GAMES ARE YOU?

So is that it? Is being a successful professional gamer as simple as just being really, really good at games? Well, yeah, in the same way that being a successful professional baseball player is as simple as just being really, really good at baseball. But let's assume that there are as many casual gamers out there as there are casual baseball players. Let's take it one step further and say that there are as many gamers interested in earning a living from playing video games as there are baseball players who want to earn a living from playing baseball.

CYBERATHLETE SPOTLIGHT: THE FRAG DOLLS

In 2004, video game publisher Ubisoft hit upon an ingenious way to draw attention to their games: have them played at public events by a team of seven incredibly hot women. And thus, the Frag Dolls were born. Since establishing the American Frag Dolls, Ubisoft has gone on to assemble Frag Doll teams in the UK and France as well.

In addition to promoting Ubisoft games, the Frag Dolls's mission statement includes drawing more females into the gaming world, which we're all for.

Now look at how many career options are out there for a professional gamer as opposed to the same options for a baseball player. The latter has 30 major league teams, plus AAA affiliates and a farm system for each, plus coaching opportunities at the professional, collegiate, and high school levels, not to mention the option of playing professionally for overseas teams. A halfway decent baseball player could probably even stop brushing his teeth, give himself a lobotomy, and head over to England to start a career in professional cricket.

But a professional gamer? Well, the number of tournaments and pro-gaming organizations is on the rise, but it's not nearly at the level of professional sports yet. Unless you count bowling as a sport. Which we don't. "Outside of the top five players in the most popular game, there isn't much endorsement money to be had," says Thresh. Turn that one over in your head for a moment. One of the most well-known and successful cyberathletes in the world says that there's only room for about five guys at the top right now. At this point, you might want to put down the controller, pick up a push broom, and start training for a career in professional curling.

Fortunately, that seems to be changing: "Until recently, it was impossible to really be established," says Dave Walsh. However, thanks to the rising number of gaming leagues and tournaments, it's becoming more possible for gamers to make a living doing what they do best. "I couldn't have done it without Major League Gaming," says Walsh. "I had been playing *Halo 2* for years, but when MLG started competitions in 2004, I got to show off my skills against the best in the world. Now I'm a part of an awesome team—Final Boss—and we won the 2004 and 2005 Championships and are currently undefeated this year. Major League Gaming just signed a $1 million contract with us." Walsh also recently signed an independent endorsement deal with Red Bull, which allows him an additional eight hours per day to train by eliminating the need for sleep.

FRAGGING LESSONS, $50/HOUR

If you've made a name for yourself in competitive play, you might want to get into the emerging market of video game training. And no, this is not a joke. At least, not to Tom "Tsquared" Taylor, CEO and founder of www.gaming-lessons.com, which offers "individual and team training to gamers of any age or skill level," according to the website.

Currently, the site offers training in *Halo 2* and *Super Smash Bros. Melee*. You can sign up for individual lessons, team training, and "scrim packages" to scrimmage the top teams in the world. Lessons run between $25 and $65 per hour, and if you want to get taken to school by an instructor barely old enough to go to school, we recommend purchasing some tutorial time with eight-year- old Victor "Lil Poison" De Leon III.

Of course, with more opportunities for professional gaming, you're going to see a higher level of competition develop. Gamers might start realizing that gaming could be a legitimate career option. So, if you want to make it to the top and stay there, you've got to train like a maniac, just like any other competitor.[4]

---

4. That's the reason we don't have an interview with Fatal1ty, possibly the most famous professional gamer in the world. When we requested one, his people informed us that he was in training for his next tournament and was completely isolating himself from all distracting influences, like us pesky media types.

SUMMARY

The best part of professional gaming is that you get to play games for a living, literally. It's also relatively easy for a talented newcomer to break in, and the concept of a cyberathlete isn't as silly sounding as it used to be.

The bad and ugly parts of pro gaming are the limited opportunities for top-tier success, meaning that only the crème de la crème will ever earn enough cash to make a living at it, and fewer still will make enough of a name for themselves to parlay it into postcompetitive ventures.

Take This Job and Love It

If you want to become a professional gamer, find yourself a tournament (see the "Get Your Game On" sidebar) and enter it. "The first day of Major League Gaming competitions is the Last Chance Qualifier—an open bracket," says Dave Walsh. "There are also online qualifying tournaments. So if you're good enough, you'll be noticed. If you're really good enough, you could win prize money, too—there's $800K up for grabs this year, and the number will continue to rise as competitive gaming moves forward."

GET YOUR GAME ON

One of the best resources for finding upcoming video game tournaments is Twin Galaxies (www.twingalaxies.com), which also features player rankings and gaming statistics.

To see if you've got what it takes to be a pro gamer, check out the following professional gaming organizations and tournaments:

- Cyberathlete Amateur League (www.caleague.com)
- Cyberathlete Professional League (www.thecpl.com/league)
- Global Gaming League (www.ggl.com)
- Major League Gaming (www.mlgpro.com)
- Professional Gamers League of America (www.thepgl.org)
- World Series of Video Games (www.thewsvg.com)

And hell, just because he's such a nice guy and gave us such a great interview, let's plug Thresh's day job one more time. Hit him up at www.xfire.com for all of your gaming social networking needs.

Enter your first tournaments with realistic expectations. Don't expect to shoot to the top in your first time out. Remember, you're playing against people who are just as determined as you are to reach the top. If you find yourself getting spanked repeatedly, don't lose heart right away. Spend more time refining your skills. That's what Walsh did. "I practiced for many years," he says. "I developed my own game style—The Claw—and that set me apart from other players. Ultimately, you just have to work hard and be excellent."

And there's more to video game training than just sitting in front of the screen playing games for nine hours a day, although that's probably going to be part of the regimen as well. Most successful pro gamers are in pretty good shape to boot. That might run contrary to the stereotypical image of a gamer, but physical fitness has a variety of fringe benefits, including increased alertness and mental stamina, both of which are vital when you're several hours into a championship tournament. A bag of Doritos might be an acceptable meal during a weekend of fragging your friends for fun, but if you're going to turn pro, proper diet and exercise are part of the deal.

SUMMARY

Look for a tournament. Enter it. Practice on your downtime. Repeat. If possible, invent a play style with a tough-sounding yet ultimately goofy name.

Conclusion

Yes, it is possible to make a living playing games professionally. You have to be very, very good, because there are limited (but growing) opportunities for pro gamers. You also have to train constantly, just like any other pro competitor.

The number of tournaments and the prize money they offer are both on the rise, but the big money is in securing endorsements from sponsors. If you make a name for yourself, you can also spin that off into other business ventures that don't require you to have a twitchy mouse-clicking finger.

*Mod Makers * Brash Young Upstarts * Genius Visionaries*

IF YOU WANT SOMETHING DONE RIGHT, DIY

How to Get Paid to Play Your Own Way, without Restrictions or Security: Doing It Yourself

SO MAYBE YOU'VE GOTTEN THIS FAR IN

the book and you're starting to worry that none of these jobs sound like anything you want to do in the video game industry. Maybe you're not cut out for college, or you don't think you can hack the corporate culture of game publishing and development...or maybe you know exactly what you want to do, and we haven't described it. Maybe you know exactly what you want but it doesn't exist yet, so it's up to you to forge your own path. If that's the case, this chapter is our best attempt at giving you the clearest idea possible of what your options are and what lies in store for you.

Let's start with a few caveats. First of all, the further you get from traditional video game jobs at established companies, the less financial stability you should expect. In fact, we're not even including the usual "Payment for Playment" sidebar in this chapter, because most people who strike out on their own start out earning somewhere between zero and significantly less than zero dollars per year until their project gets off the ground, which may be never. And even if it does, they usually wind up much closer to hand-to-mouth living than to fabulous wealth. On the flip side, being your own boss means you can do whatever the hell you want, but that can work against you if your ideas are terrible or if you have no work ethic.

Next, we've all heard the stories of the whiz kid who dropped out of school and developed the best-selling video game in his basement that earned him shedloads of cash. At the risk of costing the video game world its next visionary, we'll just say it right now—that ain't you. The surest way to a video game career is to develop your skills, network like crazy, and do the job that you want for free until someone hires you to do it. If your independent creative genius trip is part of that plan, you're on the right track. But if you're banking on whipping up the next *Doom* or *Myst* (or hell, even *Leisure Suit Larry*) and retiring from the proceeds at the ripe old age of 23, it ain't happening. Sorry, pal.

Finally, if you've been paying any attention at all, you'll know that working on or with video games—even as a hobby—is hard work. If you don't love what you're doing, you're going to burn out on it quickly. And even if you do love what you're doing, you might still burn out on it. If you strike out on your own doing something that you love and have a Plan B in case things take a turn for the worse, you'll come through okay. But if you do something that you don't really enjoy because you think it will lead to huge cash prizes, or if you put everything you've got into it and leave yourself nothing to fall back on if things go south, you're going to have your heart broken and your spirit crushed. And as much as we love saying "we told you so," we'd rather that you just looked out for yourself and tried to have as much fun along the way as possible.

As a tribute to the independent spirit, this chapter isn't set up in the usual "here's the job, here's what's good and bad about it, here's how to get it" format. Instead, we'll first tell you about a group of people who are doing their own thing with no expectation of an immediate financial reward. Next, we'll move on to an independent development team who hopes that the leap of faith they're taking ends in a pile of cash, not a bunch of jagged rocks. And finally, we'll close with some of the most valuable advice you'll read in this book, courtesy of a true independent industry legend who's seen and done it all.

It's a Mod, Mod World!

In the game design and programming chapter, we recommended mod-making as a way to put together a professional portfolio from amateur work. But what exactly is a "mod"? It's basically a home-brew endeavor by a single person or group of enthusiastic individuals to design, build, populate, and release a creative addition to a video game, using the original source code, for others to participate in. Because you need access to the game's source code, pretty much all modding takes place in PC games, although with the advent of Internet-enabled and hard drive–equipped consoles, that's likely to change.

Mods are a great way for level designers to show off their skills, or for 3-D artists to model and skin characters, or for programmers to tweak a physics engine, or anyone to make any number of innovative and dramatic changes in the hopes of earning the attention and approval of the game's fan community. And if you're lucky, you might get noticed by someone who can offer you a job.

Valve's *Half-Life* has one of the most enthusiastic mod-making communities in the entire video game industry. More than 500 major modifications and countless more alterations to the original *Half-Life* software development kit (SDK) have occurred since the original game's release. And while almost none of them are official Valve products or sanctioned by Valve, they are excellent illustrations of the creativity of those who are unpaid to play.

Mods are commonly used to pay tribute to favorite movies, TV shows, comics, or even other games, something you can't do in the legit video game world without first signing expensive licenses. And while you might be on shaky legal ground by creating *Simpsons* skins for all of the enemies in your favorite game, the odds against you getting anything worse than a cease-and-desist letter are slim.[1] As far as we know, that hasn't happened to Eric "Riddler" Beyhl, project leader for the "Battle of the Millennium" *HL* mod,[2] which takes Superman, Spider-Man, Batman, Spawn, *Dragon Ball Z*'s® Goku®, and Megaman and pits them against one another in a variety of urban locales. His class-based system allowed you to really take control of the character you loved most. No two characters were even close to being alike, and the exciting, almost chaotic gameplay made it a blast to play, time and time again.

Valve created a tribute mod of their own as a way to honor first-person-shooter pioneers id Software. In 2000, Valve released the "Deathmatch Classic" mod,[3] which included all of the original *Quake* deathmatch levels and all-new models (including new animations inside weapons). They managed it in three months. As Valve cofounder Gabe Newell told Shacknews,[4] "It really reminded us of just how kick-ass the game was, and we thought it would be a great reminder for everyone and a tribute to id's accomplishments if we were to finish it and release it." Members of the "Deathmatch Classic" team, including co-cre-

---

1. That being said, we don't endorse doing anything that might potentially violate someone else's trademark or copyright, even if you're not making money off it. If there's any question whether or not you're infringing on someone else's intellectual property, you probably are.

2. www.planethalflife.com/botm

3. www.valvesoftware.com

4. Shacknews.com, "Quake is Reborn," June 6, 2001, by Steve Gibson (www.shacknews.com/extras/e_dmc/page2.x)

ator and programmer Paolo "Nusco" Perrotta, went on to create the "Holy Wars" *HL* mod.[5]

Sometimes licensed characters wind up in mods commissioned by the characters' copyright holders. That's the case with the "Underworld: Bloodline" *HL* mod.[6] Sony Pictures needed a novel method of advertising its horror flick *Underworld* and found Black Widow Games, creators of the *HL2* mod "They Hunger." They created and delivered gothic werewolf-on-vampire combat in two months. With only two maps, characters are at least different; the vampires jump higher while the werewolves are quicker, and everyone's armed with sharp maiming equipment.

TRUE STORIES OF DIY SUCCESS, PART ONE: COUNTER-STRIKE

Here's proof that making the right mod can make your name in the video game business. In 1999, Minh "Gooseman" Le and Jess Cliffe collaborated on a total conversion mod called "Counter-Strike" that used the *Half-Life* source code as the basis for a team-based strategic first-person shooter. It wasn't the first time around the block for these modders—Le had worked on several *Quake II* mods, including "Navy Seals" and "Action Quake 2."

The "Counter-Strike" beta was released in June of 1999 to an overwhelmingly positive response from the *HL* community. So positive, in fact, that Valve Software, the developers of *Half-Life*, acquired the team and put them to work on an official stand-alone retail release of *Counter-Strike*, which hit retail shelves in November of 2000. Several sequels followed, and *CS* still ranks as one of the most popular online multiplayer games in the world.

Aspiring game creators who really want to strut their stuff come up with some very interesting mods that radically depart from the source material. That's the case with Mark "routetwo" Gornall's "International Online Soccer" mod for *Half-Life*.[7] It's exactly what it sounds like—online team-play soccer—and it propelled the game engine to new heights. Reportedly, it's also a favorite among many Valve employees. It was designed during the World Cup 2002 and was written to fill a niche for fans to play soccer online.

---

5. www.planethalflife.com/holywars
6. www.planethalflife.com/manke
7. www.planethalflife.com/ios

Jordan "Masterx" Edelson created a mod in the same spirit called "Sub Hunt,"[8] a project he worked on for the Discovery Channel. In January 2003, the Discovery Channel created a piece on him and mod-making in general. The first challenge was to create a working mod during the recording. Three weeks later, "Sub Hunt" was finished. Who would have thought that you could take a vehicle-support-lacking game like *HL* and create a mod that lets you control a submarine? Well, you did, Jordan! Stand up and take a bow.

Don't feel like you must rip out the guts of the source code in order to make a compelling mod, either. Play to your strengths, not your weaknesses. That's what Paul "PlanetSun" Ehreth did with his "Boxwar" *HL* mod,[9] widely considered one of the most unique mods ever among the *Half-Life* community. Everyone expected the character models to be humanoid, but Ehreth took a different tact. He decided to play a trick on everyone else. He compiled a three-dimensional couch and made it into a working character model, spawning an innovative attempt at camouflage combat, proving you don't need to have an aptitude for character modeling and animation.

If you can find a way to get course credit for your mod-making while in school, like one college student, that's two birds fragged with one shot. He created an amazing single-player retelling of *Half-Life*'s Black Mesa storyline from a different angle, with new environments, textures, weapons, and music. He used the game in an exhibition, which resulted in a passing grade and a college diploma.

And it's never a bad thing when you get props from the developer instead of an angry letter from their lawyers. Alan "SirAlanF" Fischer is the co-creator of a *Half-Life* mod called "Wizard Wars,"[10] which we'd describe as an unrealistic mod with comical models and bizarre weapons, but a still-enjoyable play style. Amusing play elements included the beanstalk. This was quite a unique feature, because it was basically a ladder that you could put anywhere. This innovation even resulted in applause from Valve, and the team has the e-mail to prove it.

By this point, you're probably thinking that this is all well and good but that we haven't mentioned anyone whose mod-making landed them a job. Oh ye of little faith, that's because we were saving the best for last. Steven "EraSerX" Delrue is the creator of "Case Closed,"[11] a *HL* mod in which you play through the game as janitor Bob Dewer. The plotline was straightforward enough: Get the hell out of the Black Mesa complex. We count the upside-down level and the scene in Xen with the zombie sitting at a broken desk among our favorite parts of the mod. Apparently someone at Guerrilla Games liked them, too, because Delrue was hired shortly thereafter as a level designer on the PlayStation2's *Killzone*.

---

8. www.planethalflife.com/xmod
9. www.planethalflife.com/boxwar
10. www.planethalflife.com/wizardwars
11. www.planethalflife.com/caseclosed

SUMMARY

Mods are unofficial, unsanctioned modifications to a game's source code that result in a minor or significant change to the gameplay.

As many of our interviewees have previously suggested, making mods is the best way to showcase your skills if you don't have any professional experience.

Some of the most effective mods make the game engine do things that it was never meant to do. Other successful mods make small and subtle changes that completely reinvent the gameplay.

And yes, some people really do go from making mods to working in the industry. Yes, for money. Don't you trust us?

Frag You: I Won't Do What You Tell Me

Jason Fader, Nicholas Lawson, Matthew Yaeger, and Stuart Lawson are four friends who met in college and quickly realized that their futures were meant to be closely intertwined. What we might have on our hands is the story of the earliest days of the next powerhouse video game development studio.[12]

The four men banded together as Iocaine Studios in 2003, after some convincing by Fader. "One day I sat down with a group of close friends and slowly convinced them that we have what it takes to make a game and a company," he says. "We were students at the time, so our first opportunity presented itself when we all took a game project course. After our project was successful, the team was convinced that we have what it takes."

Fader now serves as Iocaine's president, but it's not a position he lobbied for. "The team needed someone to step up and be president of the company," he says. "It was like one of those comedies where a battle commander calls for volunteers from his troop for a suicide mission by saying, 'Step forward if you want to go on this mission,' and everyone in the troop takes a step backward, except for that poor guy who wasn't paying attention. I am that poor guy."

THE DAY-TO-DAY, TODAY

The team works together in an office. Well, sort of. "As of now, we don't have an official office," says creative director Stu Lawson. "We are working part-time out of Jason's house." And that's something he's grateful for: "I can't get any substantial amount of work done if I am working at home; there are too many distractions. I need an office." He also works part-time for another company just to pay the bills, but he's looking forward to the day when that's no longer necessary. In fact, he's already training someone at his other job to take his place once Iocaine is a full-time employment option. Now that's confidence.

And you won't find a slacker amongst the four of them, either. "I find we are very busy all the time, which is good!" says Stu Lawson. Senior software

---

12. No pressure, guys.

engineer (and brother of Stu) Nick Lawson says that "the busiest times are often before patch day or before major revisions. The actual time of year and month doesn't really seem to matter."

THE BEST AND THE WORST

There's no doubt that all four of the Iocaine guys are incredibly enthusiastic about what they're doing. But that didn't prevent them from giving an honest assessment of the best and worst parts of designing an independently developed game from scratch with no financial backing.

The Best

The close bond between the four Iocaine founders shows that if you've got the right group of people, just having the chance to work together can be reward enough. Jason Fader says that the best part of the job is "creating a game with a team of great people. My entire team (all three of them) are longtime friends. I either got really lucky to have friends like these, or there is a psychic monkey in my head that has the power to influence others. I like the monkey theory." Nick Lawson concurs: "We have a really good team, so there is a lot of good cooperation at the workplace," he says. "People know each other and are able to generally work differences out smoothly."

The freedom of doing their own thing in their own way is another major source of satisfaction for Iocaine. "All of my previous jobs have paved the way for me to make the leap into such a risky venture," says software engineer Matt Yaeger. "They have shown me how much better life can be when you decide to do what you want instead of what management wants to do."

And Stu Lawson seems to enjoy just about everything about the process. "I enjoy creating something that is fun for people to play," he says. "I enjoy the creative process and seeing how I personally improve on everything I do over time. I enjoy Jason's pasta, Frappuccinos, and piña coladas! But above all, the best part of the job is working together with a team to create something that will give countless hours of fun to someone out there."

The Worst

If there's one thing that we all learned from *Team America: World Police*, it's that freedom isn't free. That applies to independent game development as well as wars on common nouns. For Iocaine Studios, the freedom to create their game their way comes at the cost of holding down a job that comes with a paycheck. "Part of being a founder of a company means having to make some sacrifices," says Matt Yaeger. "There will be no influx of money into the company until the game sells, which means there are no salaries until then as well."

That's not enough to scare off Stu Lawson. "Starting a company without funding is a risk, but what is life without taking risks?" he asks. "If you are willing to work without pay, you have to enjoy your work and have a passion for it."

And, of course, independent game development comes with many of the same drawbacks as corporate game development. Jason Fader lists a few pet peeves that you've read in other chapters: "Working within a deadline. Cutting features. Accepting that your vision is not always the final product, but most of the time, it's something better."

TRUE STORIES OF DIY SUCCESS, PART TWO: *ALIEN HOMINID*

In August of 2002, Tom Fulp and Dan "Synj" Paladin uploaded a cartoony side-scrolling Flash game called *Alien Hominid* to Macromedia's website. Gamers immediately embraced the game's old-school action and little yellow extraterrestrial protagonist, resulting in more than 10 million downloads.

Fulp and Paladin subsequently incorporated as The Behemoth with the assistance of their coworker, producer John Baez. They spent two years refining and expanding *Alien Hominid* for retail release. Since its humble freeware origins, it has appeared on the PC, PlayStation2, GameCube, Game Boy Advance, Xbox, and Xbox 360.

GOOD ADVICE

Although he's gone off and started his own development studio, that's not how Jason Fader would advise others to get their start in the industry. "My experience from Blizzard Entertainment provided invaluable knowledge to prepare me for the job I am doing now," he says. "I would highly advise anyone thinking about breaking into the industry to first work for a large game company. It will give you an insight into the world of game development, and hopefully indicate if it's really the right path for you."

Stu Lawson extols the virtues of assembling a respectable body of work before trying to strike out on your own. "I feel it has really been my own personal projects that have helped me get to where I am today," he says. "Without my own projects, I would not have the extensive portfolio that I have today. My advice to anyone who wishes to learn is to start your own projects and stick to them…. You learn the most when you set out to do something and are motivated to do it…. If you want to learn how to make a 3-D model, think about an object to create, and then solve the steps to get the job complete, one step at a time."

That's advice that applies to an aspiring software engineer as well. "Develop at least one game engine from scratch," advises Matt Yaeger. "Before using any third-party library, know how it works and know how to write one yourself to do the same thing. Some of the best experience can be gained by deciding not to use a third-party library and just writing all your own code."

If you want to head up your own company, know what you're getting into and be ready for a bumpy ride. "Make sure you have a lot of survival cash saved up if you intend to start your own company while floating in the meanwhile," says Nick Lawson. "Costco food is a must. Make sure your team is extremely good at working together. Everyone will need to jump over their normal job description and work on other tasks, so a broad experience base would be more important. Everyone must be prepared to learn. A lot."

We'll give the last word of advice to the boss-man. "Always, always, always plan," says Fader. "Know where you're going and know how to get there. If you don't know, bring on someone who can help. The president of a small company is like a superproducer. You're in charge of all the little things and big things. You're responsible for your team, their productivity, and their state of mind. If something needs to be done, and no one else has time to do it, it defaults to you. It's a thankless job, and very rarely will you feel appreciated for all you do. However, in the end, when the project is complete, and you're at your launch party, when your team raises a glass in your honor and you can see the smiles on all their faces, it's worth it."

THERE IS NO FATE BUT WHAT THEY MAKE

When it comes right down to it, Fader sums up the team's core motivation in three sentences: "It doesn't take a 200-man team to make a game. Four guys in a garage can make a great game with a very small budget. It's simply a matter of passion and talent."

So is he right? Well, that's kind of the exciting part. We don't know, and we won't know until Iocaine ships their game, *ThreadSpace: Hyperbol*, which is nearing completion. But you can follow their progress through the gaming press and their website (www.iocainestudios.com). And hey, if you're down with them from day one, and they hit it big, they might be your next employers.

SUMMARY

Forming an independent development studio means you can do your own thing, but you don't get someone else's money for doing it.

Make sure every team member has the proper experience and gets along on a personal and professional level, because you've got a ton of work ahead of you.

Before we go any further, we'd like to

TRUE STORIES OF DIY SUCCESS, PART THREE: SERIOUS SAM

TRUE STORIES OF DIY SUCCESS, PART THREE: **SERIOUS SAM** (CONT.)

apologize to all our Croatian readers for neglecting you throughout so much of this book. We hope to win you back with this sidebar, in which we relate the rags-to-riches success story of Croatia's greatest game development studio, Croteam.

Most of the gaming world wouldn't hear about Croteam until they released the beta of their first game, *Serious Sam*, in 2000 (and were subsequently interviewed by website Old Man Murray [OMM]),[13] but they'd been busy creating the game engine ("Serious Engine") since 1996. In the OMM interview, Croteam CEO Roman Ribaric described the development team: "All together, there are nine guys now. Six of us work full time, two guys work in [their] spare time (studying), and one guy is serving in the Croatian army. We have some guys who left. They thought working 10 hours [a day] for free for 4 years is not a good option and that they can make more money elsewhere."

It turns out that the joke was on them. Thanks in part to the interest generated by the OMM interview—and the fact that the game was a technological marvel of its time, with refreshingly bright and open level design—*Serious Sam: The First Encounter* and its sequel (*The Second Encounter*) were picked up and published for the PC by Gathering of Developers shortly thereafter. A third title, *Serious Sam II*, was published by Take-Two Interactive for the PC and Xbox in 2005, and Croteam shows no signs of slowing down.

Hits and *Myst*s

Rand Miller is the epitome of the DIY video game success story. While working at a bank in Texas in the early '90s, he and his brother Robyn began collaborating on kid-friendly PC adventure games, including *Manhole* and *Cosmic Osmo*. In the early '90s, Rand and Robyn relocated to Spokane, Washington, where they collaborated with friends Chris Brandkamp and Chuck Miller to form Cyan Inc. (later Cyan Worlds) and independently create the smash-hit *Myst* from their basements. *Myst* went on to sell over 10 million copies, almost single-handedly driving the PC CD-ROM drive market. Only *The Sims* has ever rivaled it for "best-selling game ever" status, and *Myst*'s critically acclaimed sequel, *Riven*, did brisk business as well, topping the 3 million mark for sales.

But Miller's Cinderella story does have a turning-back-into-a-pumpkin twist. Shortly after Cyan completed the long-awaited massively multiplayer

13. Read the interview at www.oldmanmurray.com/features/73.html. Now!

Myst spinoff *Uru Live* in late 2003, publisher Ubisoft decided not to fund further development of the ambitious title, leaving Cyan no choice but to lay off the vast majority of their employees. Fortunately, Cyan has since forged a new partnership with GameTap that seems to be as good a fit as the mythical glass slipper (just to continue this tortured metaphor), so there's hope among the faithful that *Uru Live* may have finally found its happy ending.

Miller has seen the heights and depths of the video game industry, so listen to the man. And of course, while taking his advice will probably improve your odds of success, it doesn't guarantee it. "Part of being a functional business is making your choices, to the best of your ability, and then making those choices work," says Miller. "Another way to put that is that anybody who goes into business planning on only making the right choices won't be in business for very long."

RAND'S RULES

I'm afraid I'm just going to make this very practical. If you can't just make this vision happen on your own, then you can try these steps. Be prepared to be rejected and dismissed. But don't let that get you down.

1. Define and refine your vision into something more than just an idea. Ideas are cheap. Ideas are easy. Ideas are lazy, good-for-nothin', lying fools who sit around watching TV and drinking beer, talking about how amazing they could be if someone would just give them a chance! If you are just bringing an idea, then you are bringing nothing. While you are refining, remember that you don't have to refine what you're not good at—don't do a bunch of illustrations if you're not good at art. But bring to this project what you are good at.

2. Define your "return." [This] can be a quick buck, or long-term funding, or fame and notoriety, or world peace, or being heard, or the love of a girl. What do you want out of this? Don't kid yourself—what do you really want? We have been incredibly fortunate, for the most part, to work with employees and outside companies who agreed on the "return" aspect. The return that Cyan has been based on through the years has been (not necessarily in this order): short-term money, long-term money, good will, artistic recognition, Mom's blessing. That seemed to fit well with most of our partners and (except for "Mom's blessing") was discussed up front and agreed upon. If the partners always want the same return, it's easier to work out issues of trust.

3. Go out and find three people (Mom doesn't count) who think your idea is incredible and who agree with your return. This will both validate your idea and link you with people who can help you pull it off. By the way, if in step 1 you found out that you're not really good at anything,

then step 3 is going to be very important. If you're good at everything, it's still useful to get some other opinions.

4. Define and refine your vision into something more than just an idea. Yup, step 1 all over again. You have other people and other opinions to help you refine a bit further. You want to know why this is important enough to be both step 1 and step 4? First, because you don't have enough money to build the product yourself, and this definition that you are working on is the primary tool you will use to get the money. Second, because whatever you clearly define is a little more locked down—which means that there is a greater chance that it'll make it to the final product.

5. Prepare the pitch. Take that definition that you've been working on and summarize it in a single sentence, a single paragraph, and single page. Now create something flashy and interesting (DVD, website, Flash, PowerPoint, brochure, etc.) that gets across both the defined vision and your passion for it. This needs to be equal parts well-defined vision and passion. Don't skimp on either. This step is purposely rather vague—you have to be creative enough to build the pitch into something that will be considered.

6. Find the money to make it happen. It's probably safe to assume that you haven't found a friend who is willing to pay for this massive undertaking, so you've got to reach out and connect with someone who can. Use every connection you have to get actual names of people at companies you want to work with. Send them the pitch, call them, send it again, call them again. Then ask for feedback. Take the feedback and either go to step 4 or go to step 7.

7. Get a job at a bank.

SUMMARY

Rand Miller is a very smart man. Pay attention to what he tells you. Read it twice. Then read it again.

Conclusion

The video game industry is a big enough business to produce multimillion-dollar blockbusters, but there are still enough frontier fringes of it for independent, creative types to make their mark. The essential components of DIY success in the video game world are talent, drive, passion, and a willingness to work long hours without pay. And even with all of these things, you still need a healthy dose of dumb luck to make it. There are no guarantees in life, and that goes double for working independently in the video game industry.

BASIC CABLE GUYS: MASS MEDIA PERSONALITY

How to Get Paid to Play Host in Front of Millions of Viewers: Get on Gaming TV and Explain Games to the Masses

"I find television very educating. Every time somebody turns on the set, I go into the other room and read a book."

—*Groucho Marx*

"I think that parents only get so offended by television because they rely on it as a babysitter and the sole educator of their kids."

—*Trey Parker and Matt Stone*[1]

THE VIDEO GAME HOST—PART PERFORMER,

part repository of knowledge with the ability to articulate complex video game concepts into bite-sized, digestible chunks, all with a perfectly manicured look. This is the world where charisma, hard work, and an in-depth knowledge of video games is your ticket to invading millions of homes across the country.

We'll also cover those who contribute video game columns to national newspapers.[2]

A syndicated columnist and a video game show presenter actually share many of the same qualities, the chief one being their ability to quickly convey information that the casual gamer (or parent of a gamer) might enjoy. In our quest to interview almost everyone remotely connected to video games, we tracked down four industry heavyweights—a writer for a major newspaper, and three video game TV hosts.

A Day in the Life

Ah, the world of fast cars, sexy women, rampant commercialism, and the latest in designer clothing. And when you've finished playing the latest *Need for Speed*, the reality of the job hits home: Working a mainstream gig isn't as easy as it sounds, and the hours you'll spend certainly vary. Levi Buchanan, a contributor to the *Chicago Tribune*, says he usually works from home.

MAINSTREAM VS. ENTHUSIAST: ROUND ONE—FIGHT!

There's some pretty obvious differences between "mainstream" journalism and the "enthusiast" press. Levi Buchanan notes a few of the main ones, as he's seen journalism on both sides of the fence. "Before working for the *Chicago Tribune*, I headed up GameFan Online. Don't laugh!" he tells us.

---

1. The creators of *South Park*, who said this before *Grand Theft Auto* came along and absorbed the flack from "concerned citizens" and Joe Lieberman.
2. The newspaper: an antiquated handheld device where non-interactive information is pre-downloaded on a reconstituted wooden pulp. This is read once, and then discarded. See also "book."

"The most rewarding part of that job was	MAINSTREAM VS. ENTHUSIAST: ROUND ONE—FIGHT! (CONT.)

getting accurate information out first—you earn serious street cred with your readers for being right. Bum rumors frustrate fans."

Of course, now Levi can't rely on speculation: "When writing for the newspaper, I never trafficked in information I could not back up with a firm source. Wild conjecture is just not tolerated at a newspaper, and I appreciate the respect afforded to me within the industry by being aligned with an esteemed outlet."

Levi spends around 10 to 20 hours a week on assignment with the *Chicago Tribune*, and he juggles a whole load of other freelance gigs on top of this (being a newspaper columnist only pays some of the bills).

As for the TV personalities involved in video games? They have their fingers in a whole batch of virtual pies.

WHAT'S IN A NAME?

Victor Lucas and Tommy Tallarico are two of the busiest men in video game show business. In fact, to prove this, we're revealing their full job titles, which are the longest we've ever seen and really should be submitted to the *Guinness Book of World Records*. Victor Lucas is "president and executive producer of Greedy Productions Ltd. and our properties, the *Electric Playground*, *Reviews on the Run*, the Art of Play, GameTap News, and elecplay.com."

Mr. Tallarico tops even that: He's (deep breath) "president of Tommy Tallarico Studios, Inc.,[3] executive producer/CEO of Video Games Live,[4] [and] president/founder of Game Audio Network Guild (aka GANG).[5] When he's not involved in his presidential duties, he's "the host, writer, [and] co-producer of the *Electric Playground* and *Reviews on the Run* television shows."

So, when you've got two paragraphs in this book on your titles alone, you know your day's going to be hectic. But just how hectic?

---

3. This is "the largest video game postproduction audio house." He's done music and sound design for over 250 games over the past 16 years. Find out more at tallarico.com.

4. If you want your *Final Fantasy* overtures played in a real concert hall by a real orchestra, check out videogameslive.com.

5. A "nonprofit organization raising the awareness of the importance of game audio" and boasting over 1,200 members. Last of the free plugs: audiogang.org.

HOST OR HUSK?

Are you a Pat O'Brien, or a Ryan Seacrest? We know, this could be a very difficult question to answer. We're asking the question because, like it or not, hosts like Seacrest do more than just host; they have other jobs like radio show DJ and other successful career ventures. Whereas Pat O'Brien's main outlet for host-based awesomeness is just *The Insider*. But like them or not, they've both made a name for themselves in two different ways: one concentrates on a single hosting duty, while the other combines a multitude of gigs. Both types of job have their own advantages, but we'd rather be a Seacrest; he's got more to fall back on, careerwise.

THE HARDEST-WORKING MEN IN SHOW BUSINESS

Victor Lucas says he "oversees the company on a general level and [is] responsible for all key financial and editorial decisions and directions. I also manage a staff of more than 10 people. I host, direct, produce, write, and edit content as needed as well. I work from home, the office, and on location at different events and game and content creation studios all around the world." This shows that Victor does more than look into a camrea, hold a microphone, and interview David Jaffe; he's a shrewd businessman with on-air hosting duties being only one tiny aspect of his career. And he spends upward of 60 hours every week growing this business.

Tommy Tallarico describes his day-to-day activities as "too much to list." When pressed, Tallarico reveals his true form—a workaholic vampire. It's the only possible way to explain the number of hours he puts in: "I work 20 hours a day, seven days a week. This is *not* an exaggeration. I absolutely love what I do, and I'm extremely passionate about each company I run or job I take on. I am not married and do not have any kids."

Or, to put it another way: "I've dedicated my existence to the video game industry."

So, when you're spending all hours in the pursuit of video game happiness, there's no point in asking what parts of the year are busiest, then, is there? We did anyway.

Victor Lucas is busiest during "the five months leading up to and just after E^3. We launch new seasons of our programming at this time, so we're doing a lot of production and traveling. And then as E^3 looms closer, more and more studios want us to cover their games, so production intensifies. Of course, things really get crazy through E^3 week and the two weeks after while we digest and utilize all of the fresh content we've gathered." The good news is that the reams of footage can be spliced together to form multiple shows for months afterward.

Tommy Tallarico leaves that extra can of Red Bull in the fridge in December and January "because most of the games are completed for Christmas, and the new ones haven't quite started up yet."

However, when you must fill in several inches in a national newspaper column with video game recommendations, as Levi says, you'll always find your workload ballooning in "the last three months of the year, when publishers release their biggest games in hopes of dominating the holiday shopping." Since this is when 80 percent of software sales occur, columnists are busy informing the general public about "must-buy" games.

SUMMARY

Working as a columnist usually takes place at your home. You're a freelancer, unless you're working as part of the "technology" department at a newspaper.

Working as a video game host takes you on the road, all over the world, and then to a film studio somewhere near Vancouver, Canada. It's cheaper up there.

The folks we interviewed also ran their own companies, cultivating them like plants potted in Miracle-Gro. Most were at least semi-related to the on-screen work they do, and all were video game related.

Newspaper columnists write books and other prose to keep the wolf from the door.

TV hosts with their own companies work like absolute maniacs.

Just like everyone else who doesn't sell games, those in the video game TV business are busiest around any major industry events.

Just like everyone who *does* sell games, columnists are allowed more inches during the holiday shopping season.

The Good, the Bad, and the Ugly

By now you'll either have given up your dreams of hosting anything more than a game of *Counter-Strike*, or you'll be feverishly purchasing books on journalism, strategically plucking your eyebrows, and boning up on your video game knowledge. If it's the latter, then you'll enjoy learning what the best parts of this job are, which we'll quickly follow with the more miserable aspects.

THE GOOD

According to Levi Buchanan, "being paid to play games is akin to winning the lottery—for somebody that grew up on [video games], getting a check for your efforts is sweet reward. However, there's much more to the gig than just burning [video games] all night; there are so many average writers in this racket that you really need to focus and carve out a voice for yourself."

And if you're working in television rather than writing for a newspaper, the results are equally as rewarding. Victor Lucas "loves all the aspects of my job, which include marketing and managing the sales of our programming to broadcasters and sponsors, as well as managing and working with the variety of people I'm fortunate enough to be able to build our shows with."

Victor enjoys his other job, too: "I love being on camera and interviewing people. I love traveling to different studios in different cities around the world and seeing games months before they're released. I love reviewing games. But I think the element of my job that I really enjoy the most is directing the cinematic bits in *Electric Playground*, where we incorporate performances with the game developers, one or more of our hosts, maybe some background actors, and then figure out some cool camera angles, moves, 'stunts,' and how some flashy visual effects could improve the segment."

These amusing interludes are *Electric Playground*'s trademark. If you're a developer about to be interviewed by Victor or Tommy, and your game involves dragons, then be prepared to dash around, pretending to be on fire. The flames, actual dragon, and burning flesh wounds are all added in postproduction, thankfully. "One of the most enjoyable days of my career was when I directed our *Star Wars: Battlefront* segment with Geoff Keighley hosting, and [we had] a forest filled with stormtroopers and Rebel soldiers."

Geoff Keighley is the third host we interviewed. He is the host of *Game Head* on Spike TV, the number-one video game show on American television. He's also got a vast biography,[6] and his hosting duties allow him to "set [his] own schedule and…interact and interview the biggest names in the video game business." So, if your career ambition is to interview that slightly eccentric Japanese developer you've enjoyed the work of, but you think that working *for* him might drive you crazy, then this is the gig for you. "And of course, free games!" Yep, as Geoff points out, there are grab bags full of goodies at media events.

MAINSTREAM VS. ENTHUSIAST: ROUND TWO—FIGHT!

Two things irk Levi Buchanan in his capacity as a journalist for a major newspaper. The first are overly aggressive PR agents. The second are fanboy writers: primarily website writers.

"There is a definite difference between the guys who cover [video games] for magazines such as *Time* and *Newsweek* and website writers," Levi says, quickly and importantly pointing out he's only referring to *some* website writers. "Consumer and mainstream media writers are adept at staying above fanboyism. You can enjoy serious, insightful discussion with them." But for the guy in the extra-large Capcom T-shirt, smelling slightly of wee? "There is nothing worse than the drunken "Which Mega Man is best?" argument that happens three hours after the open bar has been opened. I have seen this argument first-hand, and the results were embarassing."

---

6. Which can be viewed at his website, gameslice.com.

MAINSTREAM VS. ENTHUSIAST: ROUND TWO—FIGHT! (CONT.)

But lest you think Levi's championing the mainstream media, think again: "There is something to be said about having passion and intimate knowledge of the industry. Some mainstream outlet writers end up sounding either coolly indifferent or downright uninformed when they come at this industry without the kind of background a fan has, [who] managed to land a gig at a website or enthusiast magazine. A mainstream outlet writer wouldn't dare get the name of a White House staffer wrong, but [would] shrug off knowing the difference between Mario and Wario. That *destroys* cred with readers."

THE BAD AND THE UGLY

Being an on-air journalist isn't all about jetting off to exotic places to interview Michael Madsen/Brooke Burke/Lemmy from Motorhead about their latest voice-over work on *Reservoir Dogs/Need for Speed/Barbie's Horse Adventures*. No; for every 22 minutes you're on-screen, there's more than a week of preparation, narration, postproduction, and editing. "You have to be very self-motivated and willing to put in long hours," Geoff tells us, "both playing and writing about games. Sometimes a bit of the joy of playing games is lost because your hobby becomes a job." But what a job, eh?

MAINSTREAM VS. ENTHUSIAST: FINAL ROUND—FIGHT!

The term "play-ola" rears its ugly head again, having been mentioned in previous chapters about journalism. Levi isn't a huge fan of enthusiast press man-children taking advantage of their jobs: "There are plenty of 'playola' stories floating around, and most of them are true without exaggeration. I recall sitting across from a writer at an expensive steak dinner once [who] ordered two appetizers, a massive steak, two lobster tails, and a bottle of wine for himself, with a grin the whole time. I could tell the PR rep nearby was decidedly unamused, and so were the other writers at the table—because it reflects on all writers as a whole. However, these stories are getting fewer and [farther] between, as game companies are not throwing press events in Hawaii or in 'haunted' castles like they used to; there is some maturing going on. Press events (non-E[3]) are now more 'normal affairs,' with presentations and gameplay sessions with some food provided."

MAINSTREAM VS. ENTHUSIAST: FINAL ROUND—FIGHT! (CONT.)

So if you're getting into this career expecting to stuff your face, order only one lobster tail with your prime cut of steak.

PAYMENT FOR PLAYMENT

Although the amount of money you earn doesn't apply to our specific interviewees, TV-hosting duties vary wildly. We've heard rumors that in the early days, G4 TV hosts were paid around $500 a show. If you're "just" a host, without a company to run, expect your salary to fluctuate wildly, from the low to high five-figure range. Expect to earn more than that the more famous you become. If you're part host, part business mogul, then your other activities increase your pay. As Tommy puts it, "Because I do so many things, it would be difficult to just lump it into one sum (which varies extremely from year to year)." However, if you're syndicated, with networks buying your shows, and you're finding other ways to supplement your income, expect that income to drift into the low- to mid-six-figure territory. This is great for your retirement, because you won't have time to spend it now.

For a columnist? Don't expect much more than the going rate for newspaper prose (around 50 cents a word). The world doesn't have (or seemingly want) the video game equivalent of a Dan Savage or Paul Krugman.

PR, PAPERWORK, AND PAID-TO-PLAY PROBLEMS

A strong work ethic and a photogenic style aren't enough to be a mass-media video game personality. You also need to "[get] the video game industry (publishers, developers) to understand the importance of marketing, PR and 'thinking outside the box,'" says Tommy Tallarico. He should know; he's managed a successful career in music *and* cohosted *Electric Playground* for over 10 years. Back in 1996, Victor and Tommy were convincing game companies that they should be revealing preproduction software on television. It might seem obvious these days, but back then, PR reps and developers were extremely cagey about their games being seen.

Another tough part of the job is the paperwork. In fact, the paperwork takes a serious chunk out of his game-playing time: "Because every season and year of making our shows is based on us having all of the contracts and cash flow in place to get going, the worst part of my job is any period of uncertainty or indecision that I'm facing with a broadcaster or sponsor. I would also say, just like most jobs, that worrying about getting [together] all of the paperwork involved in delivering our programming is not that much fun at all." And when it takes time away from *World of Warcraft*, well, that's approaching an unspeakable torment.

If you've plowed through the previous chapters, you'll be bracing for the inevitable mention of what popular misconceptions outsiders have about those working in the industry. We'll let Tommy Tallarico reveal it for the eleventh time: "A common misconception is that all you do is play games and have fun." Levi fumes at the very mention of it: "That's the worst misconception and it irritates established players in the industry to no end. And even when you do play, you need to be keeping notes as you go—so while you can definitely have fun, there is always a work element involved. You need to supply specific examples in reviews to establish trust with your readers. If you read a review that deals only in generalities, chances are there is only a few hours of actual game time on the other end."

There's another matter than gets Victor's goat: "That anyone could go on television and talk about video games." While Victor is incorrect to a certain degree—anyone *can* go on television and talk about video games—most of them aren't very good at it. This is the distinction Victor is making. Creating an entertaining show about games is more than just turning up wearing a "Classically Trained" NES T-shirt. It's about keeping your sweating to a minimum, not flubbing your lines, and being genuinely interesting. Sound easy? Then download a few online videos and see what you think. Even some that the big websites publish are cringeworthy.

"While playing games is an important part of my job," says Geoff Keighley, "most of my time is spent shooting shows, reviewing scripts, recording voice-overs, planning future episodes, and speaking with game developers and publicists." He adds, "But yes, you do get free games!"

SUMMARY

You've got some games to play. Now play them until all the fun's been sucked out of them. Then go on television, give a quick two-minute review surmising all relevant points, and wait for the backlash from the fan faithful.

Or, spend 200 words explaining the game to the "nonbelievers" out there in the real world, making sure they can grasp why this game isn't going to kill their children.

Job satisfaction and security among TV hosts is highest if you can muster the winning combination of (a) knowledge, (b) charisma, and (c) the ability to read a teleprompter.

The job has a tremendous, unseen amount of work involved. For every cocktail dinner celebrating Wario's latest attempts on Mushroom Kingdom domination, there's a week's worth of preparation and other work to do.

If you own the company that's making the programs, you have to sell the series to a sponsor and a network, dozens of jobs are in the balance, and the pressure is immense.

For the eleventh time, will you listen? This job *isn't* just about being PAID TO PLAY! But we mentioned the free games, didn't we?

NO PREVIOUS GAMING KNOWLEDGE NECESSARY?

Although G4 TV remains a curious experiment in youth programming and tries to court the hip as well as the home-dweller, it has mainly steered away from hiring "gamers" as hosts for their shows. The problem is, there just aren't enough of them who could do this job. It's generally accepted rule of thumb that the more a person knows about video games, the less suited they are for appearing on camera (or in polite society in general, for that matter). Fortunately, though, there's one shining exception: Adam Sessler. Adam's knowledge is vast, and his slightly geeky, self-effacing style is in sharp contrast with "the pretty people" hosting the other shows on the network.

You're more likely to succeed in this business if you can couple a modicum of auto-cue-reading talent with a bankable knowledge of gaming. Or, if you can mask your lack of knowledge amazingly well, that works, too. Adam is a "type I" host; he knows what he's talking about.

If you're a "host" and not a "gamer," and have been hired by a network catering to those taking time out of their busy *Halo 3* marathons to watch you, you'd better have some serious charisma, or an amazingly low-cut baby-doll T-shirt. These "type II" hosts are usually female and are usually on extended basic cable to jump-start their careers. G4 TV alumni who have left (or been pushed) now work as newsreaders on CNN or hosts on HGTV or the Discovery Channel.

There's a recognizable "type III" gaming host, too: someone with the mind of an Adam Sessler and the body of a *Maxim* girl. These hosts have an X factor; they are mainly embraced by the hard-core gaming community, their opinions are valued, but they can be splashed across men's magazines from time to time to attract new viewers. Yes, we're talking about Morgan Webb.

Finally, there's a "type IV" gaming host: someone who is on a website. This could be one of the big video game sites or something cobbled together as a video blog. Usually the hosts are a pair of "Frag Doll"–like vixens (usually with the name "Vixen") who sometimes know (and strut) their stuff. Or, at the other end of the spectrum, you could be watching a video game editor nervously narrating portions of the interview he just posted online. This seems a little pointless, but website authors seem to think this is the next wave of the future.

Take This Job and Love it

Before you started this book, many of you may have imagined a career in gaming as something fantastic and wonderful. Alas, on closer inspection of this career, your illusions are shattered. But there's still some fun to be had. So here's how to get into this line of work, for better or worse.

THE GODFATHER OF GAMING TV

Victor Lucas isn't lying when he says he didn't find a job as TV host for a video game show: he created it. "I think I invented weekly behind-the-scenes TV coverage of the video game industry—at least in North America. I was an actor and a waiter, and both of these jobs helped me enormously because, since I [graduated] from the Film and Theater School [at the University of Victoria in Canada], I've been in business for myself. I've had to embrace the fact that I would have to be constantly communicating with people. This has helped me with pitching meetings, dealing with my staff, directing people, and performing in front of the camera. The other thing that has helped me is that I've always had a passion and genuine curiosity for video games and media in general."

If Victor is the godfather of video game TV in North America, then Tommy Tallarico and Geoff Keighley are his capos. But each of them had different career paths to fall back on, or as it turned out, continue to work on, after their first spell in front of the camera.

According to Geoff, "[I] started writing about video games when I was in high school and continued to do so during college. After graduating from college, I became a freelance writer/journalist. One of the things that separates me from other video game TV hosts is that I'm a working journalist, not just a host." Again, this further reinforces the notion that you must have something *other* than pearly whites and great hair to get a meaningful hosting job.

Geoff's current gig grew from a meeting with Victor Lucas: "[He's] the guy who first put me on camera as a correspondent for his show. It also helped that I live in Los Angeles, only about 15 minutes away from the main studios of G4." Geoff continued reporting for *Electric Playground*, then moved on to help with hosting duties for G4 TV, where he assistant hosted G4TV.com. "Then Spike TV took note of my work."

Tommy lists his education as "none." But he's a self-made man and naturally charismatic both on and off camera. Despite a determined drive, his only other help came from "reading inspirational and business books such as *How to Make Friends & Influence People*, *Think & Grow Rich*, etc." Oh, and then there's the networking.

NO PREVIOUS GAMING KNOWLEDGE NECESSARY?

While our interviewees exhibit an encyclopedic knowledge of video games, sometimes on a daily basis, it is general knowledge that some hosts on video game shows have been hired for, something other than their familiarity with the Konami code.[7] One of the authors of this book was interviewed a couple of E^3s back by a host of a video game TV show. Prior to the interview, the host asked about a new iteration of *Street Fighter II* that Capcom was showing.

"I met my wife over an *SF II* machine," I responded. Which was true. Then I added, "But she prefers *King of Fighters.*"

I braced for the interviewer's next question, as I had only a passing knowledge of Kyo Kusanagi and the Orochi Saga.

"*King of the* what now?" he asked.

"*King of Fighters.* You know, SNK?" I responded.

"What's an SNK?" came the reply.

We then agreed to talk about *Halo* instead.[8]

A HOST OF RECOMMENDATIONS: NETWORKING

You may be moping around, complaining that in this business it's who you know, not what you know. And you're right, to some extent. But if you *really* want a job in this industry, especially if you're cut out as a host, then you need to start meeting people. "Networking is EVERYTHING in this business," Tommy says emphatically. "Talent is ONLY 50 percent! The other 50 percent is networking and being able to sell yourself. People should spend just as much time on networking and honing their communication and 'friends' skills as practicing their talent."

When dealing with the mass market, Levi Buchanan recommends that "journalism school is a major help. Sure, you'll take the same classes with students far more interested in covering politics or the environment, but there are skills that college develops, such as work ethic and the appreciation for brevity. Enjoy the occasional fifty-cent word, but keep the flowery stuff for your novel."

Levi also recommends balance, which, according to him, is 33 percent "voice," 33 percent "charisma," and 33 percent "knowledge." This applies to any job in this chapter; you need to be recognizable, respected, or infamous, and know what the heck you're talking about. To give it 110 percent, we'd recommend you spend your remaining 11 percent on a combination of luck and chutzpah.

---

7. *Come on*, we're both strategy guide authors; "Up, Up, Down, Down, Left, Right, Left, Right, B, A, and Start" is tattooed across our bodies. We won't tell you where.

8. If you're reading this with anger slowly eating away inside you, rest assured, the guy was *really* photogenic. If you're reading this going, "Yeah, what *is* an SNK?" and you spend a larger-than-normal amount of time preening, then you're perfect for a short career in front of the camera.

Levi continues: "[Having a] more-than-passing familiarity with video games really helps you establish a voice right away. There is a big difference between game writers [who] started with an Atari 2600 or those [who] started with the first PlayStation. Having a good sense of history—but the sense to not beat your audience over the head with it (who likes a know-it-all?)—will go a long way to developing a voice and credibility."

Geoff agrees: "Really study the field of video games and think about how you'd explain games to a mainstream audience. Unlike the hard-core video game magazines, TV hosts have to be personable and figure out a way to explain video games to casual viewers who aren't reading *EGM* every month. Work on your writing skills and definitely get experience speaking in front of crowds and getting comfortable in front of the camera. It took me a few years to truly feel at home in front of the camera—but it was much easier because I knew what I was talking about and often [got] to interview my friends (and big-name game designers) on air. That immensely helped my comfort level."

Victor Lucas offers a last plan to those intent on encroaching into his territory: You have to be "good with people, articulate, educated, passionate about media and media development, comfortable on camera, and able to adapt to a variety of situations on the fly. An exhaustive knowledge about video games and the people involved in the video game industry would also be key. You can't have my job. Build your own!" he says with a smile. "Also, if anybody tells you you can't [succeed]…they're wrong."

THE TALLARICO STATUTE

Tommy Tallarico didn't become a guiding force in video game music and a reputable television host overnight. "I'd been playing piano since I was three and composing music since I was a teenager. I grew up on video games but never thought to put my two greatest loves together until I moved out to California when I turned 21. I moved out in 1991 with no money, no place to stay, no friends or family, no job…nothing! I was literally homeless and sleeping under the pier at Huntington Beach. The first day I was in California, I picked up a newspaper and got a job selling keyboards at Guitar Center. I started the next day and the first customer to walk in the store was a producer at a new video game company called Virgin Mastertronic (which later turned into Virgin Games). I was wearing a TurboGrafx-16 T-shirt, and we struck up a conversation about games. I went down to the studio and was hired the next day as the very first games tester. It was then that I decided what my career was going to be."

Needless to say, it wasn't game testing, as pretty much everyone in the "Quality Assurance" section will attest to.

THE TALLARICO STATUTE

Tommy says, "[I] wanted to help change the way people thought and felt about video game music. I didn't want it to be associated with childlike bleeps and bloops; our generation had grown up, and we were still playing games. I wanted to create thematic film score music, rock, blues, electronica, and all the music I would normally listen to."

Then, on a fateful day a few years later, Tommy Tallarico met Victor Lucas at E^3, and the on-screen duo was born.

Conclusion

Fortunately, you don't have to invent the concept of the video game TV show; Victor Lucas already did it for you. However, if you want a job like his, follow one of the paths we've laid out for you:

1. Study journalism, possibly with film and theater studies, and a side helping of business. Then form your own production company while continuing your expansive knowledge of gaming.
2. Enter the industry through one of the other disciplines. Cliffy B is a game designer, but he's been known to "rock da mike" from time to time—meaning appearing on television.
3. If this is just a stepping stone to being a newscaster, simply get yourself a headshot, an agent, and pick up a different type of career book.

Network, network, network! This isn't the same as stalk, stalk, stalk! You know the places, the websites, and the events. We won't tell you again.

Remember the four rules:

1. Voice: an identifiable writing style or way of explaining something on camera.
2. Charisma: a certain likeability that makes people sit up and take notice.
3. Knowledge: bust out that gaming encyclopedia we're sure Steve Kent should be publishing by now. Or Wikipedia your gaming series and get to know them all over again. Nothing beats playing games!
4. Luck and chutzpah: the bonus skills to write down on your character sheet.

Get up on stage, talk to a crowd, and if you haven't fainted, consider this an excellent result. Shrinking violets need not apply.

Keep plugging away at this career and weave your way into it by any means necessary. These guys did.

Games Store Clerks ∗ *Games Store Managers*
Independent Games Store Owners ∗ *Game Buyers*

SHOPPING FOR A CAREER: RETAIL

How to Get Paid to Play the Role of an Enthusiastic Game
Advisor: Working Retail in the World of Video Games

"Do you have any used dual shock controllers?"
"No, I don't."
"Yes, you do!"

"I do?"

"Right there!"

"Those are the controllers for the demo machine."

"And right there!"

"Those belong to the rental units."

"Just sell me one of those."

"And what would I use for rental machines?"

"You could open new ones for those."

"Um, no."

"Why don't you have any used controllers?"

"Because they usually only come in with a used machine. As such, I sell them with the machines."

"So sell me one of those."

"And sell the machine with no controllers? That'll go over well."

"You don't want my business!"

"How about I sell you something I have in stock like a new controller?"

"I'll take my business elsewhere."

"Would you mind? I would appreciate that."

—From **The Book of Annoyances**, scribed by Gord[1]

"This job would be great if it wasn't for the f—ing customers."
—Randal Graves, *Clerks*

YOU'VE POLISHED THE XBOX 360 DEMO

unit, taking care to cover the dents and scratches in the lockbox put there when that sniveling punk attempted to jimmy the system while his accomplice distracted you with questions about PlayStation3 backward compatibility.

All your new games are listed alphabetically—again—starting with *Aaron the Awesome Aardvark* in the top-left corner and ending with *Zytron Wars* in the bottom right.

You've got your list from the head office: there are 10 subscriptions to *Video Game Aficionado* that need pushing on your customers today, and preorders of *ZombieTown II: Corpse and Robbers* aren't up to the numbers that the regional manager (who never talks to you) was shouting at your boss. Oh well.

---

1. Gord, the nickname for a Canadian game store owner, who wrote his daily dealing with customers, Revelations-style, in his website, actsofgord.com.

No one's looking. Time to crack open your DS.

Welcome to the world of the game store clerk. If we've spent 11 chapters methodically charting the ceaseless daily toil of those inside games development, it seems only fitting to finish up chronicling whether the folks *selling* the product have the same enthusiasm for the job that people outside the retail world expect them to. After all, if you work at a game store, all you do is talk about games all day, break out the 360 every hour for 15-minute sessions of the hottest titles, and wow customers with your incredible knowledge of warp zones on *Super Mario Bros. 3*.

Right?

Wrong. And to prove it, we've enlisted the help of a half-dozen game store employees, ranging from the sales associate all the way up to the district manager. There's even a "game buyer," a job title that sounds almost as fantastic as "bikini inspector."

All of them work for big-name retailers. Naturally, when you're part of these types of organizations, you can't talk frankly about your job or, you know, you might lose it. Therefore, all of them spoke on condition of anonymity. So, we code-named them all after the ghosts from *Pac-Man*.

Then there's Lew Halboth, the president of Game Force, one of the last surviving mom-and-pop store chains in the country. He, too, is concerned about corporate overlords, but in an entirely different way. He's here to remind those of you reading this book in 2016 what the term "mom and pop" meant and how difficult it was for the independent retailer in 2006. He'll later reveal some shocking home truths that are likely to depress any entrepreneur.

A Day in the Life

The day-to-day world of the store clerk is one of action, positive reactions, and more action. There's little time for dozing.

WHAT'S IN STORE?

For the staff on the floor of a games store, there's one overriding goal: "Selling, selling, and more selling is what is most expected," Pinky, a sales associate, tells us. In addition, there's "organizing, receiving, record-keeping, and following up with whatever changes come down the corporate pipeline."

One step up from sales associate is the store manager. As Inky tells us, in addition to associate duties, there's "hiring, filing, transfering product, straightening the store, cleaning, helping customers, alphabetizing product, getting 'stats,' phone service, trade-ins, testing machines, problem solving, scheduling, [and] daily inventories." And that's before lunch. Managers are in charge of a single store, and must take great pride in all aspects of it: from the clean sidewalk outside to the rows of games meticulously arranged to the constant inventory updates.

GET ME THREE SUBSCRIPTIONS, SEVEN PREORDERS, AND A PREOWNED! STAT!

"Stats." Anyone who's in sales knows that dreaded word. It refers to a key number of merchandise that stores must shift every week in order to keep a giant company even more profitable. The company bigwigs send sales figures for new, used, pre-order, and "pushed" software to each store (which are often difficult to obtain), and it's up to the staff to match or beat them, or die trying.

The three major elements to push are subscriptions, preorders, and preowned. Subscriptions are often hawked with a year's worth of a video game magazine, like GameStop's *Game Informer*. Customers are also beckoned in with deals, like "Most Valuable Player" cards. These allow you to purchase games for lower prices than normal: preowned games, naturally.

Then there are preorders. Every store gets word from a buyer—a major software publisher—that they've *got* to entice customers into pre-ordering for a forthcoming game. This is great if it's a high-profile game, but if it's not, the presell gets a lot more stressful.

Finally, there are preowned games.

If you buy a new game at a store for $60, then between two and five percent of that goes to the store (more on that later). The rest of the cost pays for production, development, and shipping. The publisher takes a cut, too. However, if you buy that same game with a slightly scuffed instruction booklet for $55, then the entire amount, minus the cost of buying the game from the gamer who brought it in, goes into the store's coffers.

Needless to say, software publishers are pretty fed up with the situation. Why else are they introducing downloadable content you can only get from a "marketplace"? They need to increase their profits, keep so many gamers from selling back their games, but not alienate the stores that sell their hardware. It's a situation that's likely to heat up over the coming years.

All of this sounds overwhelming, so Blinky tells us the manager doesn't do all this work himself: "On a day-to-day basis, the store manager takes the general resposibilities and prioritizes them by delegating them, in different parts, to the staff." This frees up more time for managers to worry about how the store looks, while also maintaining "excellent customer service [and] profitability, [and] developing and training staff."

Almost every aspect of running a store can be taxing, but if the customer is a fan of the team running the place, they're likely to return, helping, unknowingly or otherwise, to up a store's stats. "It's great to know the answers to every gamer's questions," says Inky, "but you won't, so know *how* to find the answers, because gamers can be lazy and 'know it all' at the same time."

Frantically searching for release dates, phoning other stores to find a rare game, plugging strategy guides and magazines, and getting online to answer a particularly difficult customer question is all part of the job.

The district manager (Clyde, as we call him) is the store manager's boss. His role is to manage the managers. Every day, Clyde "supervises, coaches, and trains store managers." He also "increases store sales and profitability through store managers." This is another way of telling a store manager how profitable that store needs to be on a weekly basis and helping them achieve that through ideas and threats. But mainly ideas. A district manager is also in charge of making sure company policy is carried out on a wider scale.

Clyde usually has over a dozen stores to manage, which gets difficult when store reviews "to identify problems, concerns, and opportunities for improvement" take place.

If all this sounds pretty far away from sitting around playing video games and chatting to customers, that's because it is. Working at a games store is becoming more like working at any other retail outlet, except your Mario and Luigi tattoos are less likely to scare off the customers. But there's a dress code, a piercings code, and a code for not swearing in front of customers, even the idiotic ones, or the ones who didn't preorder a much-antipated game and think it's the store's fault for not having enough copies.

That would be the game buyer's fault, wouldn't it? Well, technically no, it wouldn't. At least, not usually. You see, the game buyer—who we code-named "Kratos" because we ran out of ghosts—at the major retailer we spoke to can buy only as much stock as his budget, and the game publisher, allows. "I manage the purchasing, marketing, and inventory of the products that I am responsible for. Additionally, I need to stay updated on competing products (that I am not the buyer for) so that I have a frame of reference to compare the titles that I am buying against. This will help me order the right amount of products to meet customer demand."

Spotting trends is also key so you don't overstock, and end up with hundreds of copies of a poor-selling game that you lose money on. Any unsold software is sent back to be repackaged, or destroyed, but this is a rare occurrence; after 20 years, companies are pretty good at judging how many copies of a game they will sell. And the game buyers from different companies tell them this, months before the ship date. "My 'homework,'" says Kratos, after agreeing to the numbers on his latest game shipments, "entails reading as many video game magazines as I can so that I'm as knowledgeable as I can be on the products."

It's also been around 20 years since Lew Halboth started his independent video game emporium, Game Force. He's responsible for more than just the store; as president of the company, he manages absolutely *everything* for his business, "from start-up [costs for a new store] to day-to-day operations. [There's] lease negotiations, budget for product, employees, taxes and licenses, deposits, payroll, etc.... I'm one guy [with] many jobs!"

'TIS THE SEASON TO BE OVERWORKED

Store clerks—aka senior game consultants—work hourly and get a modicum of health benefits if they can scramble for 20 to 40 hours per week. In fact, this is a great way to get health care. Managers, and the game buyer we asked, worked around 40 to 50 hours per week, while district managers spend most of their day driving, shouting into their BlackBerries, and asking why store #347 smells bad. They do this for around 60 to 70 hours per week. For the independent game store owner, workload can be as much as 90 hours a week, but mainly tops out at around 55.

These hours are prone to massive increases during October through January. Store hours are extended during this time, which is when around 80 percent of all software and shopping (and returns) are done for the holiday season. Pinky says, "There are a lot more customers in the store—many of whom do not know much about games or gaming and therefore need help selecting appropriate gifts for their nieces, nephews, grandchildren, etc."

Store workers can't relax until after the end of the year. Pinky explains that "the least busy time of the year begins in mid-January and runs through February and into March. The release schedule is extremely light, and people start to get those postholiday credit card bills and are less likely to come in to shop."

Lew Halboth has a different take on when Game Force is at full-force: "Wednesdays, [which are] release dates [for new games at mom-and-pop games stores], and the first and 15th of each month, [which are] payroll days for our customers." This is a game store in America's heartland, where good, honest, blue-collar workers head in after a hard day's working. They're searching for a fun, wholesome game to relax to.

SUMMARY

- Your main focus as a game store person is making sure all those games and accessories on the shelves are exchanged for great wads of cash as quickly as possible.
- Then, when the corporate office calls with a special promotion to presell a game, you shift as many units of that as you can, using your witty banter and enthusiasm, and keeping threats down to a minimum.
- Then there's all the additional organizational, bookkeeping, and corporate red tape that a manager has to deal with. If managers aren't pulling their weight, they get it in the neck from the district manager, whose job it is to drive around to a dozen or more stores and make sure they're all fully functional, then fix problems if they aren't.
- A game buyer purchases large quantities of games, based mainly on guessing how well the game will sell.
- An independent game shop owner has the additional concerns of paying the rent on the place, the electrical bills, and all the payroll.

- Game stores love their preused games, as the profits they can make are either ridiculous for big store chains, or if you're a mom-and-pop store, just enough to keep you from bankruptcy.
- Like some sort of ironic torture test, you're surrounded all day by the latest gaming goodies, and you've no time to play any of them, without getting told off.

The Good, the Bad, and the Ugly

Working at a game store isn't the best way to get into gaming. Heck, it's not even the best way to get into retail. However, it's a path that anyone without serious mental or social problems can use as a means to an end. If that end is "working at a games store," then congratulations, my friend, you've made it! If that end is "getting a college degree," then this is a great way to stay on top of the gaming scene, talk to like-minded gamers, and then ostracize yourself from them after getting them to preorder a game that turns out to be a complete turkey. Welcome to the section where we crush that industrialist spirit of yours.

THE GOOD

Do you feel the need to change the general public's concept of video gaming, one customer at a time? Do the young kids flock around your counter, needling you for gaming knowledge? Can you keep the deprecating comments to yourself or make them subtle enough so only your coworkers get the joke and high-five you afterward?

Then you can experience some of the benefits of being paid to take pay from other people who want to play. Pinky loves this part of the job: "[It's] very high energy and dynamic. If you enjoy talking to people and talking about games in an informative, friendly way, then this would be a good position." But don't take it too far: "If you tend to become pedantic and abrasive when discussing your favorite games, look elsewhere; no one wants to buy anything from 'Comic Book Guy.'"

For Inky, a self-confessed gaming novice, store management allowed him to increase his knowledge about games: "Now, after six months in the 'gaming world,' I'm somewhere between a parent who comes in seeking the newest Monopoly board game (we don't sell these) and the guy who comes in every day to buy a new video game, because nothing will ever replace his *Final Fantasy VII*." Blinky concurs: "The ability to interact with people and discussing video games [is] an interest that I enjoy."

In addition, district managers enjoy the flexibility of the job. "I can travel between any location at any time," says Clyde. For Kratos, his greatest job-related task is "being able to work with the video game publishers to provide ideas and suggestions on things we would like to see in future products and promotions."

For the lone independent, holding out against the corporations, it's all about the family. Lew says the best part is "the guys that I work with. I say work *with* and not work *for*, because we are like a family. I see a lot of the guys that have worked with me over the last 17 years and they are still like my kids." Lew also gets a kick "watching former employees having success in the industry I introduced them into."

Big Chains vs. Mom-and-Pop Stores

Big chain stores aren't able to offer the customer service some game stores pride themselves on, a fact that Inky definitely sees as an asset. "You get to know customers' names. You get to spend a lot of time with the customer. The people who I work with know tons about video games. We have more games than [a big-box store], and used games are a plus! 'Cheap' is the word! While occasionally, the big retail stores will have crazy sales, usually our sales are crazier and way more people-friendly. Plus, you don't have to walk for ten minutes just to find the video games; it only takes a second and you are surrounded by them, with your personal game advisor at hand."

The manager at the game store doesn't seem unduly worried about large "one-stop shops" influencing their bottom line (the goal of acquiring larger and larger quantities of cash). And it's a similar story among the independents. Lew Halboth tells us, "They aren't hard to compete with from within the store: Competent help behind the counter has always been a secret to the mom-and-pop stores' success. I would go into big-box stores and leave business cards for their employees to send customers to us, and they did. Other than their buying power, they are *no* competition when it comes to selling games to gamers. Our atmosphere is built around the gamer; my two guys have over 25 years behind the counter in my store. You won't find anyone working with me [who] will be working in housewares tomorrow. We just sell games!"

PAYMENT FOR PLAYMENT

Store associates at a game store make the least amount of money out of anyone even connected with the gaming industry—less than $25,000 a year, and usually more like $8 an hour. Store managers and game buyers fare a little better, starting off in the mid to high $20,000 range, and topping out at around $40,000 after years of experience. District mangers are where it's at, though; aside from company PDAs and compensation on vehicle mileage, expect a wage of between $60,000 to $80,000 a year, which should be just enough to cover the hospital visits after your ulcer bursts.

When we asked our independent retailer, "Salary?" he replied, "Yes, please, but only with ranch dressing." But as he's had to close a couple of stores in the last few months, we'll let that horrific pun slide. This business is tough.

THE BAD

When Marshall Field said, "Right or wrong, the customer is always right," he didn't have to deal with some of the gaming flotsam and jetsam floating into a game store on a daily basis.

"Contact with the public can be a big drawback," says Pinky. "People can be jerks, and you have to keep your cool and remain professional in the face of some pretty rotten stuff sometimes." Inky agrees: "Occasionally, the guest who doesn't bathe can be a real nuisance. I could go on and on about awful customers, but those people know who they are."

Store managers also have additional feelings of hopelessness, sometimes among their own staff. Inky says, "If you're the boss, like me, when no one can cover a shift, you're stuck with it because, by gosh, you care too much! Being on salary sometimes sucks, because you end up making two-thirds of what you're supposed to." However, if you're a sales associate, "the pay is abysmal, retail hours generally stink (though they can be good for students), and the burnout rate is pretty high," Pinky tells us.

As the game shops become much more goal-orientated, extra stress is piled on store teams. "Deadlines are tight and are given as if miracles happen daily," says Inky. The stats are sent over to the district managers from their regional bigwigs, who then tell their managers, in no uncertain terms, that these goals must be made. The managers in turn then have to motivate their sales crew as if this low-paying job was a military conquest.

Or, as Inky points out, "Meeting business goals [is] challenging when good titles are being made and as gaming systems become more expensive and the cheaper ones rarer." There's only so much disposable income the general public can fritter away on video games.

Pinky backs Inky up, saying, "The corporate retail environment can be very stressful, with the folks back at the home office trying to cut expenses and expand profit margins, which means things are always being cut back, while sales goal expectations are simultaneously increased."

As for Blinky? He's more concerned with that pungent aroma coming from the back room: "The worst part of this job is probably the cleaning aspect; that toilet doesn't clean itself."[2]

What about the independent guy? He's more concerned with being screwed over royally by publishers and distributors. "Not getting the product through distribution for release on Tuesday, and having to overnight the product to try and meet the consumer demand" is the worst part of going it alone in the wonderful world of corporate retail.

---

2. Unless it's one of those Japanese robotic ones.

CAN YOU GO FROM RETAIL TO A SOFTWARE STUDIO?

Dan Hsu had "a brief stint working in retail for Electronics Boutique…[but] that didn't really help or hinder my chances of working for *Electronic Gaming Monthly*," he says.

Conversely, Matt Ibbs, a QA manager for Rockpool Games, got a job from his chance encounter with a developer who was buying games from the store Matt worked at. "If you want to be an actor, you should work in a theater. I think the same applies if you want to work on games. Apart from the working in a theater bit. I mean, get a job in a video game store. Getting a job in a theater if you want to work on games would probably be a waste of your time." Thanks for clearing that up, Matt.

But Matt is the exception to the rule. Unless you're working at the Electronics Boutique that everyone from Valve vists, don't expect to ask them how Gordon Freeman's next outing is going and parlay that into a ham-handed attempt at a job interview. You could, we suppose, go online and talk about your work, rent out games and play them, start a blog, become a writer, and leave your game store forever when some script supervisor or editor in chief e-mails you, wanting more of your prose. But your game store job still wouldn't have been a factor.

So, a career in retail gaming stores generally only prepares you for a career in retail, not a career inside the gaming industry itself.

THE UGLY

Apparently, you *don't* get to play games all day at this job. We've said it 11 times previously, but we'll let Pinky state it once more: "Many of our customers (particularly the teen boys who come in and spend hours on our demo units) think that it would be the best job ever—all you have to do is come to work, play games, talk to people about games, and run a cash register."

Some might feel we've flogged this dead horse enough. Most probably think we've flogged it, resurrected it, shot it through the head, zombified it, ridden it around the paddock, out into the field, and off a cliff into a ravine, and then separated its brain from its spinal column.[3] But it bears repeating again: getting paid to play games for a living is the biggest lie since Santa Claus.

As Inky explains, this perception continues with applicants for a job in a game store, who soon find their world crumbling around them. It starts off with an interviewee exclaiming this must be "the coolest job ever!" Then they continue with "I've been playing video games all of my life. I know everything!" Once the job

---

3. It's the only way to ensure zombies stay dead. Equine or not.

description has been amended from "sits around playing *World of Warcraft*" to "stacks shelves and sells like a maniac," the enthusiasm lessens slightly. But their eyes are still on the prize. Inky explains, "It goes more like this: 'No, I've never had a job! No, I've never actually worked with a cash register, or cleaned my room. No, I don't have any nice clothes to wear. But I want all the hours I can get!'"

Others looking for a career in game retail are "customers who like to 'shoot the shit' with the workers here, and they think that's all the job entails. However, it's about finding out the needs of each customer and maximizing that particular sale! It's about selling, promoting, and organizing video games. If you're a hard-core gamer, then all you can hope for is part time in a retail video game store," says Inky.

As soul-crushing as this may be, it gets worse if you're after a store manager role: "If you don't mind *not* playing *World of Warcraft* every day, then being a store manager might be for you. You just won't have enough time outside of work to play all the video games that come through the door, so don't expect you will."

What about the awesome discount? "No, not really; this isn't Wal-Mart," says Inky, with a slightly exasperated look on his face, since employees at Wal-Mart get a better discount than at the specialized game stores.

SUMMARY

The Good

There's plenty of room for both big-box retailers and specialized game stores; they aren't killing independent game sellers. The battle is more of a playful mauling. The reason why is simple: Most gamers want to chat with knowledgeable staff or score deals on used games. Game stores and independent chains have them both.

- Expert staff can change a customer's mind-set about the games they buy: *No, this game you're about to spend $70 on is actually appalling! Buy this instead!*
- There's camaraderie, and this is most visible at independent stores that don't ritually sacrifice the sales associate straggler with the least number of stats.
- Game buyers get to talk to publishers about marketing strategies and some times affect how a game is pushed to the public.

The Bad and the Ugly

Customers range from the polite to the brain dead. Some are rude. Others are stupid. Many are irritable, unpleasant, and abusive. Grin and bear it, then write about them on your *anonymous* blog. Attacking them using a pair of nunchakus usually results in your dismissal.

Ready to have your spirits utterly crushed? Then try out at a video game store with the expectation that you're there to be paid to play games all the time. You won't last the day.

- Burnout is horrific. Just look at the staff turnover at most games stores.
- Flipping burgers or tipping customers off about that new God of War game pays the same. The smell of grease is only slightly less intense.
- The job's stressful, and if you haven't had a previous career in sales, you won't be expecting the high-pressure zeal that's needed to keep your stats high.

Take This Job and Love It

So far, we've learned the eye-opening facts about what game store personnel *really* have to deal with. The reality is far removed from the fantasy. It isn't that bad: you get games to rent and a staff discount.

BUSINESS CASUAL: A CAREER IN RETAIL

"Showering. The ability to not be a jackass. The ability to show up on time and follow directions. Some degree of self-motivation." These are all skills a potential store manager is looking for. Writing your own name on the questionaire you're usually given instead of scrawling an "X" usually works well, too. And like it or not—and you won't like it if you're a big fan of video games—"retail and customer service experience count for a lot more than general video game knowledge," Pinky says. Other skills are more basic: Abilities like multiplication, addition, and division are helpful. In your head, not using a calculator. No, we're serious; some people actually turn up having never learned how to multiply. And these people shouldn't be allowed to multiply.

Blinky offers up another way to stand out in your interview: "Lots of people who apply do so because they like to play video games. Be different; highlight your other skills." Does Pinky have any final words of encouragement for those about to attempt a basic career in game retail sales? "Yeah, don't expect to make a career of this, but if you take this job, it can be a fun environment—hey, games are fun, remember?!—if you can work with a smile on your face." What's more, you don't need any education, aside from a high school diploma or GED.

When you reach a store manager position, a previous career path in retail management is definitely a plus. Inky had seven and a half years' experience in another field. Although Inky completed a BA at college, this wasn't necessary when he took the game store job. According to him, you definitely need "previous retail management. Working your way up to store manager is also preferrable if you are younger. Whether you like it or not, you have to prove yourself through work experience, not a college degree."

If you can demonstrate to the district manager interviewing you that you possess basic managerial skills—leadership, organization, salesmanship, problem-solving ability, cooperation, positivity, initiative, communication, and staying calm during a crisis—you should be running your own store in no time, and hopefully not into the ground.

Blinky, another store manager, concurs: "All my previous jobs had some sort of customer service aspect involved, and most jobs had some sort of sales involved as well. I've been in customer service for over 17 years, 10 of which were in management." Plus, you also need to prove that you held your own at a previous retailer, rather than larked around all day: "Previous management experience and a track record of successful sales performance" is also the key.

When you reach district manager level, like Clyde, "previous district managerial experience in retail and entertainment industries" is a must. You won't ever step into this position overnight; strong sales staff are promoted to managers. Strong managers are given their own store for a year or two, then they're trained and promoted from within. Or they do all of this at another company, then jump ship. Either way, expect a three-year-minimum wait, at the very least. Blinky also recommendes an "ability to relocate; [it] will open more options that become available." This is because there's always openings for game store managers and district managers in Alaska. Or anywhere else in the United States with a lot of bears, snow, and humans stuck indoors.

District managers must also cope with "working variable hours, including evenings and weekends, and [traveling] extensively. [They must have the] ability to communicate clearly and concisely, both orally and written, and [be] able to balance multiple priorities and meet deadlines. Be able to influence others!" Clyde tells us from his company sedan, typing furiously on his mobile PC.

By the time you've gotten to this level in a company, the job features absolutely *zero* game-playing time, and a job of a district manager at Game Crazy, for example, could be done by a Borders district manager relatively easily. So, we recommend a career book on business if you're heading off down that road. The same goes for a game buyer; you're a merchandizing expert who knows how many units to purchase and who has the time and personnel management skills to back this up. "I would rather work with people [who] are organized, efficient, timely, and team-oriented than the person who is only intersted in the video games themselves," says Kratos.

ENTER THE ENTREPRENEUR

Lew Halboth started selling used games in 1989, which saved his business: "If I had to just carry new games, you wouldn't have read this interview," he tells us. He is currently a major windfall for the bigger chains and shares with us what additional skills he thinks you need in order to run an independent game store. "Patience, patience, and more patience. To be honest, the used-cars industry is a mirror of what you need to be successful in this business. Know what to buy it for, trade it for, and sell it for." Don't expect your business to flourish. It's more likely to lie withering on the ground. What about those who really want their own game store? Take from someone with over 17 years in the business: "Think twice!! The competition is higher than ever before, and the margins are smaller than ever before. [Big name] game stores are on every corner of intersections, sometimes two per shopping center."

Lew is unique. He has something that the bigger chains find very difficult to cultivate: true customer appreciation. "Thank you to my customers," says Lew, in what we hope isn't a farewell speech. "I sold games to your parents, you, and now your kids. Thank you. Please support independent retailers in your area. YOUR business is important to us!"

You're more than a statistic to Lew: "When you are in an independent retailer, you are treasured and respected. If you are in the gaming community and reading this, visit the independent retailer in your area, and let them know you appreciate their efforts. Some of us paved the road for where the industry is today!"

Seventeen years ago, Lew was "selling *Skate or Die* and *Super Mario Bros. 2* on the NES. I just wish I had a dollar for every time somebody has told me this industry was a fad. I would be Bill Gates."

WHY PUBLISHERS ARE PULVERIZING MOM AND POP

Lew's getting into the swing of things, so we asked him whether he was getting preferential treatment due to his independent status. You know, an extra helping hand so he isn't eventually driven out of business. "Rolling on the floor, laughing my ass off!" came the reply. "Really, go to E^3 and tell them you have one store, and see how far you get into the booth." But you're allowed into the back room to check out the games and obtain free samples, right? "You might get a button or bag to carry around with you." Oh well, a button's pretty cool.

"First, we were the 'dark side' of the industry; we sold used games. No one wanted to sell to 'used-game stores.' Next, the mall stores finally figured out they couldn't compete with easy-access stores in strip malls. They also started carrying used games, but their size made it impossible for manufacturers to do anything but accept this practice. Everything you see being done at retail today, I was doing on February 1, 1989."

"I want to try and remain positive," says Lew Halboth about the future of mom-and-pop game stores, "but these last few questions are making it really hard. I also want to say that I made ALL the decisions along the way for my company and have been right many times and wrong more times than I want to admit.

"I was asked recently by a business broker if I would recommend this business to anyone, and my answer was a resounding NO. That being said, I cannot see myself being in any other business than this. If I had to look into my crystal ball and predict [the future], I would have to say that in the bigger cities, [independent stores] will face tough competition and get nothing for their advertising dollar.

WHY PUBLISHERS ARE PULVERIZING MOM AND POP (CONT.)

"If you want to get into this business with a retail store, choose a market that is small enough for you to be a major player. This is the key for the mom-and-pop stores.

"The key is, [get] your advertising [to] reach a higher percentage of customers, and then you have to whoop the competition with outstanding customer service and timely delivery of the product."

Conclusion

A career in gaming retail is all about the retail and less about the games; an employee with shop-floor experience is likely to be preferred over a *Halo* player.

Getting a job in a games store is straightforward. In fact, one of our authors did something similar, for about the same pay, too.

You like games, you can complete simple math in your head, and you're literate? Great, you start tomorrow.

If you're manager material, be prepared for at least a year's worth of positive stats for your store and a good working relationship with your crew.

College? No need, except for those wanting to progress through the company. Merchandizing courses (for a game buyer), business courses, and perhaps psychology courses are a plus. Retail management courses are nowhere near as important as real-world experience in the game store trenches.

Managers spend less time worrying about playing games and all their time worrying about making money; you're learning skills that are interchangeable with other retail outlets, which is excellent if a rogue meteor shower targets all the game stores in the continental United States, or if you decide you want to work at Macy's.

And, finally, and rather sadly, if you're wanting to start a business selling games yourself, don't. It's likely to all end in tears unless you're offering something that no one else has, like Japanese imports, really obscure Turbo Grafix titles, or those "adult" games we don't know anything about.

MEN ARE FROM THE MUSHROOM KINGDOM, WOMEN ARE FROM HYRULE: WOMEN IN GAMING

How to Get Paid to Play Well with the Sometimes Socially Awkward Boys: Does Being Female Matter in a Male-Dominated Industry?

"If women had a little more fun in online worlds, or played games that involved killing folks, they would do better at their jobs."

—*Professor Justine Cassell*[1]

YOU'RE A HUGE FAN OF VIDEO GAMES;

you're constantly kicking all kinds of booty on Xbox Live, you have a gigantic collection of action figures, and when you're not playing games, you're instigating threads on gaming forums. In fact, you're toying with the idea of making your hobby your career. But you're different from 65 percent[2] of other gamers out there: You are female.

Quite understandably, many women aren't overly keen on a career in what appears to be a male-dominated industry, with past overtures of sexism, pasty-faced programmers keeping to themselves, and little room for advancement still lingering. Fortunately, the role of women within the gaming industry, and the integral role they're playing in shaping what female (and male) gamers play, has never been more advanced. But just how advanced? What can recent female gaming graduates expect to find in the workplace? What jobs do women usually migrate to? Is there equality? Is an office full of pale, sweaty men a good or bad thing?

To answer almost all of those questions, we asked those in the know—nine industry folk, ranging from editors in chief to newly hired designers,[3] all of whom just happen to be female.

It's a Man's, Man's, Man's World. Or Is It?

"On a male-to-female strict ratio in the development, and especially the media, end of the business, men make up the overwhelming majority of decision makers, creative talent, and wordsmiths," says Francesca Reyes, the editor in chief of the *Official Xbox Magazine*.

Jane Pinckard from 1up.com wholeheartedly agrees: "Yes, absolutely it is—that's why the GDC has sessions every year on how to attract more women in game development; video game journalism is very similar, although there have been some high-profile female writers, [such as] J. C. Hertz [and] Van Burnham."[4]

---

1. From a paper titled, "On Underdetermined Technology, Social Norms, and the Gender Politics of Mobility" by Professor Justine Cassell. Courtesy of Ruth Shalit.
2. According to a study by the IDSA, women make up 43 percent of all PC gamers and 35 percent of console gamers. That sounds incredibly promising, and it is, as long as you realize they're including games like *Jeopardy* and backgammon here, too.
3. We even tracked down a couple of female programmers, a position previously thought to have been extinct.
4. Know your female gaming luminaries: J. C. Hertz is the author of *Joystick Nation: How Videogames Ate Our Quarters, Won Our Hearts, and Rewired Our Minds*. Van Burnham is the author of *Supercade: A Visual History of the Videogame Age 1971–1984* and writes for *Wired*. According to her website, she can kick your butt at *Galaga*.

Lisa Mason, a high-profile female writer from *Game Informer* magazine, echoes these sentiments: "I think [the games industry] is male-dominated, in that many of the people working in games are men, but I don't think that it's a big problem for women getting involved."

Currently, it's actually a tiny little bit easier for women to get their foot in the door compared to their male counterparts—if they're any good. It's just there aren't enough ladies out there. Lisa continues with her point, that "developers, publishers, [and] media, etc., are much more interested in hiring people who know and love games, and less interested in maintaining the stereotypes that mainstream media seems to have about who a gamer is: that is, a loser dude living in his mom's basement—an idea so far from the reality of most developers that it always cracks me up."

YOU SEXIST THING, YOU

Jane Pinckard still encounters sexist murmurings from the less enlightened, more Neanderthal members of the industry: "I encounter versions of 'Girls and women just aren't that good at games,' or, even worse, 'aren't that good at math and science and programming.' This is an issue, of course, that reaches way beyond video games."

CHILD'S PLAY: FOR BOYS ONLY?

Research has shown that young girls don't utilize the computer nearly as often as young boys, a claim Professor Justine Cassell supports: "From the age of two on, boys spend more time than girls on the computer—and that the magnitude of the gap increases with age. What we see is that, as early as kindergarten, both girls and boys consider the computer to be a boy's toy."[5]

Tasha Harris of Double Fine software agrees: "When I was growing up, young girls were not expected to have an interest in computers or technical things and so were not encouraged in this direction. Hopefully this is changing with computers being more commonplace, but many stereotypes about gender roles are slow to change—if you look at most toy and video game advertising you will see that there are still very clear-cut roles." Or, to put it another way, if you're playing *Barbie Horse Adventures*, you're either Seanbaby working on an EGM article, or a seven-year-old girl trying in vain to back up a pony and about to lose all interest in video gaming.

Fortunately, for the sake of the gaming industry, this problem is likely to lessen in the years to come. These "innate differences," as Jane calls them, or perceptions thereof, begin at home: So, future parents, get that young tyke away

---

5. Justine Cassell is a professor in the departments of communication studies and computer science at Northwestern University, where she is also director of technology and social behavior.

from *Bob the Builder* and set her in front of the latest 3-D world builder on your PC instead. The call is out: nurture future female gamers.

It looks like this is occurring, too. Jane says, "Every day I see more young women and girls interested in computer science classes, programming, in making games. Conferences like the GDC and even E^3 achieve better gender balance every year. And most men I've met are in favor of this change."

GAME GIRLS: ADVANCE!

But what about the women who are on the front line of game development? The male domination is abundantly clear, as Anna Kipnis, a programmer at Double Fine testifies to: "This is especially true of production staff on a development team. Although you do see slightly more female modelers and animators working in games these days, the ratio very much favors the men. There are barely any women programmers in the business—significantly fewer, I'd say, than in other tech industries."

The situation is even worse in the United Kingdom. Emmeline Dobson, a QA technician at Ninja Theory, tells us, "[We have a] lower ratio of female workers in the games industry compared with the USA and Japan. Not only in terms of workplace statistics, but out of eight projects that the studio I've been employed in has been working on, one was aimed at young girls, four were 'gender neutral,' and three were aimed mainly at young adult and adult men."

Josie Nutter, content engineer for Snowblind Studios, reinforces this notion stateside: "At every game studio I have worked for, men have definitely outnumbered women. There are very few studios run by women. I can count on one hand the number of female executives I've worked under." So where are the highest concentrations of females and males? Christa Morse, a junior game designer for Pronto Games, gives us a quick rundown based on her observations: "Human resources and non-industry-specific jobs [are] staffed by women regularly. From what I've seen, art is 50/50. It's a fierce competition for talent and any woman who has a good demo reel can get an art job. Engineering has a very high concentration of males. I'd attribute this to the general societal qualm that girls just aren't encouraged to go into sciences. I have seen quite a few female associate and midlevel producers, but not so many executive producers. It's a demanding job and it's possible that women might turn down a high-powered job like that to raise kids, unlike a man."

STICKING WITH STEREOTYPING

Anna agrees about the concentration of women as producers, and other nontechnical disciplines: "[One] of the very few areas in the industry that is female-dominated is PR for games, most likely because the video game press, with whom PR must maintain a strong relationship, is male-dominated." So why is public relations such a haven for women? Because many women try a career in public relations in the general sense; spreading the word on a variety of products, not all of them video game related; and this skillset can be transferred to another PR job easily. The frighteningly exact knowledge of gaming isn't necessary; it's the PR skills themselves that are valued. This is why companies drag a much more knowledgeable producer or designer into a room full of journalists and let *them* do the talking at gaming events.

As much as many people would like to ignore this fact, an attractive PR woman is a real treat for some of the less-seasoned, more freakish male freelance writers out there.

For every woman in gaming that doesn't need, or want, a gigantic encyclopedia of gaming facts to succeed, there are many other jobs where this knowledge is more relevant and sometimes essential.

GAME GIRLS: RETREAT!

Journalism is another area of the industry where there doesn't seem to be significant room for female career progress. Fran Reyes is the exception rather than the rule, at least according to Cindy Lum, senior public relations specialist at Ubisoft: "Having worked in both the editorial and publishing side of the video game public relations business, I do believe that within video game journalism there is more of a glass ceiling. [Fran Reyes is the] only one other woman who made it to an executive editor position. You would be hard pressed to find women in a position higher than managing editor within video game editorial." But for the rest of the industry, the times are a-changing.

Gradually.

Josie Nutter sums up the collective feelings of women gamers in general: "Slowly but inevitably, I think we will see more women joining the ranks as time goes on. It makes me think of the early days of the tech industry in general. Younger women are much more accepting of computers and technology these days. Interest is not as strong or widespread as I'd like it to be, but it's coming along."

SUMMARY

- The video game industry is crying out for quality candidates, and although women are encouraged, getting the job is almost entirely based on your qualifications.
- Growing up, women don't statistically get to play with computers as much as boys, and thus aren't getting as many opportunities to hone skills useful to many aspects of the video game world.
- But as time marches on, that is changing, and more female candidates for video game jobs should have the skills necessary to compete with their male counterparts.

- There's a significant shortage of women in key roles (especially in the programming and technical disciplines), and as companies attempt to expand their demographic, they're looking for a female perspective.
- So yes, the video game industry is still primarily a "man's world," but it would be nothing "without female counterparts." Or, in this case, to compete with on an even keel.

A Few Good Women: Unique Challenges Facing Gaming Females

So, ladies, are you still interested in joining the gaming industry? You'll face a few unique challenges before, during, and after you land a job. The good news is that in the late 1990s a mind-set shift occurred, where women were more openly embraced in the industry. Although, according to Alison Beasley, of Lincoln Beasley PR & Marketing, comments like, "'Of course you like *The Sims*; that's a dollhouse simulation,'" still occur from time to time.

For Fran Reyes, the switch came after years of dealing with public relations people: "Many of the marketing and PR folks working several years back when I started were so used to dealing with guys, that they [mainly] catered their promotional media kits, tours, junkets, etc., to males. After all, booth babes and the possibility of interviewing, say, porn stars, aren't nearly as tempting for a straight female games journalist as it would be for a straight male games journalist."

Fran encountered many instances where well-meaning but slightly ignorant developers and marketing people attempted to explain a game to her as if she was a simpleton: "There was some hesitance to trust that a female gamer would understand the tech lingo or knowledge associated with games and their history." But this has lessened considerably, and Fran thinks she knows why: "Games companies are becoming more driven to cater to all audiences, and not necessarily just the entrenched hardcore converted (which also claims plenty of female gamers, mind you), so the language and general attitude has become way more inclusive rather than exclusive overall. And that's brilliant for either males or females, really."

While Fran Reyes's initial hurdles seemed high, Lisa Mason's hurdles were more manageable and mainly about "proving your knowledge and appreciation of the medium. That's the same for men and women, but there have been times where I felt that I had to prove myself a little bit more than a guy in my position. Then again, I used to do IT for a long time, and I had more resistance and requirement to prove I knew my stuff from coworkers, employers, and customers in that field than I ever have in video games."

CHALLENGES OF PERCEPTION

All our interviewees experience what Jane Pinckard calls "challenges of perception." For Jane, it was from "fans, from some male colleagues, and even, I'm sorry to say, from some female colleagues. One of the most insidious perceptions of women in game journalism is that it's 'so much easier for them' because they 'stand out'; even worse, that they only got the job because they're women and therefore their talents must be less than men's."

Elizabeth Ellis, an editor and translator for *Hardcore Gamer Magazine*, has also seen "accusations that we're only hired because a team needs a 'token female,' so our competence often comes under deeper scrutiny from critics." But, in order to muddy the waters still further, Elizabeth has also seen evidence that some women use their sexuality to their advantage: "Because female gamers are so rare, they're often in high demand—so we all face the question of how much we can and should use our sexuality to try and get ahead. Some do this more than others, of course, but I think that whether or not you do it consciously, it's going to be a factor in any woman's professional life."

In the game development community, according to Jane Pinckard, the challenge to women may not be quite as problematic, as there's mainly just your team to deal with, and "game development is so competitive that I doubt anyone, male or female, could survive long if she's truly incompetent."

Anna Kipnis cites a comprehensive survey,[6]—which, although applied to hacker subcultures, applies to gaming and development, too—with slightly more unexpected findings: "In short, women are considered unusual in the gaming industry, and so they are not readily accepted as members of the development community. Unless she's doing PR, a woman entering the biz must be prepared that a lot of attention will be paid to her gender. If she is doing development, especially programming, doubt will be cast on her abilities and understanding of games, and she will be under significantly higher pressure to prove herself to her peers and superiors than a man at her very same skill level. Having a family— something that is important to many women—will be a huge challenge, because the hours developers often have to work are brutal." As Alison Beasley puts it: "The reality will always be that, in general, women don't want to be programmers, and our biology means that we get pregnant and have kids, which makes a big dent in our career paths—all worthwhile, but still an issue that men clearly don't face, even if they take paternity leave."

There's a resounding "afraid so" to the question of women having to prove themselves to a greater extent than men. Cindy Lum states, "Oftentimes, others assume you must be in public relations. No one really expects a woman to be in a position that perhaps would require someone to be a hardcore gamer. It often comes with a jaw drop and look of disbelief when a woman says she's a programmer, producer, or even video game journalist. Because of this, women may

---

6. Which was undertaken by Flosspols.org, a gaming research company based in the Netherlands.

feel like they have to constantly prove something to their male counterparts, which sadly, I don't think is unique to the video game industry."

Josie Nutter agrees: "As in any traditionally male-dominated field, there is some resistance to the idea that a woman can be just as capable as a man—especially in fields involving math and science. Women in the games industry have to work really hard to prove themselves."

DOWN ON THE CUBICLE FARM

Then there's the crazy day-to-day social experiment that places one or two women in a giant cubicle farm with dozens of men, with often manic office hours and a free Ping-Pong table. How do women deal with this semifraternity?

Emmeline Dobson says, "I think there are challenges. I can fit into a male environment and be quite 'tomboyish,' but when starting out in games, a job that you invest time and passion into, [you're in] a different environment [than] what you're used to."

And if some of the male team members have limited life experiences with the ladies, that can also lead to uncomfortable situations. Josie Nutter has met "quite a few men in the games industry [who] have never had the experience of working with women on a professional level. Social ineptitude combined with the stereotypical male behavior of some individuals can potentially create a hostile work environment. As a woman, you sort of have to come into a company expecting some of that ([it] doesn't mean you need to endure inappropriate behavior without complaint, of course)."

Josie Nutter's outlook is the same as Emmeline's: "Whenever I go to a new studio, I make it a high priority to become just 'one of the guys.' In my experience, it helps remove any gender-conscious awkwardness from working relationships." But don't take it too far, Alison Beasley says: "Have a laugh with the guys—you don't have to act like a lad/ladette to be accepted; in fact, they're likely to think less of you for that, but don't be afraid to tackle the guys on issues that bother you."

It also helps to bring a sense of humor to work. Josie says, "I'm very easygoing, do not wear revealing/suggestive clothing to work, and rarely find crude humor seriously offensive…all of which I'm sure helps." Tasha Harris has the same understanding, too: "A sense of humor and being more laid-back about things definitely helps. If you are able to laugh at a female character's skimpy outfit or 'bounce physics' rather than getting offended at little things, [when] you do speak up about something you have an issue with, people are more likely to pay attention."

FEAR AND LOATHING AND RETAIL: ISOLATION

Women in game development can also feel slightly isolated. Or even that green-eyed monster, envy. Jane Pinckard noticed it "between female colleagues—because it's such a male-dominated world. I really think some women survived for a long time being the *only* woman on a team, and got used to it, and when another woman comes along, there's sometimes a sense of feeling threatened. Of course, that's only sometimes, with some people. In my experience, the women who seek out the company and support of other women are vastly in the majority. Who doesn't like to have a girlfriend at work to go get lunch with?"

Emmeline agrees: "Sometimes at work, I desire some female-style friendship, sympathy, and support, but these can be absent or handled inappropriately. Inevitably, being one of few females leads to situations to deal with that you wouldn't have to if you were another man, which can be a stress factor. Fortunately, some of the time this works to your advantage or the game's advantage, such as getting a chance to consult on how to remove barriers for female players to all around improve a project!"

One of our interviewees, having experienced narrow-minded attitudes from the men, didn't expect the same treatment from the women: "I, personally, experienced some social stigma from other (especially older) women, [who felt] game development [was] unserious, unglamorous, and immature."

Coaxing women into the field of video gaming is also a problem on a wider scale, because the industry still has to wrap their heads, and their focus-group budgets, around a fact no one's bothered to rectify: more women need to be attracted to the industry. Elizabeth Ellis says, "Ninety percent of what we're playing, reviewing, or creating isn't being marketed at us at all. A lot of women enjoy male-targeted genres like first-person shooters and real-time strategy regardless, but they're still not being made for us."

Which gives further weight to what many women have suspected all along: most management at gaming companies don't have a clue how to market to women, or at the very least, have executives who sometimes make laughingly inept comments amid the recognizable "market research" data when attempting to address this issue.

SUMMARY

- Ignorant workers exist, and you'll need to prove your knowledge, rather than have it taken for granted. Prepare for accusations that you're a "token" or that you used your cleavage to get a job. Some women do, and don't last long. But this shouldn't be a factor when you get your job.
- Having a family and a game development job is a huge challenge.
- When at work, mingle with the men. Become an integral part of the team, rather than becoming ostracized.
- A laid-back attitude is best. Be prepared for testosterone, but speak up if there's a real issue.
- Fellow females provide a support group to combat certain feelings of isolation, but don't necessarily rely only on a female teammate; jealousy can rear its ugly head.
- Games still aren't properly marketed to women.

■ Overall, the "old boy's club" has mostly disappeared. Women are recognized as workers and leaders in this industry. And this will continue to improve.

You Go (Get a Job in Video Gaming), Girlfriend!

If all these obstacles are making you think twice about a career in gaming, then stop right there and heed the advice from five of our interviewees: "Go for it!"

WHERE THERE'S A WILL, THERE'S A WAY: PERSEVERANCE

These women have plans for you, beginning with Fran Reyes: "If you have a passion for games, the talent for executing an idea, and an open-minded attitude, then there's no reason to hesitate. The people in this business are amazing, smart, and driven—and above all, they're not as exclusionary as the media would have you think."[7]

Being strong-willed also helps, too: "There's really nothing stopping you except other people's perceptions," says Jane. "And if you have the talent and believe in yourself, do you need to listen to what other people say?"[8]

In fact, now's the best time ever to be a career-oriented female gamer. "There's a lot of enthusiasm for recruiting more women," Alison Beasley says, "particularly in development and journalism. Go for a well-established company that will have a good structure and policy [for women] in place."

Anna Kipnis encourages you to think ahead: "Be prepared for difficult, awesome work, rad people, long hours you'll be spending with them at work, and dirty jokes."

WOMEN ON TOP: KEY ADVICE

Emmeline Dobson has, perhaps, the best advice of all: "Pay close attention to all the advice in this book from all contributors about the games industry, regardless of gender."

Tasha Harris has advice you'll love: "Play a lot of games." But then she goes on to spoil it: "Read gaming industry news websites, [and] go to school with teachers that have experience in the industry."[9]

Anna Kipnis says to also make subtle attempts to cultivate gamers out of those you associate with: "Get your girlfriends to play games with you, especially those who've never played a video game in their life. Keep playing games yourself, because they will give you perspective on your own work."

---

7. Remember, Fran has been a pioneer for females in this business for over 10 years; she knows what she's talking about.

8. We'd only recommend listening to what other people say when you're reading quotes from our respondents. That's allowed and encouraged.

9. Once again, accredited colleges with courses that actually help you are recommended. Being sucked in by late-night infomercials from places where students "can't believe we play games for a living" are not.

This training doesn't just stop when you finally land a job in gaming, either, says Josie Nutter: "If you like novelty, working in games is definitely the way to go. Technology is constantly changing, so you always get to learn new, fun things. There are a few downsides, however. Depending on the studio you work at, hours can be pretty long—especially during the final month(s) of a project. Try to find a company that values proper preproduction and realistic scheduling to avoid the worst of that."

Josie goes on to say, "Be prepared to work hard to prove yourself worthy of your title. An open mind and laid-back attitude will help you fit better with the guys, personality-wise. Most importantly, have fun! You get to help create something that brings enjoyment to people all over the world!"

Where else could you work, where "only one project in fifteen is cancelled, your views are welcomed as you contribute actively to an energetic and co-operative team, and everything runs smoothly to a well-managed staffing and budget plan"? Emmeline says; then she offers a caveat: "But it doesn't always happen that way!" Still, despite the odd mishap, for most, this is a wonderful industry.

But you'll need perseverance: "Stay motivated as you investigate the industry. Make effort to shine at your work, and sometimes be prepared to champion your own contribution to the project," says Emmeline. "Take up networking opportunities (both with men and women) because friends in other companies can be a helpful morale support, and treasure any mentor-type relationships if you're lucky to find them! Be aware that there are plenty of successful and talented women working with, shaping the future of, and going down in the history of games today!" Emmeline adds. You should know this by now; we've been interviewing them.

Need to find networking opportunities? Then check out our following list of websites, starting with the IGDA.

VIDEO GAME WEBSITES

www.igda.org/women: This is basically the nexus for the vast majority of information pertaining to nonmale gaming

http://womengamers.com: Helping the industry create "a female-friendly gaming space"

http://evergreenevents.org: Organize female-centric conferences

http://womeningamesinternational.org: For international lady gamers

http://gamegirladvance.com: Jane Pinckard's always-entertaining website

AND FINALLY: DON'T FEAR THE CHAUVINIST

If you're interacting with other women, play nice, says Cindy Lum: "Sometimes you'll come across women who don't like other women in the industry, whether that's because they've had so much to prove to the men that it's a badge of honor to only associate with men in the industry or whether it's just because they don't like other girls in general. But there really aren't that many of us females in the industry, and it just makes the good times that more fun and the hard times that more bearable when you have the support and friendship of other women."

And don't fear the chauvinist, says Lisa Mason: "People in the industry never ask what it's like to be 'the only chick in the office'; it's always people outside of gaming that think it's weird. The development community is small, but delightfully short on judgmental people who will assume you aren't qualified because of gender."

In the end, however, it's your talent that will ultimately take you on this wild, roller-coaster ride of a career. And men can help, too, says Jane Pinckard: "There are plenty of men in all areas of game development and in games journalism who want to welcome talented women to their team and learn from them, collaborate with them. It's a matter of finding where you fit in. Take criticism well, but ignore the haters."

We'll give Fran Reyes the last word of encouragement: "The good news is that this is a young industry and it's constantly changing—I don't believe anything is impossible in gaming as long as you've got the ideas, the talent, and the passion. If there are any restrictions, they're not gender-based and are entirely up to you to shatter."

Conclusion

You've got to be open-minded and, ideally, strong-willed. And talented. And able to take criticism. And suffer through long hours. Wait, is this job for a human or a protocol droid?

Make sure the company you're applying for doesn't have "pants optional" Fridays; progressive developers who treat everyone well are your best bets.

Keep cultivating those thumb calluses; play games that inspire you.

Get a great degree from an accredited school, network like a social butterfly, and hang on to a good mentor.

Ignore those who offer unconstructive criticism.

You love games and want an exciting career? Go for it!

GETTING A JOB

If you've made it this far, you should have a pretty good idea of the wide range of video game jobs out there and a short list of the types of jobs that appeal to you.[1] Congratulations! You're one step closer to silencing that nagging parent/spouse/voice in your head that insists that spending your days dreaming up more efficient ways to slay orcs doesn't constitute "doing something with your life." Now it's time to take that dream job and make it a reality. If you follow the advice presented in this chapter, we *absolutely guarantee* (not really) that you'll soon have the job you want in the field you love.

Earning Experience Points

As you begin hunting for your first job in the video game business, be prepared for a fair amount of disappointment and frustration. Most jobs require that you have previous experience in the field, and the only way to get that experience is by having held a similar position, which you need previous job experience to get, and so on. However, if you're crafty and persistent, you can find ways around this Catch-22. Which we'll tell you about. Starting right now.

BLOGAMANIA IS RUNNING WILD!

These days, everyone's got a blog, which our primitive ancestors referred to as a *Weblog*, an online repository for your thoughts, ideas, and pictures of your cats doing the cutest things! But in the right hands, a blog can be used for good instead of evil.[2] If you're an aspiring video game journalist, start blogging about the games you're playing and review them. If you have an interest in game design, you can blog about the features you like and hate about recent games, showing that you actually put time and effort into thinking about this stuff.

If it were possible to throw a rock in the online world, you wouldn't be able to do it without hitting a site that allows you to blog for free. We don't specifically endorse any of the following sites, but they seem to be pretty popular:

- Blogger.com: Powered by Google and extremely customizable. It can be embedded in existing websites.
- Blogdrive.com: Choose from the basic free service or pay to subscribe to different levels for added benefits.
- MySpace.com: Not as versatile as the first two but extremely popular. It's also ideal for virtual bullying of high school students.
- Livejournal.com: Similar to MySpace, but 20 percent more self-indulgent.

If you need something a little more versatile or if you're as sick of the word *blog* as we are, register a domain name and build yourself a website. This is

---

1. This assumes that you started on page 1 and read each page in sequence.
2. "Good" here meaning getting a job and "evil" meaning posting lame demo songs that your friends will only pretend to have listened to out of politeness.

essential for anyone hoping to land a visual design job, as a website is the fastest and easiest way to showcase your portfolio to potential employers. Visual artists should have sites with attractive layouts and a strong design.

Always seize the opportunity to prove that you can do the job you want to get, even if it means doing the job for free. Building that *Legend of Zelda* fan site might not get you a job at Nintendo, but it might help you land a game-review assignment or website design job. Your home-brewed online game mag might not be as polished as GameSpot or IGN, but no one's expecting that it will be—regular updates of solid content matter more than a slick interface. Strategy guide publishers rarely hire completely unproven writers, but banging out an FAQ for the latest Japanese RPG in two weeks and posting it on www.GameFAQs.com might be enough to get your name put on the list of authors to call when they get desperate.

Remember, just because you're not getting a paycheck for your work doesn't necessarily mean you're wasting your time. Everyone's got to pay their dues.

TRUE STORIES OF ONLINE SUCCESS

If you don't believe that the right website can launch your video game career, let us refer you to Jerry "Tycho" Holkins and Mike "Gabe" Krahulik of Penny Arcade (www.penny-arcade.com). In November of 1998, the duo unleashed their webcomic on an unsuspecting online world that quickly embraced them and elevated them to such heights of popularity that our product manager had to beg them piteously for three days (dressed as both Twisp and Catsby) to get them to illustrate this book.

Or consider the case of Seanbaby, the Handsome Face of Geek Culture™ who parlayed the success of his website (www.seanbaby.com) into frequent guest-host spots on G4 TV and a regular column in *Electronic Gaming Monthly*.

Scott Bonds launched a website (the now defunct www.iwant-toworkatea.com) in the hopes of getting a job at Electronic Arts. "It occurred to me that if I changed my default e-mail to iwanttoworkatea.com, it would be a nice, unobtrusive way to tell everyone I e-mailed that I was looking for game industry introductions," he says. He used the website itself to blog about his experiences looking for work in the industry. And in one of those quirky twists of fate usually reserved for Disney Channel films, it wasn't long before EA took notice, offering him a production internship on *The Godfather*. Six months later, he was promoted to Assistant Producer, and now, two years after getting his break, he manages the game development team for EA's Pogo.com.

TRUE STORIES OF ONLINE SUCCESS (CONT.)

Be warned, however, that the Internet is a cruel and unforgiving place. If you open yourself up to public feedback, you'll find out pretty quickly if you don't impress your audience. For every Penny Arcade, there are 50 sites like The Mushroom,[3] whose only saving grace is their ability to provide fodder for punch lines for snarky jerks like us.

WILL TEST FOR FOOD

One of the lowest rungs on the video game ladder is QA—quality assurance—also known as *testing*. These are the folks who play the same unfinished, bug-ridden code for up to 12 hours a day in the final months of a game's development in an attempt to find and squash all of its glitches. It's tedious, unglamorous work, but it's a job that you can get straight out of high school. Sometimes it even comes with a paycheck, albeit a very small one, and all the pizza and Mountain Dew you can consume.

QA is the proverbial foot in the door for the game biz, but even this low-level grunt position can be competitive. So the first thing you should do is sign up for open beta tests of upcoming PC games. This almost never pays a dime, but it's something that looks good on an otherwise empty résumé. Plus, if you put in the hours and do good work, you stand a chance of getting noticed by someone who has the ability to put in a good word for you down the line, and that never hurts.

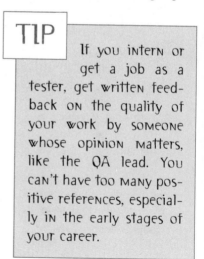

TIP If you intern or get a job as a tester, get written feedback on the quality of your work by someone whose opinion matters, like the QA lead. You can't have too many positive references, especially in the early stages of your career.

GIT YERSELF SOME LEARNIN'

More and more colleges and universities are offering courses of study in game design (see the back of this book for a partial list). Are some of these programs hastily-thrown-together attempts to jump on the video game money train? Absolutely. Does that mean that they're entirely worthless? Not at all.

---

3. A site so incredibly not funny that it has been wiped from the collective video game consciousness. Trust us, you're glad you missed this one.

Let's face it: If you can get Mom and Dad to subsidize four years of LAN parties and *World of Warcraft*, that's a sweet deal, and you'd be a fool to turn it down. But if you actually want to wind up with a job after school, use that time to hone your skills and make yourself as attractive[4] a candidate as possible for the job you want to get once they stick a diploma in your hand and boot you into the real world.

The same goes for non–video game courses of study (aka, "real college"). If your school doesn't offer a game design program, focus on computer science, a writing program, or some other skill that you can apply to the video game industry. In your spare time, review games on your blog, write FAQs, design deathmatch levels, or do whatever it takes to prove that you're capable of doing that job for money.

Not college-bound? In the video game industry, this is less of an issue than it is in many other more-traditional fields. Because the games business is still a relatively young field, your real-world experience is much more important than the degrees you can list after your name. A high school diploma is pretty much a must in this day and age, but a sizable body of quality work—amateur or professional—is often enough to convince an employer that you're worth taking a chance on.

Finding the Job

Preparing yourself for your fancy new career in video games is only half the battle. The next step is to actually find a job opening in the field you want to work in.

APPLYING ONLINE

The easiest way to find a job opening is to scour industry websites that specialize in posting game jobs. The three big ones to visit regularly are:

- www.gamesindustry.biz
- www.gamasutra.com
- www.gamejobs.com

The only problem with this method is that everyone else in the world is using it, too, and the competition for jobs posted on these sites is fierce. Don't let that discourage you from making the attempt, but don't base everything on kick-starting your career with an e-mailed résumé.

> **TIP**
> If you live in an area that has several video game companies, such as Los Angeles, Seattle, or San Francisco, check out Craigslist (www.craigslist.com) regularly for local job postings.

---

4. Not physically attractive, mind you. No one here cares about that.

IT'S WHO YOU KNOW

Most of the job openings in the video game business are never listed publicly. If a producer needs another game designer, for example, he'll usually offer the job to people he or his team members have worked with in the past. Networking—making connections in the industry—is your best bet at moving your career forward.

If you're not in the industry but know people who are, ask them for help. But don't be obnoxious about it, and don't expect them to help you land a job just because they're your friend. Odds are you'll be working with them on any job they help you get, and they're not going to want to pull more than their fair share of the weight if you're not qualified for the job.

NOTE

Schmoozing is a big part of networking, but another big part is just doing your job well and making sure that people notice it. When you start making some inroads in the industry, be flexible, easy to work with, and hardworking. Above all, learn what it means to be professional. If you want to be a gaming journalist, learn how to be a "real" journalist first; don't accept gifts from the people whose products you're reviewing. There's a lot of adolescent boy behavior in the games industry, especially at the entry level. The people who move up from there are the ones who quickly move beyond that and can be trusted to represent the company without embarrassing it or themselves.

If you've had any experience whatsoever in the video game industry, make contacts with people who have the jobs you want. The best source of advice is someone who came from the position you're currently at and has moved into the spot you want. They can tell you how to get there, and they can share the mistakes they've made so that you don't make them.

If you're not in the industry and don't know anyone who is, your best bet at networking is to regularly post on the video game forums on which game developers post.

TIP

Here are eight of the best places to network, or a place to start when locating specific developer forums. Construct an avatar, name yourself something semi-hilarious, and get on board at one of these locations:

Gamedev.net
Indiegamer.com
DevMaster.net
Igda.org
Gamasutra.com
Sumea.com.au
Thechaosengine.com
Gaming-age.com

INDUSTRY EVENTS

One way to do a lot of networking very quickly is to attend industry events. Many events require you to have some existing industry credentials to get in, but professional-looking amateur work might be enough to get you in the door. Your school's career counselors or department head may be able to help you gain admission as well.

Come armed with résumés, business cards, a professional appearance, and a firm handshake. Introduce yourself to anyone who will give you the time of day and tell them that you're new to the industry and looking for an internship or entry-level position. Be sure to collect business cards. Above all, understand that this is a place where business is conducted, and any time someone gives you is a favor. Be polite and professional at all times.

Follow up after the show with an engaging cover letter and another copy of your résumé. Try to schedule an informational interview[5] either over the phone, through e-mail, or in person. Be persistent but not creepy. Stalkers don't get jobs in this business. Daily e-mails are a big no-no. If you are told that there's nothing for you at the moment, ask when would be a good time to follow up.

JILL ZINNER, VIDEO GAME INDUSTRY RECRUITER

For 14 years, Jill Zinner has been a video game industry recruiter. She is currently president of Premier Search, Inc. (www.premier-search.net). We asked her about the best schools and degrees to have on a résumé for the video game industry. Here's what she said:

With design I think a good degree would be in writing or English. However, sociology and psychology are also good. Someone in behavior sciences will most probably be able to know the minds of gamers and what they will like.

Art: Well of course take courses in art, a degree in fine arts, and so on. Communications: Get a degree in communications.

Of course, in programming, [get] a BS in computer science and a minor or even a dual degree in physics and higher math.

Production (producers): [Get] a degree in business and business management, and even a masters degree (MBA) would be good too. A degree in communication and in a behavior science (sociology and psychology) are good areas to concentrate in.

Then, after [earning a] degree from a college or university (even an AA degree is better than nothing), [you] can consider one

---

5. See the next chapter for an explanation of what an informational interview is, exactly, courtesy of a real-life career counselor-type.

JILL ZINNER, VIDEO GAME INDUSTRY RECRUITER (CONT.)

of the special schools for making computer games. I really like Guildhall at SMU. They try to really help their people find a job in the industry.

There are some good schools out there, but in my opinion, none of them are outstanding. Some of the people teaching have never even made a game. They're gamers, and they know lots of people, but they have no idea what it really takes [to be] in the trenches. Some of them made games, like, eons ago and things have changed drastically even in the past 5 years, much less 10 or 15 years ago.

The best way for these people to get a job is to show the potential employer a game or game level that they made; get together with others on a team and then make something. They need to have something to show. The coders need to show code, the artists need to show art, the designers need to show a demo. These projects are called "mods."

The artists have the most competition. Usually their work is just so-so, and, [therefore], many times I've seen people put their portfolio together in a haphazard manner. Someone needs to tell these people that making a good first impression is **very** important. [It is difficult] going after [a company that has already passed] on a candidate. Short demos that are really good are worth a lot. If the hiring manager likes what he/she sees and wants to see more, then the person may have an opportunity to do a test or an assignment to show off more of the talent or skills.

Networking is so very important. Finding a mentor within the industry, someone who can give advice or even make a personal referral, is worth a lot. Going to GDC, joining a local branch of the IGDA (International Game Developers Association), or reading up on industry news and stuff like that is so important. Make sure you know what the studio makes, and if you are going to make a friend in the company, make sure you know what they do, [and] what credits they have on games they have made.

Networking

The good news about a career in video games is, once your foot is in the door, you can usually use every job you hold to get more work in the industry. After you've been around for a few years and have held a couple of positions, you're practically tenured in the industry. There might be periods when the work is a little lean, but if you're good at your job and willing to move to where the work is, you shouldn't have trouble finding any.

Unfortunately, getting that first job can be a royal pain. The vast majority of video game jobs are never posted to the general public. And because there's a lot of money to be made in video games and the work seems like fun, competition for available positions is intense. Most producers assemble teams from people they or their team members have worked with in the past, and the same goes for just about every non-game development job as well.

For these reasons, to get your career started and to keep it moving forward, network with other video game professionals; use them as references and information sources. However, unless you're already in the industry, or you're lucky enough to already know a pro who doesn't mind sharing time and advice with you, networking can be tricky. But there are two networking strategies that just about anyone can use: attending industry events and going on information interviews.

INDUSTRY EVENTS

The best way to meet a lot of industry professionals at once is to attend the events where they gather. The following list details the most important video game industry events:

- **Classic Gaming Expo**: Celebrates the history of video games and is open to the public, which makes it a great opportunity for amateurs to network (www.cgexpo.com).
- **Consumer Electronics Show (CES)**: Not strictly a video game event, this trade show covers all aspects of consumer electronics (www.cesweb.org).
- **Electronic Entertainment Expo (E^3)**: The granddaddy of all video game industry events, E^3 is where *everyone* in the industry winds up every May. Because it's a trade show, you must be a video game professional to attend, and you must be 18 years of age or older (www.e3expo.com).
- **Game Developers Conference (GDC)**: This trade show is for game developers only, with plenty of seminars and opportunities to network with professionals (www.gdconf.com).
- **SIGGRAPH**: An animation and graphics trade show, with seminars and great networking opportunities (www.siggraph.org).

EUROPEAN INDUSTRY EVENTS

And lest we be accused of forgetting our friends across the pond, here are a couple of trade shows that cater to European video game pros:

EUROPEAN INDUSTRY EVENTS (CONT.)

- **European Computer Trade Show (ECTS):** Europe's largest interactive entertainment expo; think of it as the European E^3 (which presumably would make it E^4) (www.ects.com).
- **MILIA:** European entertainment consumer software trade show, open to the general public (www.milia.com).

How to Get In

Most of the aforementioned industry events are trade shows; this means they're open only to people working in the video game industry. However, if you've done some professional-looking amateur work that is posted online, it might be good enough to let you pass for a pro. If you're in school, your advisor or guidance department might be able to grease the wheels a bit and get you in. As a last resort, you can visit the event's website and plead your case via e-mail.

Once You're In

Tell as many people as possible that you are new to the industry and are researching careers. Be as specific about your field of interest as possible. Tell everyone that you meet what you're interested in, and listen to what they have to say.

Meet with representatives behind the exhibition tables. Ask them who would be a good person to talk to about careers in your interest area. Ask for their business cards and follow up with an engaging cover letter (see following) after the show.

POSTSHOW COVER LETTER

Hi [NAME],

My name is [NAME], and I met you at [EVENT] (or [PERSON] recommended I contact you for an information interview). I'm currently a [STUDENT AT; EMPLOYEE OF; INTERN AT;] and I'm excited to learn more about your organization. I have a background working with [RELATED EXPERIENCE] and I'm very interested in [FIELD OF INTEREST].

I'd like to connect with you to learn how I may be a resource for [COMPANY] in the future. Would you be available for a brief phone meeting in the next two weeks? I promise to respect your time. Even 15 minutes would be great, or perhaps I could take you out for lunch. Let me know what would be a good time for you to meet.

Best Regards,
[NAME]
[CONTACT INFO]

NOTE

Use the sample cover letter as a reference for your own cover letter and customize it.

INFORMATION INTERVIEWS

Make sure you take action and follow through. After you send the cover letter, follow up and schedule an information interview, either in person or over the phone, to get the ball rolling.

NOTE

Be determined! Don't get discouraged, but don't be a stalker, either. If you send more than two consecutive unanswered messages, you risk alienating the people you're trying to get help from.

Information interviews aren't job interviews. Your objective isn't to land a position with the company but rather to find out more about what the jobs require. In conducting these information interviews, you're also making fledgling professional connections that you can use to get your own insider information on breaking into the field, or discovering if it's really the right fit for you.

Keep in touch with your contacts while you are in school or launching your video game career. This dramatically increases your chance of landing a competitive job or internship. Drop a line to your contacts at least two or three times a year. Keep them updated on your progress and what you are excelling in as it relates to the video game industry.

Questions to Ask

Unlike a job interview, at an information interview, you're the one asking most of the questions. Here are a few to get you started (be sure to add your own to the list):

1. How did you get into this field?

2. What training or education did you have?

3. What is a typical day or week like?

4. What do you like most and least about your job?

5. What are the skills most critical for success in this field?

6. What are your organization's/department's most pressing, significant, and immediate goals? What obstacles are getting in the way of achieving these goals?

7. What professional association do you recommend for this field?

8. Given my background, how well do you think I'd fit into this profession (or your organization)? What are my strengths and skill gaps?

9. Who else should I talk to?

NOTE

Bring a copy of your résumé to the information interview, and respect the time given to you. A half hour is the average length of an information interview.

Follow Up

Follow up with a thank-you note to everyone you met during your career exploration. Let them know specifically how they helped you.

Keep in touch with them. Even if their career area is not suitable for you, let them know what career area you've decided to investigate and ask if they know someone in that field.

PROFESSIONAL ORGANIZATIONS

There are several professional organizations in the video game industry that can possibly assist you. Go to the association mixer events, get business cards, and follow up with your cover letter requesting an informational interview or internship.

- Association for Computing Machinery (www.acm.org/)
- San Francisco ACM SIGGRAPH (http://san-francisco.siggraph.org/)
- San Francisco Bay CHI, ACM SIGCHI (www.baychi.org/)
- San Francisco Bay Area ACM Chapter (www.sfbayacm.org)
- Silicon Valley ACM SIGGRAPH (www.silicon-valley.siggraph.org)
- Digital Games Research Association (www.digra.org/)
- International Game Developers Association (www.igda.org/)
- International Journal of Computer Game Research (www.gamestudies.org/)
- International Simulation and Gaming Association (www.isaga.info/)
- Game Developers Network (www.gamedev.net)

Applying

If you're applying for a job, the two most important things you need are a professional-looking résumé and a concise, engaging cover letter.

RÉSUMÉ

There are many general career advice books out there that can help you put together your résumé, and there are several different ways to correctly create a résumé, but a good résumé should contain most or all of the following sections.

NOTE

If you're in the early stages of your video game career, your résumé should fit on one standard 8.5 x 11 piece of paper with 1-inch margins. Only after you have had several positions and years of experience should it go beyond a single page.

Header

The first thing any employer should see is your name at the top of the résumé, followed by your contact information (mailing address, phone number, e-mail address, website).

Summary

Describe yourself in two or three sentences. Example: "A highly skilled strategy guide writer with seven years of experience authoring over 40 guides, as well as a variety of freelance writing for a number of publishers. Especially effective at time management and self-motivation. A strong problem-solver who anticipates small issues before they become big ones."

Professional Knowledge

Include here any special classes, certificates, or skills relating to your objective. Use phrases such as "professionally certified in," "exceptionally skilled at," "highly knowledgeable in," "excel at," "capable of," "able to," and so on.

Accomplishments

Include brief descriptions of two or three of your greatest achievements, such as important, related school achievements or internships, and leisure or work projects you successfully completed.

Experience

List here your relevant job experience, in chronological order from most recent to least. If you do not have any experience yet, list relevant volunteer work or school projects. Internships also count as work experience. Your experiences should be formatted as follows:

Job title: Company name, city, state. Month/year to month/year
Description of duties, tasks performed, skills utilized, special recognition or promotion received

Education

In this section, list any formal education you've had, beginning with the most recent. Don't go any lower than high school. Even if you didn't complete the course of study or receive a degree, mention what you did accomplish. Use the following format:

> Degree or semesters attended, school name, city, state, years attended or year of graduation
>
> Brief description of course work
>
> Relevant extracurricular activities
>
> Awards received
>
> GPA (only if outstanding)

Training

If you've completed any nonacademic training, such as seminars or certification courses, list them here in the following format:

> Seminar title, organization name, year completed

Affiliations

Here you list relevant professional associations. Do not include any religious or political organizations. Use the following format:

> Society name, offices held (if any), description of activities (if any)

NOTE

For international jobs, you may be asked for a CV (curriculum vitae). This is a longer résumé that includes personal information, hobbies, interests, and publications, and is typically three to five pages long.

RÉSUMÉ TIPS FROM THE PROS

1. After you enroll in college (or a trade school), list this degree and place your education section at the top of your résumé, right under your objective (i.e., **BA in Computer Animation**, DiGiPen Institute, Redmond, WA [in progress]). If your résumé is electronically scanned, the optical scanner will read your degree acronym (BA, BS, MA, MS), and you'll have an easier time getting in to interview for jobs and internships.

2. Make sure all the buzz words in the job ad are reflected in your résumé's summary section. For example: If you are applying for a software engineer position with Activision, and the job asks that applicants be "fluent in C++, with strong communication skills," make sure your résumé includes that language. This is how optical scanners work. The system searches for key words, and if your résumé doesn't have them, it might not ever be read by human eyes.

3. Having a website with samples of your work is very important for designers and artists, but don't send a demo of your work along with your résumé. For legal reasons, it's much safer for a prospective employer to visit your website and see your work than it is for them to have a copy of your code. At most companies, unless you sign some legal documentation in advance, unsolicited demos will be destroyed, sight unseen.

4. If you've got a website (and you really should), don't just list the address at the top of your résumé. Refer to it again in the summary (i.e., "Expert ability in 3-D character animation—see www.IAMGREAT.com for samples of my work").

5. Balance your passion for gaming with your professional credentials, because both are important. If you dropped out of school because you stayed up every night playing *Quake II* deathmatches, that can actually work to your advantage in the video game industry, provided that you can point to professional qualifications as well.

SAMPLE RÉSUMÉS

What follows are two real-world examples of résumés from actual video game professionals. Only the names, dates, and places have been changed to protect the applicants' privacy.

The first résumé is from an inexperienced applicant who's fresh out of college and is applying for a game design job. The second is from a very experienced professional who's been in the business for years. Use these for guidance as you assemble your own résumé.

Inexperienced Sample Résumé

642 W INVENTED ST. • PORTLAND, OR 76543
PHONE (456) 789-0123 • FAX (456) 237-8901
E-MAIL CWANNABE@ZIPMAIL.NET
WWW.IWANNABEAGAMEPRO.COM

CHRIS WANNABE

Summary

An aspiring video game designer with a diverse array of strong skills and significant entry-level experience in game testing. A self-motivated multitasker who masters new concepts and responsibilities quickly and with ease.

Education

| 2002–2006 | Burlington College | Burlington, VT |

BA Computer Science
- 3.97 GPA
- Recipient of the Arthur Q. Frink Prize for excellence in science
- Minor in English (Creative Writing)

Work experience

| Summer 2006 | Gee Whiz Games | Los Angeles, CA |

Quality Assurance Tester
- Beta-tested *The Turgid Adventures of Thurston the Turtle*

| Summer 2005 | Gee Whiz Games | Los Angeles, CA |

Production Intern
- Provided support for production team on *Ninja Strippers 4*
- Offered input on design process
- Served on QA (testing) team

| 2002–2006 | The Burlington *Campus* | Burlington, VT |

Columnist
- Wrote a biweekly column on gaming news and reviews for student newspaper; over 50 articles published.

Experienced Sample Résumé

JIM GAMESMAN
123 Fake Street
San Francisco, CA 98765

Office Telephone: (123) 456-7890
Cell Phone: (123) 098-7654
E-mail: jgamesman@nosuchaddress.net

SUMMARY

A versatile and prolific game producer experienced in developing electronic entertainment, games, and toys. Over 5.5 million units sold, generating more than $176 million in sales ($37.7 million in profits.) Expertise includes outstanding project management, communication, and design skills.

EXPERIENCE

Game Consultant/Author/Speaker, Los Angeles, California   2000-present

Consulted for game developers, publishers, and educational institutions internationally; wrote articles for books and magazines; gave lectures; maintained website where free information was offered to game industry aspirants. Previous clients include (partial list) Megaworks, Sunburst Games, AAA Games, Intelligent Designs, Montage, Libra Media, and Simple Plan Software.

MegaGameWorks, Inc., Irvine, California   1988-2000

Creative Director (2000)
Executive Producer (1999-2000)
Senior Producer (1992-1999)
Marketing Specialist (1990, Japan)
Producer (1988-1992)

Produced and designed software products totaling 4.2 million units, representing $141.6 million in sales and $24.3 million in profits. Accomplishments include:

- Produced 36 game titles generating $48.4 million in sales.
- Designed 6 games generating $32.5 million in retail sales.
- Significant participation in additional 53 game projects (multiple platforms, OEM, licenses, and international versions) resulting in $60.7 million in retail sales.
- Participated in the acquisitions of games from Japan, Australia, and England. Brand-managed the Dora the Dolphin series across international and domestic licenses. During this period, Dora sold 1.9 million units with $9.4 million in profit.

Fizzle Games Corporation, Phoenix, Arizona   1986-1987

Director of Product Development
Produced 20 games for the WhizBang 32 and 32e games systems.
Participated in licensing of game properties. Created developers' manual.

Pester Your Parents Inc., San Francisco, California

Toy Consultant   1986
Created and executed mechanical models for electronic toys for Pester
Your Parents Inc. and Tubular Inc.

Scimitar Design, San Diego, California   1985-1986

Senior Project Engineer
Created working prototypes and mechanical drawings of game and toy
concepts. Participated in the development of board games.

The Truth About Hoagie, Los Angeles, California

Toy Consultant   1985
Designed an original board game based on *The Truth About Hoagie*
TV series for Beefeater Products. Made mechanical designs for Scimitar
Design.

Kurutaro Enterprises Inc., Los Angeles, California   1984

Game Designer
Managed external game developers in the conversion of arcade games
for home entertainment systems.

Binarix Inc., Santa Monica, California   1983

Game Designer/Programmer
Programmed two original computer games in Z80 Assembly language.
Assisted in the development of 3-D games for the Cyborex System.

EDUCATION

<u>Master in Fine Arts,</u> **University of St. Paul,** St. Paul, Minnesota (in progress)

<u>BA English,</u> **State University of Washington,** Olympia, Washington

<u>Additional:</u> Courses in Supervision, Japanese, Screenwriting, Storytelling,
Negotiating, and Entertainment Law.

NOTE

If applying for jobs in Europe and Canada, a Curriculum Vitae (CV) is the norm, as opposed to the one- to two-page "American" résumé. A CV is typically four to five pages long and may include these additional sections: "Awards," "Professional Associations," "Publications," and "Speaking Engagements." If it's a Journalist's résumé, then use "Interviews" and "Personal Section" (to include where born, hobbies, interests).

TIP

It is recommended that you only show the last 15 years of professional experience in your résumé. If experience prior to the last 15 years is significant to the objective, then create an "Additional Experience" header, list relevant experience, and leave off the dates. This tactic helps protect against age discrimination.

COVER LETTER

When you send off your résumé, you should also include a cover letter that briefly introduces yourself and states your objective. Use the following sample cover letter as a template for your own, but be sure to customize yours.

APPLICATION COVER LETTER TEMPLATE

Date

Name of contact person, if applicable
Company
Company address

Dear [NAME],

I am enclosing my résumé for the [NAME OF POSITION] position I saw advertised in [LOCATION]. I am very interested in the position and feel my experience and educational background make me an excellent candidate.
[INSERT 1–2 PARAGRAPHS DESCRIBING RELEVANT SKILLS].
I would welcome the opportunity to work for your organization and make a contribution to its success. I look forward to hearing from you to further discuss my qualifications.

Sincerely,
Signature
Your name
Your contact info

Enclosure (résumé)

SAMPLE APPLICATION COVER LETTER

August 21, 2006

Rita Barnsworth
Electronic Arts
12345 Canal Blvd.
Foster City, CA 94306

Dear Rita Barnsworth,

I am enclosing my résumé for the Tester position I saw advertised on GameJobs.com. I am very interested in the position and feel my previous testing experience and computer science educational background make me an excellent candidate. Specifically, I have experience testing prerelease games, creating detailed bug reports, setting up videocapture using PhotoShop, and verifying all aspects of a game are aligned with company standards.

I would welcome the opportunity to work for your organization and make a contribution to its success. I look forward to hearing from you to further discuss my qualifications.

Sincerely,

R. Abbott

Ron Abbott
(650) 356-5555

Enclosure (résumé)

USING RECRUITERS

There are recruiters who specialize in placing people in video game jobs. However, they're only useful if you already have some experience in the industry. Recruiters are paid only if they place you in a job, so don't contact them until you have properly prepared yourself for a non-entry-level position.

When you are ready to consider having a recruiter work for you, go to www.peer-org.com for a list of recruiters.

TIPS FROM A VIDEO GAME RECRUITER

A veteran video game industry recruiter in Southern California answered a few questions about getting paid to play:

Q: How does one find a job in video games?
A: Use a recruiter like myself (go to www.peer-org.net for a list of recruiters). Also go to college job boards, university job fairs, and find a mentor—or many mentors—through networking.

Q: How else can I find a job?
A: It is always best to know what you are looking for when you apply. Make sure you know what you are applying for and that you target your actual skills to what the employer needs. *Do not* just send the résumé in without understanding the requirements.

First impressions are so very important. They post the job descriptions because they want to find people with those particular skills. Can you imagine what they think when a job requires C or C++ and you only have Basic? What if they ask for an environmental artist and you do modeling of buildings and vehicles? Do you honestly think they will consider the résumé? Or maybe they will think you can't read!

She also advises the following:

- Know the companies that are your most likely prospective employers.
- Get to know people in the companies through networking and information interviewing.
- Learn about the position you want to have.
- Find out through informational interviewing who provides on-the-job training for that position.
- Obtain a degree in a relevant field, not just a set of specialized skills.
- Apprentice or intern for experience.
- Network with various professional associations (GDA, Academy of Interactive Arts and Science/AIAS, etc.).
- Become informed about the business of video games. Go to industry business websites (Gamasutra, Games Industry.Biz, Game Daily News, IGDA Newsletter, IGN, Game Developer Magazine, Gamer NationTV.com).
- Check out the credits on the games you play. Who published the game? What studio made the game?
- Contact companies you admire and find out about on-the-job training opportunities.

Interviewing

The big day has come. You've learned the right skills, made the right connections, and sent off the right résumé. Now it's time to seal the deal with a killer job interview.

WHAT TO WEAR

Just because you might be hoping for a job where you can wear ratty jeans and a Led Zeppelin T-shirt to work, don't dress that way for the interview. For creative jobs and entry-level positions, business casual dress is fine (slacks, button-down shirt, tie optional, no jacket). Three-piece suits are probably too dressy for any non-managerial job interviews. Most game companies are staffed by younger, hipper employees, so your piercings and tattoos probably won't be the drawback that they'd be in more conventional industries, especially if you're going for an art job. But, when in doubt, err on the side of caution and remove them or cover them up.

Finally, but most importantly, good hygiene goes a long way. The morning before your interview, be sure to shower, wash your hair, brush your teeth, clean your ears, trim your fingernails, shave, and wear deodorant. The people interviewing you are going to spend a lot of time in close proximity to whoever they hire. If you come in smelling like a rugby team, that person isn't going to be you.

YOUR PORTFOLIO

Come to the interview prepared to show off samples of what you've done. If you're an artist, bring digital and printed versions of your work. Programmers should have a demo of code that they can present. Writers should have samples of their work that reflect the appropriate type of writing (for example, aspiring journalists shouldn't offer up their *Star Trek* fan fiction).

Your portfolio should be a careful selection of the best examples of your work. Don't throw everything you've ever done into it. Instead, carefully select 5 to 10 pieces that can be reviewed in as many minutes. If you have more work that you believe is of the same quality, bring it and offer it to the interviewer if they're interested in seeing more of your work, but don't water down the overall quality of your portfolio just for the sake of padding it.

THE "PSR" FORMULA

The best way to shine in an interview is to tell real-life stories about challenges you've faced in previous jobs and how you overcame them. Merely stating that you have "good problem-solving skills" is not as impressive as describing specific problems and how you solved them.

Before the interview, carefully review the job posting and research what skills the job calls for. Make a list of these skills and come up with 15 "PSR" (problem-solution-result) stories about how you've used these skills previously in your own life. Use these stories in the interview to clearly demonstrate that you're the best person for the job.

Problem

The problem is the setup of the story. Include your job title at the time and how long ago it was.

Example: "Last year when I worked for a video production company as an intern and office manager, I was supporting fifty staff members, all with simultaneous deadlines for projects they needed my help with. I needed strong multitasking skills."

Solution

The solution is where you describe, step by step, exactly what you did to resolve the problem.

Example: "So, I prioritized each project on a spreadsheet, and I communicated regularly with all fifty staff members, telling them that for any project they needed my help on, I needed a seven-day projected lead time."

Result

The result describes the positive effects that the solution had on the company, the individuals, and so on.

Example: "And it resulted in my consistently being able to meet everyone's deadlines, with minimum conflict. Everyone felt taken care of equally, and with this lead-time schedule, I was then able to handle and take on more emergency projects, which resulted in my greater flexibility and productivity."

INTERVIEW QUESTIONS TO ASK

At the end of most interviews, the interviewer will ask if you have any questions. Asking the right questions shows that you have a high level of interest in the position. The following are excellent questions to ask:

- In your opinion, what skills are critical to be successful in this job?
- What would be my performance goals, for the first 30/60/90 days?
- Can you tell me why this position is open? Is it newly created?
- How is outstanding performance recognized?

INTERVIEW QUESTIONS TO ASK (CONT.)

Do not ask questions about the exact salary or benefits for the position until it is offered to you. If they ask you for your salary requirements or history, ask them what salary range they have budgeted for the position and let them know if that is in line with your history and expectations.

Conclusion

Well, that's it, folks. You've reached the end of the book and have absorbed the knowledge that we have to impart to you. With information from over 100 industry types, ranging from the tester, to the sharp-suited director, we're leaving the most important step to you: using all this information to get the career you always wanted.

After your dreams of sitting on a couch playing the next *Grand Theft Auto* while you're drip-fed Mountain Dew have been toned-down, and after the realization that there's long hours, dedication, and hard work behind the fancy graphics and addictive gameplay, you're still on the brink of a career that most people would cut off a thumb for (not a good idea in this field).

Your plans for video game industry domination don't end here. You should network, use the tools and insider knowledge we've given you to make those valuable connections, and seek out meetings with people who work in the industry. Most people (85 percent, according to the Bureau of Labor Statistics) obtain their jobs through who they know or through the hidden job market.

Keep the momentum going! Then maybe in a few years, we'll be interviewing you. Good luck!

About the Authors

With over 11 years in the video game industry, David S] Hodgson has helped launch five different magazine publications in both his native England and in the US. Hodgson has written close to 1,000 game reviews, and interviewed some of the biggest names of the industry, including Toru Iwatani (inventor of Pac-Man), Hideo Kojima (Metal Gear Solid), and Gabe Newell (Half-Life). He has worked closely with over 50 video game development studios in the last nine years of writing strategy guides, and was recently featured in the New York Times and on National Public Radio.

Photo by Katherine Hopkins

Now in his eighth year in the video game industry Bryan Stratton, has worked with virtually every major player in the business, including Nintendo, Sony, Microsoft, THQ, Electronic Arts, id Software, Cyan Worlds, and LucasArts. A script writer for THQ's *WWE SmackDown* franchise, he has recently accepted a full-time game design position with THQ. His writing has appeared in a variety of video game publications, including *Computer Gaming World*, *Electronic Gaming Monthly*, *Official Xbox Magazine* and *GameSpy.com*, and he is the author of a bunch of Prima strategy guides, including *Legend of Zelda: The Wind Waker*, *Doom 3*, and *Uru: Ages Beyond Myst*. This is like his 40th book or something. He's lost track.

Alice Rush, MA, RPCC, MCC is a certified registered career counselor and founder of CareerU counseling practice. She has over 15 years experience in career development, consulting with Fortune 100 companies and providing career counseling services to the general public Projects she has worked on have been documented in *Harvard Business Review*, *Fortune*, *Personnel Journal*, *Training Magazine*, and televised on PBS.